I0823045

CHARLATANS

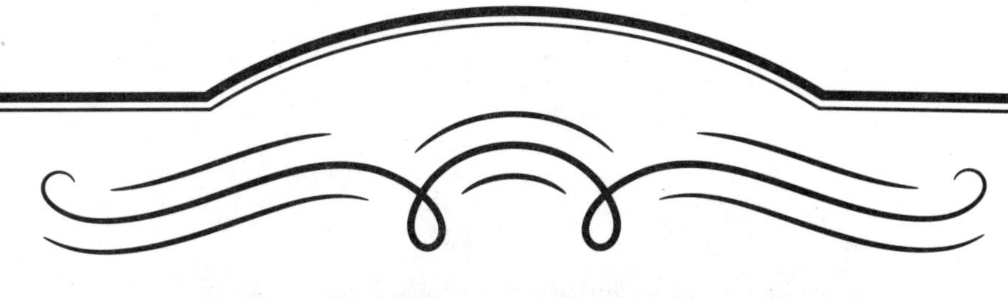

CHARLATANS

HOW GRIFTERS, SWINDLERS, AND HUCKSTERS BAMBOOZLE THE MEDIA, THE MARKETS, AND THE MASSES

MOISÉS NAÍM & QUICO TORO

BASIC BOOKS
New York

Cover design by Chin-Yee Lai
Cover images © Daboost / Shutterstock.com; © Ruediger Geisler via Getty Images; © Noli Molly / Shutterstock.com; © Vasya Kobelev / Shutterstock.com

Basic Books
Hachette Book Group
1290 Avenue of the Americas, New York, NY 10104
www.basicbooks.com

Printed in the United States of America

First Edition: October 2025

Published by Basic Books, an imprint of Hachette Book Group, Inc. The Basic Books name and logo is a registered trademark of the Hachette Book Group.

The Hachette Speakers Bureau provides a wide range of authors for speaking events. To find out more, go to hachettespeakersbureau.com or email HachetteSpeakers@hbgusa.com.

Basic books may be purchased in bulk for business, educational, or promotional use. For more information, please contact your local bookseller or the Hachette Book Group Special Markets Department at special.markets@hbgusa.com.

The publisher is not responsible for websites (or their content) that are not owned by the publisher.

Print book interior design by Amy Quinn.

Library of Congress Cataloging-in-Publication Data

Names: Naím, Moisés author | Toro, Francisco author
Title: Charlatans : how grifters, swindlers, and hucksters bamboozle the media, the markets, and the masses / Moisés Naím and Quico Toro.
Description: First edition. | New York : Basic Books, 2025. | Includes index.
Identifiers: LCCN 2025001592 (print) | LCCN 2025001593 (ebook) | ISBN 9781541606517 hardcover | ISBN 9781541606524 ebook
Subjects: LCSH: Swindlers and swindling | Quacks and quackery | Fraud
Classification: LCC HV6691 .N33 2025 (print) | LCC HV6691 (ebook) | DDC 364.16/3—dc23/eng/20250707
LC record available at https://lccn.loc.gov/2025001592
LC ebook record available at https://lccn.loc.gov/2025001593

ISBNs: 9781541606517 (hardcover), 9781541606524 (ebook)

LSC-C

Printing 1, 2025

To Susana

◇◇◇◇◇

To Kanako

◇◇◇◇◇◇

Contents

Preface

In November 1589 the senate of Venice elected a new official alchemist for their Most Serene Republic. He came from Cyprus and introduced himself as Marco Bragadino. Whispers had it his real name was Mamugnà.

His charisma was spellbinding, and stories about him abounded. That was no accident: Mamugnà had spent years carefully seeding rumors that he had finally cracked the age-old secret of turning base metal into gold.

This caught the senators' attention. Venice was in the middle of a fiscal crisis—its trade with the east was undercut by new long-distance shipping from Portugal and Spain to Asia and the Americas. The old city on the lagoon, once a Mediterranean superpower, had been slowly losing power for three generations: only a miracle could turn its fortunes. And the senate decided Mamugnà would be that miracle.

They put him up in a lavish palazzo on the island of Giudecca, at city expense. There, Mamugnà cultivated an air of mystery while making a show of enormous wealth. He didn't explicitly claim he could make gold, but the shocking ease with which he spent money left little room for doubt. The newcomer threw balls of such opulence, flaunted his money with such astounding openhandedness that no one dared doubt him.

In a spectacular public demonstration, the alchemist showed the amazed patricians how he could heat a small amount of base metal, add to it an amount of a secret substance, and, with a flash and a bang, transmute it into a solid nugget of gold.

Contemporary accounts describe a man of magnetic charm, who often referred obliquely to the secret insights garnered from his youth in the mystical East, in far-off Cyprus. He needed only time, he said, to make the process work at a scale large enough to solve the city's budget crisis.

How much time?

A smidgeon under eight years, he said.

In the meantime, naturally, Mamugnà would live a life of decadent luxury on the city's dime. Noblemen paraded through his drawing room, families in tow, dreaming of marrying their daughters off to the man who could literally make gold. Mamugnà partied like it was 1599, his palazzo becoming a focal point of the city's feasting culture. City fathers tied themselves up in knots to keep him happy; at any hint of disapproval over his extravagant lifestyle, Mamugnà would rage, threatening to defect to one of Venice's rivals.

That kept them in line.

He was not short of offers. The Grand Duke of Tuscany made a bid to secure his services, as did the city fathers of Padua, Venice's old mainland rival. The pope himself tried to win Mamugnà over to Rome. Nobody in Venice dared go against the mysterious Cypriot . . . imagine being the man who squandered Venice's chance to restore its glory.

The story, laid out in Grete De Francesco's magisterial 1939 tome, *The Power of the Charlatan*, captures a man who had the measure of his marks.[1] Venice's noblemen would not let go of their dream of global power and glory. They had been brought up to believe it was their city's destiny to rule the Mediterranean and stand at the pinnacle of the Western world's wealth and power. The world they knew made sense only if Venice led it, as it had done for centuries.

Mamugnà exploited that dream ruthlessly; he made it synonymous with support for *him*. And because their identities were wound up with that dream, his supporters in the senate went far—very far—to protect him. He employed psychological jujitsu to trick them into believing protecting *him* meant protecting *it*—the dream of restoring Venice's power and glory.

He took them for an amazing ride—but he didn't have to *convince* them of anything. They wanted to believe, so they convinced themselves.

This is a book about public figures who have a knack for manipulating groups of people into trusting them, and who then use that trust to exploit those people without overt coercion. The first, in our opinion, are charlatans. The people they victimize are their marks, who come to trust the charlatans so completely that they become enthusiastic participants in their own exploitation.

Charlatanism is an age-old phenomenon, and the techniques used today by the most talented charlatans aren't all that different from the techniques Mamugnà used to bamboozle Venice's noblemen. And yet, even if the techniques aren't different, the landscape in which charlatans ply their trade is completely transformed.

In the twenty-first century, charlatans have access to many more marks—or victims—than was ever before possible. Some of them rely on television to beam their pitches into their marks' homes. But new technologies enable schemes that are digital, viral, scalable, and potentially global in scope. They're leveraging new technologies in fundamentally new ways to target more marks with a greater variety of pitches than was historically possible.

The variety is truly bewildering: In Chapter 2, we'll see how a daring charlatan targeted middle-class Istanbul moms by championing the dream of Turkish rural simplicity. In Chapter 5, we'll meet a charlatan who specifically crafted her digital-marketing campaign to reach people actively considering suicide. You may never have suspected that many city dwellers in Turkey long for a simpler agricultural past; it may never have occurred to you that the suicidal could be targeted for exploitation. But there are hucksters out there who spotted these people as gaps in the market and crafted pitches that earned them a devoted following—as well as millions of dollars.

Charlatanism used to be on the sidelines of society. It is moving to the center. In 2025 a tsunami of charlatans descended on Washington, taking control of the governing institutions of the world's only superpower. Understanding charlatanism has never been more urgent.

It is not only the supply side of charlatanry that has been upended in the twenty-first century. The same technologies that make it easier to target people also render them more socially isolated, leaving them more vulnerable because they lack the social connections that might otherwise have protected them from charlatans. In 2023 the US surgeon general published an advisory warning that an epidemic of loneliness and social isolation was leading to a sharp deterioration across measures of social well-being. The report notes that "from 2003 to 2020, the average time that young people spent in person with friends declined by nearly 70 percent."[2] It presents evidence that the increasing use of technology to mediate social relationships "displaces in-person engagement, monopolizes our attention, reduces the quality of our interactions, and even diminishes our self-esteem," which can "lead to greater loneliness, fear of missing out, conflict, and reduced social connection."[3]

This is an evolving area of research, but in many of the charlatan stories that follow, social isolation seems to play a key role in laying victims open to exploitation. We'll meet isolated immigrants cut off from social connections back home who are swindled out of thousands of dollars by storefront astrologers, devout Christians disconnected from local church communities who are victimized by scammy televangelists peddling an absurd prosperity gospel, and the thousands of Trump enthusiasts who substituted the imagined bonds of the QAnon community for the local bonds they lack.

Socially isolated people are ripe for the picking by charlatans. And charlatans have an uncanny knack for turning socially isolated people into their own worst enemies. But how? What exactly is it that leaves people vulnerable to this type of victimization?

In the first chapter, we discuss how charlatans have found a way to hack into people's *dreams*: they identify some key belief a group of people is passionately committed to and secure their trust by championing that belief with zeal and charisma. Mamugnà *knew* Venice's nobles were desperate to believe their city's power and glory could be restored, so he positioned himself as the only one able to make that happen. Venice's noblemen wanted to believe in that dream, so they wanted to believe in him.

In earlier eras, before technology made it simple to microtarget people according to their specific dreams, charlatans had to confine themselves to just a couple of tried-and-true niches proven to have wide appeal. The word *charlatan* comes down to us from seventeenth-century Italy, where sketchy *ciarlatani*—roughly "loud mouths"—went from town to town hawking miracle cures to treat the health problems that no doctor could tame. Similar swindlers arose in many different places over the centuries. A rich lore exists around the snake oil salesmen who plied their trade across the old West, telling tall tales about the curative power of the dubious concoctions they hawked.

In fact, until recently, almost all charlatans haven't been able to microtarget their marks, so they've had to specialize in just a handful of fields with very wide appeal. People have always dreamed of sudden riches, and they've always dreamed of regaining their lost health. These simplest of scams are the hardy perennials of charlatanism, and as we'll see, they're still popular among the panoply of twenty-first-century charlatan schemes.

But today, search algorithms powered by artificial intelligence make it easier to burrow into many more types of dreams: dreams of perfect union with a love mate; dreams of cosmic connection with divinity; dreams of overcoming death; dreams of spiritual growth and frictionless community; dreams of racial reconciliation or, alternatively, of racial purity; dreams of connecting with the nation's agricultural soil; and dreams of transcending money altogether.

These kinds of dreams were far too niche for previous generations of charlatans to target: How would you even find enough people to exploit who share such dreams? Modern technology solves this problem, resulting—among many other things—in a kind of golden age of charlatanism, where any dream you have, no matter how recondite it may feel, can become a vulnerability a talented charlatan uses to exploit you.

Modern charlatans use the same kinds of techniques the ciarlatani used centuries ago. They exploit the same weak points in human cognition as the snake oil salesmen of the old West. They earn their mark's trust. They skillfully manipulate them by championing their dreams with passion and charisma. Then they exploit them. And the marks fall for it, again and again, just as often now as they did then.

And yet charlatans today can cause much wider harm.

Soon, a nearly limitless supply of charlatans will be able to target marks *individually*. As historian Yuval Harari has argued, new forms of artificial intelligence allow anyone to "mass-produce intimacy," with bots now confidently playing the role of confidant, of mentor, of priest.[4] The internet made charlatanry digital, social media made it viral, and AI is making charlatanry scalable in ways it had never been before. Already, a few of the most successful charlatans operate at a global scale, and AI is creating the conditions for many more to join them.

The advent of the AI charlatan is the logical conclusion of trends that have been in play for decades. Over the first three decades of this century, charlatans acquired tools that mock borders and geographies, putting the machinery of twenty-first-century surveillance capitalism to the worst of ends.[5] Their pool of potential marks has multiplied from the few dozen people a ciarlatano might be able to gather in front of his soapbox on market day to literally billions spread worldwide.

The power of the digital technologies charlatans now wield, together with the shift to an online-based social life, creates ideal conditions for them to operate in. Rather than having to rely on a few universal themes like the cure-alls of thirteenth-century Italy or the American West, they can specialize in fulfilling—or pretending to be able to fulfill—dreams based on a much wider array of human needs. This works because the dreams charlatans exploit have their roots in things everyone needs: health, wealth, love, security, and connection.

Charlatans, by definition, are exploitative: they specialize in convincing people to do things that go against their own interests. This leaves marks in a peculiarly contradictory position: they are victims who are happy to be victimized, victims who reliably end up among the charlatan's biggest supporters and most convinced defenders—and often play a lead role in recruiting yet more marks for the charlatan.

All this happens even though the charlatan is saying things that in any ordinary context would sound really quite crazy: claiming exclusive access to secret knowledge, special powers, and secret insights in ways that would normally set all your alarm bells ringing. Charlatans regularly convince marks to take extreme measures: to cut off their relationships with their dearest family members, to sleep with people they would never have dreamed of sleeping with, and, of course, to give all their money to them.

How can people be so gullible? How can they be so completely taken in?

These are the questions that kept coming to us as we studied the charlatans that you will read about in the pages ahead. They're not very charitable questions. On hearing a charlatan story, almost everyone's first instinct is to be quite dismissive of the charlatan's victims.

Marks must just not be very smart. Or perhaps they're not very well educated. The image that tends to come to mind is of older, poorer, less educated, simpler people. Maybe they are too needy, or too insecure, or just too ignorant. Perhaps they lack the family, friends, or community that might shelter them from the advances of the charlatans. Perhaps it's unrequited love, the loss of a loved one, a spiritual crisis, or financial woes that make them easy prey for unscrupulous people smarter than they are. One way or another, we want to believe there is something *wrong* with them.

But that can't be right. Just think about the victims of some of the century's most notorious charlatans: Elizabeth Holmes, of the blood-testing scam company Theranos, or the financier Bernie Madoff, whose investment scam cost investors billions. Nobody can call their victims stupid or unsophisticated. Holmes snookered the most celebrated brains in America, putting the likes of former US secretaries of state Henry Kissinger and George Shultz, alongside a who's who of former four-star generals, former high-ranking cabinet members, and top public health executives on her company's board. Bernie Madoff swindled everyone from Steven Spielberg's charitable foundation to Kevin Bacon to Nobel Peace Laureate Elie Wiesel.

What the rich and powerful people who fell for these charlatans have in common with the everyday victims is that both have needs. Different kinds of needs. Normal needs. Legitimate needs. And those needs express themselves through deep, abiding wants, the kind of driving wishes that you organize your identity, indeed, your whole life around. We call those deep longings "dreams."

To dream is human; the human capacity to dream is endless. Anyone who has been sick has dreamed of health. Anyone who has been heartbroken has dreamed of love. Anyone who has been poor has dreamed of wealth. And anyone who has been lonely has dreamed of connection.

In the first chapter, we'll go into considerable detail on the specific mechanisms charlatans exploit to prey on people's dreams, whatever those dreams might be. We'll see how they treat our dreams as a vulnerability they can exploit for profit. We'll see how some common cognitive biases create openings that charlatans can take advantage of to gain power over their marks.

In the chapters that follow, we'll look at the story of twenty-four supremely successful contemporary charlatans. They come from all around the world. They exploit rich people and poor people, young people and old people, men and women, religious people and secular people.

Our approach has been to pick a broad selection of charlatans from all walks of life, from different geographies and ages, actively manipulating all kinds of dreams. We will present you with charlatans from rich countries and poor, charlatans who target illiterate people and PhDs, charlatans everyone has heard of and charlatans no one has heard of, even charlatans who collaboratively deceive one another as a group.

Inevitably, most of them will be charlatans whose pitches hold no appeal to you, and you'll recognize their pitches right away as scams or manipulative swindles. One startling regularity we've found when reporting these stories is that to people outside a charlatan's target group, their pitches very often sound entirely preposterous. The problem isn't spotting charlatans who are out to exploit others. The hard part is spotting the ones out to swindle you.

If we have done this well, there'll be at least one charlatan who might have taken you in. Perhaps we even wrote about a charlatan who *has* taken you in. If so, maybe seeing the story of your tormentor alongside so many other stories of charlatans you can simply laugh at will help you see him, or her, in a new light.

We wrote this book to call attention to new forms of deception and manipulation that don't quite fit into our usual categories for talking about such things. Charlatans aren't mere scammers or fraudsters, like the ones behind the robocalls trying to steal your identity you probably get quite often: charlatans are public figures who keep one foot on the legal, above-board world while also developing exploitative swindles.

We'll meet a charlatan who controls a billion-dollar empire but pretends to be a holy yogi who owns no property, a charlatan who convinced millions of Turkish people to invest their life savings in digital farms, charlatans who scam daytime TV viewers in America to buy worthless vitamin supplements, and others who convince their marks that the only way into the kingdom of heaven is to give them all their money. We'll meet so many charlatans in so many fields, by the end you'll start to suspect what we suspect: nobody is safe.

Governments, universities, hospitals, the military, churches, corporations, and the media are failing miserably to protect vulnerable people from charlatans. That's not surprising. Charlatans move at the speed of electrons, while the institutions meant to police them work at the pace of bureaucracy. They struggle to collaborate across international borders and are fundamentally flummoxed by the problem of patrolling a form of exploitation that turns victims into enthusiastic champions for the very hucksters victimizing them. When exploitation involves neither violence nor overt coercion, our usual mechanisms for fighting it seize up and stop functioning. And this too is baked into the charlatan's calculation.

We wrote this book because we realized spotting the charlatan out to exploit your dream has become a key survival skill for the twenty-first century. It's time to name charlatanism as the scourge of our age, because you can't solve a problem until you've addressed it, and you can't address it until you've named it.

Of course, Mamugnà had no secret method that would transmute base metal into gold.

The demonstration he had used with the flash, the bang, and the nugget of gold was just sleight of hand, the same kind of trick magicians use at children's birthday parties today, a craft Mamugnà had studied much more carefully than alchemy. Not long before his death, Mamugnà confessed that the gold nugget was hidden up his sleeve and released while the astonished viewers' attention was fixed on an unrelated chemical explosion.

In 1590, after missing a series of deadlines the Venetians had set for him to show his progress, Mamugnà saw the writing on the wall and bolted for a different court. He wrote to the King of France offering his services, but he was declined. He lay low with a noble family in Padua for a while until he struck it rich in Munich, where Duke Wilhelm V of Bavaria was facing outright bankruptcy. The duke, whom contemporary accounts paint as an imbecile, was no match for Mamugnà, who won him over almost instantly. Alarmed, a group of Bavarian noblemen seized the Cypriot one night, interrogated him, extracted a confession, and put him to death before the duke could intervene.

Mamugnà's story feels distant. Yet, all the way back in the sixteenth century we already find all the elements of the charlatan's art; every charlatan's basic business model is, at heart, the same. Like Mamugnà, they identify a *dream*—an idea so important to some people that they cannot bear for it to be called into question—and they champion it confidently, authoritatively, eloquently. They champion it so ably that the people who share that dream can't help but believe in them, to the point that their belief in the dream gets all jumbled up with their belief in the charlatan, until the two come to seem inseparable.

Mamugnà never persuaded Venice's city fathers of anything; he didn't have to. He championed their dream of wealth and glory to them and portrayed himself as the key to making it a reality. After that, he didn't even have to ask them for their praise, their palaces, or their daughters: they lined up to offer them to him.

1

Hacking HumanOS

To understand how charlatans turn people into their own worst enemies, we'll need to take a detour through the fascinating, fast-moving world of cognitive psychology, the science of how we think. The upshot is that, despite all the vast technological upheavals between his time and ours, the vulnerabilities that modern charlatans exploit are the same that Mamugnà targeted centuries ago. And these vulnerabilities are hard-baked into the way our brains work: we're pretty much stuck with them.

Just like a new computer, humans ship with a kind of cognitive operating system preinstalled in their minds, a framework for thinking built deep into the brain's architecture. We think of it as the Human Operating System, or HumanOS for short. As an operating system, HumanOS doesn't determine *what* we think, but it does determine *how* we think.

For the most part, HumanOS is great software: it allows people to accomplish amazing feats, from reading this sentence, to designing a spaceship, to writing a symphony.

But like all software, HumanOS has its share of bugs and vulnerabilities too—places where it misfires in ways that can get you into trouble. In the same way a hacker who can identify the vulnerabilities in computer code can get the computer to do things that aren't in its owner's interest, the bugs in HumanOS lay us open to attack from people who want to turn our minds into weapons against us.

When it comes to charlatans, a couple of vulnerabilities in HumanOS are especially relevant. They're built into the architecture of the way we think, so we all share them. The first one is *confirmation bias*: our tendency to want to confirm, rather than falsify, our hunches. This is a universal feature of human thinking that expresses itself most powerfully when our most cherished beliefs are at stake. In those cases, people show a marked tendency to engage in *motivated reasoning*: beginning with a cherished conclusion, and reasoning backward from there to look for the reasons they hold it.

A second set of vulnerabilities involves herd mentality: our instinctive sense that if a lot of people like us believe something, we ought to believe it too. Social psychologists and marketers know this as *social proof*: our tendency to substitute the judgment of others for our own. This, we'll see, is often paired with techniques to get us to first make a small commitment to a charlatan's schemes, which is then ratcheted up gradually, one step at a time. Such *commitment ladders* reliably get people to stay committed to a charlatan, becoming ever more enthusiastic participants in their own exploitation.

To be sure, Mamugnà had never heard about any of this; the terms themselves were all coined hundreds of years after his time. It didn't matter, because he had an intuitive sense for the timeless human traits the terms attempt to capture. More important, he had a knack for exploiting the vulnerabilities these traits create. Modern charlatans do exactly the same thing, only with the benefit of powerful new technologies that allow them to amplify both their reach and the damage they inflict.

Like charlatans of every age, Mamugnà's craft, his art, consisted in getting people to believe things that it was not in their objective interest to believe. He knew that to do that, he needed to earn their trust. Once he had that, he would not need to coerce anyone to get them to give him what he wanted. Money, sex, power . . . Venice's august senators lined up to offer them up freely to him.

Whether they're in the field of religion, politics, business, health, wellness, or anything else, charlatans' stories all rely on a single structure, a kind of universal grammar of charlatanry. Charlatans forge a deep connection with their marks on the basis of their deepest beliefs, the things their marks most fervently *need* to be true: their *dreams.*

People hang on to their dreams tenaciously. Charlatans know this, which is why they interpose themselves between marks and their dreams, by convincing marks that they, and only they, can make their dreams come true. This is how charlatans achieve a remarkable feat: they turn people's deepest desires into weapons against them.

To understand precisely how they do this, it is helpful to review what the research on cognitive psychology has identified as the way our minds work. This will help us see that what charlatans are really doing is exploiting some of the best-understood glitches in the way we process information.

Glitches in HumanOS

HumanOS is an amazingly powerful piece of software. We use it to run a huge number of mental applications, each catering to a different sort of human need. Much of it runs in the background, without our conscious awareness: HumanOS keeps us breathing, keeps our balance, and keeps our digestion going without the need for input from us at all. Awareness comes in only when HumanOS is running higher-level programs, such as those that keep us fed and clothed, those that keep us connected to our families and our communities, and those that make sense of the world around us.

But even here, much of the nuts and bolts of the OS are hidden away from the user: we perform many of our operations without any conscious awareness of what we're doing. And just like any OS, HumanOS has its share of flaws. It does some things well and other things badly. And some of the things it does badly create vulnerabilities to malicious intruders: hackers determined to turn your resources against you.

The vulnerabilities we're talking about aren't a disease. They are not a moral failing. And they're the opposite of unique. They are sources of systematic error in human thinking that psychologists have studied for generations. They call them cognitive biases, and we all share them.

Yes, you do too.

The granddaddy of these vulnerabilities is known as *confirmation bias*: our tendency to process new information in ways that are consistent with what we already believe, whether we have any good reason to believe it.

Confirmation bias is a basic feature of the way humans think, and it's one of the best-documented vulnerabilities in HumanOS. Over the last five decades *thousands* of studies have been aimed at understanding it precisely. The literature is vast, and its findings are subtle. The basic insight has been replicated across a huge variety of settings: study after study has found that confirmation bias is pervasive and powerful. Confirmation bias operates unconsciously, or rather *pre*consciously, before we've even had time to deliberate on what we think.

It happens, that is, at the level of intuition.

For an insight that explains so much about what humans think, confirmation bias has a pretty clunky name. It got that name through a quirk of first usage. Back in 1960 British cognitive psychologist Peter Wason at University College London was investigating a narrow technical question about people's strategies for finding information to either confirm or refute a given hypothesis. Let's look at that original work, now a classic study with the less-than-spellbinding title "On the Failure to Eliminate Hypotheses in a Conceptual Task."[1]

Wason took a group of undergraduates into a lab and showed them a simple series of three numbers: 2-4-6.

He told them that this sequence follows a particular rule. Their job was to infer what the rule was.

He invited them to propose their own sequences of three numbers, saying he would tell them whether the sequences they proposed did or did not follow the rule he had in mind. Participants could propose as many sets of three numbers as they wanted to check their hunches. Once they were confident they had understood the underlying rule, they could declare it to check whether they were correct.

Try it! What three-number sequence would you propose first to see if it follows the same rule as 2-4-6? Almost everyone intuits that the underlying rule is probably "add 2 to the previous number." That's natural enough.

What's interesting, though, is what people do next. Time and again, participants first try to check their intuition by proposing sequences like 4-6-8 or 10-12-14—that is, other sequences that *also* follow the rule they had in mind. Their goal, it appeared, is to get a "yes" out of the experimenter. When they do, they interpret that yes as *confirming* their hypothesis.

In fact, the underlying rule Wason had in mind was "any set of ascending numbers."

So, 4-6-8 *does* follow the rule. But so does 4-6-7. And 0-1-894. Yet few checked sequences like those.

A few of Wason's participants thought the rule might be "multiples of the base number." But then they proposed sequences that conformed to the rule suggested by their intuition, sequences like 3-6-9 or 4-8-12. They too looked first for evidence to *confirm* that their intuition was right through what Wason called "enumerative induction"—just testing more and more sequences that followed the rule they intuited.

Why is this an issue? To a logician, enumerative induction is a terrible strategy for checking whether your intuition is right. The smart way to check the "+2" hypothesis is to propose a sequence like 2-4-5. If you propose 2-4-5 and you're told it *also* follows the hidden rule, then you can unambiguously discard the hypothesis you'd intuited.

As philosopher Karl Popper famously demonstrated, piling on confirmation can never prove a hypothesis is right.[2] Scientific reasoning works by *falsifying* hypotheses that are wrong, not by confirming those that are right. Well, the sequence 2-4-5 unambiguously *falsifies* the "+2" hypothesis in a way that proposing 4-6-8 can never do. A scientist tests a hypothesis by trying to falsify it. Wason's insight was that, out there in the real world, virtually no one tests hypotheses the way Popper thought they should.

HumanOS is bad at scientific reasoning. When people try to prove a hypothesis, their gut tells them to try to confirm, not to falsify. That might seem like a technical point, but it isn't, because people's flawed intuition about how to test a hypothesis has perverse effects: people who imagine themselves to be thinking logically reliably end up *deepening* their confidence in conclusions that are just plain wrong.

In the seven decades since Wason's original study, psychologists have conducted thousands of experiments to understand the mechanism in detail. They've strapped subjects into sophisticated brain scanners to measure which areas are activated as people try to evaluate evidence. They've altered the details in any number of different ways. One researcher who reviewed the large body of research stimulated by Wason's original ideas summed up his findings: "A great deal of empirical evidence supports the idea that the confirmation bias is extensive and strong and that it appears in many guises. The evidence also supports the view that once one has taken a position on an issue, one's primary purpose becomes that of defending or justifying that position. This is to say that regardless of whether one's treatment of evidence was even handed before the stand was taken, it can become highly biased afterward."[3]

When people first hear about confirmation bias, they tend to think of it as a *mistake* people make when evaluating evidence. That's the wrong way to think about it. A *bias* is not a *mistake*. A mistake involves making an effort at solving a problem but still getting the answer wrong. A bias takes no effort at all. The thing that makes glitches in HumanOS so useful to malicious attackers is that they are *unconscious*: they're embedded into processes that run in the background. In other words, we do it without knowing we're doing it.

In 2002 Daniel Kahneman won the Nobel Prize in Economics for his insights into some of the implications of confirmation bias. Seeking to explain his findings to the world, he asserted that there was a regularity to the source of many such errors: they're the result of *fast thinking*.[4]

When we showed you the sequence 2-4-6 and asked you to think of a rule that might produce such a sequence, the "+2" rule very likely popped right into your head.

It came to you instantly.

You didn't *arrive* at the "+2" rule by carefully weighing the evidence; your hunch wasn't the result of any conscious thinking at all. That's what we mean by "intuition"—the ideas that pop right into our heads, as it seems, instantly. *Before* we've had a chance to think about them consciously.

Of course, intuition only *feels* instant. In reality, a short lapse of time must pass before you can formulate it. In the lab, researchers have begun to understand what exactly happens in that split second it takes us to formulate a hunch. The specific order of events undergone in the human mind in the four-tenths of a second after it is exposed to a new stimulus is a subject of intense scientific research.[5] The pattern from recognition to searching for local emotional associations with the stimulus moves faster than our fastest thinking process. How we feel about a stimulus is available to our consciousness *before* we're able to have even a first thought about it.

What research has found is startling. The first step in this process takes barely two hundred milliseconds to play out—a fifth of a second. In that time, we compare the new cognition to our emotionally significant associations. The result of that comparison isn't a thought. It's an intuitive *feeling*.

This all happens much faster than the time it takes to form a conscious thought. It's counterintuitive, but research shows that we know how we *feel* about a new idea before we know what we *think* about it.

Given a second or two, we do indeed come up with reasons to back up our feelings. But those reasons come *after* the feeling. Their role is to justify and defend a conclusion we arrive at *before* we have thought about it. Reasoning takes the form of rationalization much more often than we like to admit to ourselves.

Grasping the implications of this glitch is the first key to understanding how charlatans earn their marks' trust.

Charlatans know people are always inclined to accept evidence to confirm their beliefs—indeed, we can't help it. That's why charlatans never set out to change a mark's beliefs. Persuasion never enters into the equation.

Instead, charlatans latch on to what their marks *already* believe, and they confirm those beliefs again and again. By doing so, they earn their marks' trust.

And it all happens before we've had time to *think*.

Motivated Reasoning

Confirmation bias isn't so much a single vulnerability in HumanOS as it is a whole family of vulnerabilities—in fact, while psychologists have proposed dozens of separate cognitive biases, some researchers argue that they all can be traced back to "the combination of a fundamental prior belief and humans' tendency toward belief-consistent information processing"—in effect, that every cognitive bias turns out to be some flavor of confirmation bias.[6]

Hundreds of studies show that even on matters for which nobody cares very much what the real answer is, people have a profound tendency to process new information in a way that's consistent with prior beliefs. But when you take people out of the realm of abstract reasoning and ask them about things they personally care about, that tendency becomes *much* more pronounced.

Indeed, confirmation bias seems to be optimized to work in the context of things we really do care about. Laboratory experiments show that strong feelings "arise automatically within a few milliseconds of exposure to a familiar sociopolitical object or event."[7]

These nearly instantaneous intuitive feelings are all the stronger when the object is emotionally powerful, and more so still when it's people's most cherished beliefs we're talking about. Confirmation bias is turbocharged when we're dealing with our *dreams*.

Charlatans know this, and they exploit it ruthlessly.

When their emotional commitments are in question, people are *strongly* motivated to process new information in ways that allow them to uphold their prior beliefs. That is why psychologists call it *motivated reasoning*—reasoning that works backward; from a desired conclusion we are motivated to search for the reasons we hold that conclusion.

Reason doesn't come out looking very reasonable in this interpretation of HumanOS, but the research is pretty emphatic about what happens when we try to reason about emotionally or politically motivated topics. Rather than being the driving force, reason is a "yes-man" to our intuitions. In Jonathan Haidt's version, reason acts like the "press secretary to our intuition": like a good press flack, its job is to look for evidence to make the boss look good. Our intuitions are firmly in charge; our reason comes in later to suggest why our intuition was right all along.[8]

We find it easy—indeed, effortless—to think up reasons why our intuition must be right, but painful and effortful to entertain the possibility that it might be wrong. To question our intuition takes what Daniel Kahneman calls *slow thinking*: a deliberate process that questions our intuition rather than pandering to it. Slow thinking is effortful. It's a slog. As for purposefully *seeking* to disconfirm our beliefs, people find it almost painful.

Fast thinking is never awkward. It is intuitive, automatic, effortless, and—most important—it is out of our conscious control. That very automaticity seems to be the source of its amazing power to lead us into error and keep us mired there.

Turns out that to enlist the power of fast thinking to his cause, all a charlatan has to do is espouse our dreams. To tell us boldly, passionately that they *can* come true and *will* come true. Due to confirmation bias, we trust people who do this before we quite know why, which is why reflecting marks' dreams back to them is step one in every charlatan's repertoire.

Motivated reasoning is "a central theoretical concept in academic discourse across the fields of psychology, political science, and mass communication."[9] When sensitive topics come up, we reliably fall into motivated reasoning's clutches in a number of ways: "Psychological research consistently demonstrates that [people] have an easier time recruiting evidence supporting what they want to be true than evidence supporting what they want to be false."[10] People also interpret the evidence before them in biased ways to support their preferred conclusion. When facing a proposition they want to agree with, they tend to ask themselves, "Can I believe this?" Of course, as Nicholas Epley and Thomas Gilovich note, "This evidentiary standard is rather easy to meet; after all, some evidence can usually be found even for highly dubious propositions."[11]

When faced with a proposition they would prefer to think is false, by contrast, they ask themselves, "*Must* I believe this? This evidentiary standard is harder to meet; after all, some contradictory evidence can be found for almost any proposition."[12]

What is true of social and moral ideas in general is doubly true when you ask people about their deepest commitments, about their *dreams*. Here, the effect becomes overwhelming, blinding us to incongruencies that seem wholly glaring to anyone who doesn't share our particular dream.

We begin to appreciate why, far from being recondite technical glitches in HumanOS, confirmation bias and motivated reasoning are key vulnerabilities that charlatans can exploit. These cognitive biases make us prone to systematic error—not just any kind of error, but the kind of grave, life-blighting blunder that charlatans talk us into again and again.

The literature on motivated thinking is almost as vast as that on confirmation bias, and it is every bit as depressing. Motivated-reasoning errors aren't just pervasive; they're serious. You can elicit them reliably by priming people to think in certain ways. The more you stress an idea's roots in a person's identity, the stronger the effect seems to get.

In a landmark 1979 study, researchers asked students at Stanford University if they tended to be in favor of or against the death penalty.[13] They then showed the subjects one of two articles—both fake—one seeming to show evidence in support of the death penalty's effectiveness, and another that seemed to show the death penalty didn't really deter crime. Like clockwork, students found the article that confirmed their beliefs convincing, strong, and accurate. But they found all manner of faults with the study that ran against the grain of their beliefs. The researchers concluded that subjects "are apt to accept 'confirming' evidence at face value while subjecting 'disconfirming' evidence to critical evaluation, and, as a result, draw undue support for their initial positions from mixed or random empirical findings."

Worse, by the end of the experiment, students who had been shown research that ran against their prior beliefs reported being *more* convinced of their original belief than at the start . . . as though being exposed to disconfirming evidence entrenched them deeper in their convictions. This finding came to be known as the "backfire effect," and it spawned its own research literature.[14]

The more that people are thinking in political terms, the stronger the effect seems to be. Prompt US Republicans to think of their partisan identity, for instance, and their evaluation of the US Affordable Care Act (better known as "Obamacare") is much more negative than if you prompt them to think about health issues.[15]

Politicians themselves are prone to the same effect: A study of Danish politicians found them clinging to previous beliefs just as tenaciously as the people who elect them. Worse, the more information they received, the more stubbornly they stuck by their prior beliefs.[16]

But we don't need a stack of academic papers to convince us of this. We just need a little introspection. It pains us to see the truths we've built our identity around being desecrated. It feels like a personal attack, an injury. It hurts. Our instinct is to fight back.

This is especially the case when our sense of identity derives from feeling as though we're part of a community of people who share that belief—one reason why many of the charlatans we describe in this book seem to veer into cult territory. People value that sense of membership in a tight-knit group of like-minded people.

Motivated reasoning has its roots in our identities. The more powerfully a person's identity is associated to a given claim, the stronger the pull of motivated reasoning, and the bigger an opportunity they present to a charlatan.

People *love* to see their own dreams championed, because they love to see their identity affirmed. Nothing is as convincing as someone telling us the truths at the root of our identity are vital and correct. This is the reason social media companies with a strong monetary incentive to keep our eyes glued to their pages know to pander to our dreams, to feed us content that confirms our most cherished beliefs.

We're suckers for it.

They've noticed.

Confirmation bias and motivated reasoning are HumanOS vulnerabilities with dire real-world consequences. How dire will become only too apparent as you read through the cases we'll discuss in the pages ahead. So central are these phenomena that you soon learn to see them as being much more than cognitive glitches, bugs in HumanOS. They are better thought of as the defense mechanism we deploy to defend our sense of identity: our deep-down, bottom-line sense of who we are and how the world works.

Social Proof

There's one more quirk in HumanOS we need to keep in mind to understand how charlatans get us. Like most cognitive biases, it's adaptive most of the time but can turn into a vulnerability, one that charlatans have used against us for centuries, and one that explains some of the strangest, most self-destructive behavior we'll see in the chapters to come.

Imagine this: You're walking down a busy New York City sidewalk when you notice a person staring up at a building across the road. What do you do? If you're like most people, you just keep right on walking. But what if it's a little group of five people looking up at a building? Now you're much more likely to stop. Intuitively, you sense that if they are all looking up, there must be something interesting to look at. What if fifteen people are looking up? Now you are *much* more likely to stop and look: the very fact that so many people are behaving this way becomes social proof—a powerful reason for you to copy them.

The original street-corner experiment that established social proof as a psychological concept dates all the way back to 1969.[17] In the decades since, social proof has been extensively studied—and much research has confirmed that herd mentality has a powerful influence on us. When we see people like us behaving in a certain way, we are much more likely to behave that way ourselves.

Studies have found evidence of the power of social proof in all kinds of unexpected places. One famous study showed that when you tell hotel guests that *most other* hotel guests reuse their towels before sending them to be washed, they're much more likely to reuse them than if you give them a message about the environmental costs of extra towel washing.[18]

Another well-known study found that by far the most effective message you can give someone to motivate them to vote is to tell them that most of their neighbors vote.[19]

In situations where the correct course of action is ambiguous, people look for clues in the behavior of people around them. The outcomes can be good, or they can be bad. One experiment, carried out at the Arizona Petrified Forest, showed how making bad behavior seem normal can encourage it. Experimenters put up signs asking people not to take petrified wood home from the park, adding that many park visitors had been ruining the natural beauty of the park by doing so. In the following weeks, three times as many visitors began stealing petrified wood from the park as before. When you make a behavior seem "normal," you encourage it, whether you want to or not.[20]

Of course, marketers have long grasped the way social proof can be used to juice sales—messages about how popular a product is have long proven effective in advertising. The entire ecosystem of online commerce—with its five-star ratings and its user reviews—works by digitizing social proof: giving us clues that purchasing a given product is "normal" for people like us.

It works! People are social creatures. We want to fit into our group, and copying the behavior of those around us is a surefire way to avoid standing out. Social proof, in other words, is built deep into HumanOS.

Alas, what we perceive as normal behavior can be manipulated or even manufactured, which means social proof introduces a vulnerability that can be hacked by malicious intruders. And this is something the most successful charlatans grasp intuitively. Their pitches, we'll see, very often feature claims about how the charlatan has benefited "people like you." These messages can be enormously effective at overcoming resistance to that first step in committing to the charlatan's message. And that first step is crucial, because charlatans have techniques up their sleeves to ensure that once it has been taken, it's the first of many.

Charlatans know they can't ask too much of a mark too soon, which is why they often structure their schemes to build gradually. Marketers call this "a commitment ladder": a succession of bigger and bigger requests made of customers . . . or of marks.

Commitment ladders work because once they've put their foot on the bottom rung, people will go to great lengths to avoid admitting they've made a mistake. It is always easier to climb one step up the ladder than to take one step down. Charlatans know this intuitively and leverage the phenomenon to their advantage.

They do this by gradually getting us to make larger and deeper commitments to them. In a well-thought-out commitment ladder, no step feels too great, each step feels safe, and at each step, it feels easier to go one step higher than to begin to climb down.

Charlatans know that as we climb higher and higher up the commitment ladder, the psychic cost associated with turning back keeps rising. Motivated reasoning ensures the ladder works to their advantage: once we're on it, it means we work harder and harder to convince ourselves that taking that step was the right decision.

Commitment ladders and social proof work hand in hand: commitment ladders are often structured to be public, with a community of fellow believers all traveling up the ladder together and urging one another on. When people we identify with decide to take one more step up the ladder, social proof reassures us that doing this makes sense for us too.

For the Venetian noblemen intrigued by Mamugnà's pitch, expressing skepticism about his claims was relatively low stakes at first. Once they'd climbed onto the commitment ladder, though, they found it devilishly hard to get off. Once they'd invited Mamugnà to their city, the psychic cost of admitting they'd been bamboozled began to build up. After they had put him up in one of the city's most famous palaces, it climbed higher still. As they gawked, dazzled, at his whiz-bang demonstration, the psychic cost of accepting they'd been duped kept climbing. And after they'd gone to a few of his balls and tried to entice him to marry one of their daughters, it had become unimaginable. Mamugnà manipulated the perception of what "people like you" (Venetian noblemen, in this case) *act* like, and when each Venetian senator saw all the other senators kowtowing to him, they did likewise: a startling example of the way social proof and commitment ladders work in tandem to lure people into making ever-worse decisions.

Commitment ladders work by locking people into defending a previous bad decision by making a subsequent decision that's even worse. On each rung, the mark's determination to avoid the anguish of admitting they've been bamboozled grows. As it does, the mental gymnastics they'll be willing to undertake to defend their initial choice will grow ever more contorted. As long as they continue to see other people "like them" defer to the charlatan, they'll let that social proof guide them.

In this book we will introduce charlatans who expertly craft commitment ladders and use social-proof techniques to get their marks on board. The techniques work as well today as they did 450 years ago.

These three closely related vulnerabilities—confirmation bias, motivated reasoning, and social proof—are all you need to understand why people have fallen prey to charlatans with such regularity across the centuries. The pleasure we get from feeling we're right and the pain we get from feeling we're wrong are some of the most thoroughly studied features of human cognition. But they induce us to commit some errors again and again, predictably. They create vulnerabilities that a skilled attacker can turn against us. And that, we will show you, is what charlatans do.

And this is the real answer to the question we began with: Why are we so gullible? Faced with stories of people being led to do self-destructive things in defense of patently absurd beliefs, we can't help but ask ourselves, "How could anyone have persuaded them to do something so stupid?"

By now, you should have a hunch about the answer to that question. Persuasion plays no part in it. The one thing no skilled charlatan will ever do is try to change your mind. Charlatans manipulate us not by getting us to change our prior beliefs but by pandering to them. They earn our trust by championing our priors—they hold us prisoners inside a cell made of our own commitments.

Picture Mamugnà in his opulent Venetian palace. He took in the entire elite of a major (if declining) European power without ever really having to persuade anyone of anything. Venice's senators gave him all the material he needed to work with in the form of their prior beliefs. They were *already* convinced iron could be turned into gold. They desperately wanted to avoid facing the reality that Venice's glory days were in the past. And once treating Mamugnà with deference became the "done thing" among their group, each of them joined the herd, reasoning that if everyone else was doing it, it must be right.

All Mamugnà had to do was reflect his marks' dream back to them. He championed their dream. He did it charismatically, eloquently, and persistently. The more he championed their dream, the more they wanted to believe him.

And the more they believed him, the more power he had over them.

That, in short, is the *structure* of every charlatan story—the universal grammar of the charlatan's craft. Charlatans never seek to persuade anyone; they don't need to. They don't want to. They know they can't. Persuasion is never the point.

Charlatans grasp that they sound preposterous to those who don't share the dream they build their act around. That doesn't matter to them. All that matters is that they champion a dream that some section of the public sees as central to their identity.

Championing the mark's dream creates a powerful sense of identification. It primes marks for what comes next. It leaves them ready to believe that the charlatan really is *special*, that he has some unique insight into the true nature of things that eludes lesser mortals. So, when he makes a claim to special knowledge or special power, he finds a group of people ready to believe.

Once our dreams have been hacked in this way, we become our own worst enemies: people unable to distinguish our own interests from our exploiter's interests. In the pages ahead, we will show you how this formula can be applied to any kind of dream. Virtuous dreams and vicious ones. Widespread dreams and others that are quite specific. It really doesn't matter what the dream is.

What Is a Charlatan?

The time has now come for us to propose a definition: A charlatan is a public figure who manipulatively champions the dream that a group of people share in order to exploit them without overt coercion, turning those marks into enthusiastic participants in their own exploitation.

This definition is both broad and narrow. It's broad in that it encompasses the wide variety of different types of charlatans we have compiled in the following chapters. It includes both wholesale charlatans who cast their nets wide and exploit an entire nation and retail charlatans happy to burrow deep into the lives of a handful of followers. It includes both convicted criminals and those whose conduct stays within the bounds of the law.

But it's also narrow in helping us see who a charlatan is *not*. A charlatan is different from a fraudster in that he's a public figure: the people you'll meet in this book don't need to use pseudonyms or fake identities. They do not hide; they are out in the open, often operating in an ambiguous gray area between legitimacy and illegality. And their marks are not just passive victims of a con; they are evangelists for the charlatan's gospel. Time and again, we'll see marks turn out to be a charlatan's biggest asset: his top recruiting agents and his most loyal defenders.

If this kind of exploitation reappears century after century, in all kinds of different settings and guises, it is because the mechanisms this formula exploits are here to stay. The glitches charlatans exploit are deeply ingrained in HumanOS; the whole organization of human cognition renders us vulnerable to them.

Having laid down the theory, we're ready to dive in. The charlatans we'll meet throughout the rest of the book are all quite different on the surface, but they're very similar deeper down.

2

The Dark Side of Entrepreneurship

EVERYONE HAS, AT ONE POINT OR ANOTHER, DREAMED OF WHAT IT would be like to be rich. Poor people do it, middle-class people do it, even rich people dream of what it would be like to be richer still. And where there's a dream, there'll be charlatans looking to bamboozle those who share it.

Like all dreams, this one has its roots in a legitimate human need. We all need resources to live, and more to thrive. Those resources are scarce, and to get them we need money—nothing could be more natural, therefore, than to strive to make that money.

That striving becomes a dream to some. In fact, few dreams are older. The get-rich-quick fantasy sustains lotteries and casinos around the world. In the hands of a charlatan, widely shared dreams like these make for an inviting target.

And so charlatans have been pitching marks on get-rich-quick schemes for as long as marks have been around. When they do so, they nearly always accomplish this by pretending to be what they're not: legitimate entrepreneurs.

It's the perfect cover. Entrepreneurs have an excellent image in today's world. Entrepreneurship is widely recognized for what it is: the engine that drives the prosperity of modern societies. Convince people you're a legitimate entrepreneur with a special system for making a lot of cash, and they'll line up around the block to hand you their money.

For the ordinary person, telling a legitimate entrepreneur apart from a charlatan is not easy. From afar, the two can look remarkably similar. The skills you need to succeed as an entrepreneur are awfully useful to a charlatan. To succeed, entrepreneurs need to be original thinkers who are also highly charismatic and comfortable taking risks. They need to be leaders as well as gifted at selling a dream. In the hands of ethical people, these traits are a huge engine of human progress. In the hands of charlatans, they're the road to ruin.

Today's charlatans can't succeed without an entrepreneurial streak.

And, indeed, in some ways the two are similar: both legitimate entrepreneurs and business charlatans are in it to try to make as much money as possible.

But there's a difference. Entrepreneurs understand they need to create something of value to the people they sell to. Charlatans focus on creating the impression of something of value, often with little regard for the substance needed to sustain that impression.

In this chapter, we're going to look in detail at three charlatans who ended up in trouble for promoting dreams of quick riches they must, at some point, have realized they could never deliver on. We're going to present them in order of scale: from the young Turkish IT visionary who scammed patriotic Turks out of tens of millions of dollars, to the would-be Hollywood hunk who scammed investors out of hundreds of millions, to a giant of world finance now accused of leaving some of the world's most sophisticated investors *billions* worse off.

These are three very different figures in some ways, yet their stories are eerily similar. In all three cases the charlatan ended up pulling off some version of a family of scams that shall forever be associated with one Italian ne'er-do-well. To understand what they did, we have to start by understanding what he did.

Charles Ponzi

He was born in a small town in Italy's northern Emilia-Romagna region and christened Carlo Pietro Giovanni Guglielmo Tebaldo Ponzi, but history would come to know him as Charles Ponzi. At first glance there was little to set him apart from the hundreds of thousands of Italians who were pouring into the United States each year at the start of the twentieth century. A law school dropout, he hustled his way around banks in the United States and Canada for a few years, refining in his mind the sprawling fraud that would forever bear his name.

Ponzi realized he was surrounded by struggling Italian immigrants who were under intense pressure to make money quickly to help the loved ones they'd left in dire poverty back in the old country. Their dream to make money fast was grounded in a real, pressing need, and Charles Ponzi sensed that by manipulating it, he could get them to hand over all the money they had.

He pitched them on a complicated investment scheme few of them could really grasp. He was careful to pay out eye-popping dividends to his early investors. Their stories got around and brought in many, many new investors. The catch was that the money he was paying out wasn't coming out of profits, but directly out of the cash he was raising from new investors. This worked great until he ran out of new investors to keep pumping cash into his ruse. It was nothing but a giant pyramid scheme. When it all collapsed—as pyramid schemes must—it left thousands of poor investors even poorer than they had been going in.

Often forgotten in the story of Ponzi's exploits is that at the outset, he did indeed have a nugget of a sound business idea. He had come up with a legal idea that, in the hands of an honest man, could have been the basis of a moderately profitable business.

Back in the era of mass European immigration to the United States—the 1910s and '20s—people wrote letters to family in the old country as the only way of staying in touch. But international postage was expensive. Poor relations back in Europe would often be financially hard-pressed, upon receiving mail from a brother or son in America, to pay for the postage needed to write back. To address this, postal systems on both sides of the Atlantic introduced a system of international reply coupons (IRCs). The coupons enabled the sender of a letter to pay for the cost of replying to that letter: a popular, welcome, and fully legal service.

Charles Ponzi was the first to realize that the IRC system could be profitably hacked. European currencies had lost much of their value in the wake of the Great War, but the relative prices of IRCs had remained pegged at yesteryear's exchange rates. Ponzi quickly caught on that you could buy an IRC in Naples for much less money than the identical IRC cost in New York.

Doing the math, Ponzi realized that in Italy, one dollar would buy you the same number of IRCs you'd need two dollars to buy in the United States. To turn a profit, all he'd have to do is buy IRCs in bulk in Europe, ship them to America, and turn them into US postage at the prevailing American rate—allowed by IRC rules—then sell the stamps at their face value.

Nothing about this idea was illegal, and, in principle, the profits to be had from this kind of arbitrage are large, not to mention risk free.

To make it all work, Ponzi would need money up front—and to get it, he had to offer investors eye-watering returns.

He quickly amassed an investment pot—$1,800 from eighteen investors—and just as quickly realized the actual logistics of transferring that money to Italy, using it to buy IRCs, shipping the IRCs back to the States, and selling them as postage would be a terrible hassle. It took a long time and quite a bit of complicated office work.

Time was short, though. Ponzi needed to show his early investors returns right away to attract more money and maybe, just maybe, he thought he could fake it 'til he made it: pay off the first investors with money from later investors rather than with profits from the IRC scheme. That would be much simpler. Only once he started doing that, stopping doing it proved devilishly hard.

To be clear, many Ponzi schemes are just straight-up criminal frauds from the word go. Charles Ponzi, for one, seems to have been fully aware that he was running a scam from the start.

Others, though, slide into criminality almost despite themselves: a slick entrepreneur with more ambition than scruples starts out with a business idea he believes in but soon realizes the illusion of a good business is much easier to deliver than the real thing.

It's no wonder charlatans reliably end up at the heads of schemes like these: fueled by dreams, fed by words, watered by the cash of dupes, Ponzi schemes are perfect for people with big dreams and even bigger charisma.

People, in other words, like Mehmet Aydın.

Mehmet Aydın

The first thing everybody notices about Mehmet Aydın is his baby face. It's not just that he's a chubby guy; it's that his face has a certain *look*, all round and soft and cherubic, and he just looks like he wouldn't hurt a fly. Aydın knew his face could be his superpower: an instantly irrefutable proof of his good intentions.

But there was always more to Aydın than his aw-shucks dimples. Deep inside, he was a bad boy. Before he bought his Ferrari and his yacht, before his company set off a craze that gripped all of Turkey, before he became a household name in his country and an obsession of tabloid journalists, before all that, from around 2012, Mehmet Aydın had a dream: to become a Turkish hip-hop superstar.

He didn't have a lot going for him: a twentysomething religious-school dropout from a small provincial city in Turkey doesn't have an obvious entry point into show business. Making it takes money, and he didn't have any. To make some, he reportedly dabbled with peddling phony "X-ray glasses" that supposedly showed people naked, but he soon realized this was a dead end.[1] So, he got by on dishwashing jobs or waiting on tables at a café in town. He'd get back home late, tired, and lay down some rap tracks on his laptop before heading to sleep.[2]

That, or he'd play FarmVille.

Do you remember FarmVille? It was all the rage on Facebook back in 2013–2015. Technically described as a "farming simulator," FarmVille let bored people all over the world dream of their own pastoral future. For a kid like Mehmet, who grew up in a farming family in Bursa, two hours south of Istanbul, there was something soothing about this digital rural idyll: like a slice of the most comforting memories of his childhood served up in digital form.

Soon, Aydın got to thinking. FarmVille wasn't bad, but something was missing. It was all digital, all plastic, all fake. There weren't any real cows there, or crops, or chickens—just pixels. What if, he thought, you could have a FarmVille that came with a real-world counterpart? What if the cows on the screen were digital representations, screen doubles of real cows on a real pasture on a real farm in the real world?

If FarmVille were addictive, wouldn't a real-world FarmVille be ten times more addictive?

Aydın didn't know how to program a computer game, but he had friends who did. Soon, the chubby kid with big hip-hop dreams was running a little squad of coders putting together a FarmVille clone. On the surface, Çiftlik Bank—Turkish for Farm Bank—was little more than a FarmVille rip-off; the functionality for tending to digital crops and livestock was lifted more or less straight from their competitor. But Farm Bank would be different, because it would have a real-world dimension. The company announced it would run real farms, which Farm Bank players could invest in by putting real-world money into their fake-world app. And, in what should have been the first red flag, players would also receive a small real-money payoff for each new player they brought into Farm Bank.[3]

Launched early in 2016, Çiftlik Bank was a hit. The game was fun, and word soon got around that the money you could make from the farm side was mind-blowing. Early investors would get fat checks in the mail once a month: the dividends, they were told, from Farm Bank's real-world farming operation. It all seemed real enough: the company's young CEO, Mehmet Aydın, was in the media cutting ribbons on big commercial farms. The events were lavishly covered in the media: photos showed the young, rosy-cheeked Aydın flanked by provincial officials cutting ceremonial ribbons on muddy farm fields.

And it wasn't just the farms; it was the distribution network too. All around Turkey, Farm Bank produce stands were popping up. For about 100,000 Turkish lira (some $30,000 at the time), you could buy a Farm Bank franchise and open up a shop selling sausage, cheese, butter, honey, and other Turkish farm staples.

The products all bore Farm Bank's unmistakably Facebookesque logo: a big-eyed cartoon cow on a lush farm surrounded by jagged mountain peaks. At its height in 2017, there were 150 Farm Bank deli counters slinging cheese that supposedly came from the company's farms. (None of it did.) And Farm Bank investors were getting their dividends in two streams: 95 percent was in cash, and the other 5 percent was in coupons, to be spent at Farm Bank deli counters.

Mehmet Aydın would later claim that he'd never intended for things to get so far out of hand: he was just a farm boy who'd dreamed of making a fun new way for Turks to invest in their country's agriculture. Maybe so. But if so, that original dream did not last long in the face of the torrent of money that soon started flooding his way.

All through 2016 and 2017, Farm Bank grew at a startling rate. The company Aydın founded prized growth in membership above everything else, and for good reason. In good old Ponzi style, he was paying old investors' dividends directly out of the money new investors were putting in. And when you're in Ponziville, the prime directive is clear: keep the dream going as long as you can and keep new investors coming in at any cost.

Farm Bank invested heavily in advertising online and made sure each new player knew full well they would get paid for bringing in still more players. When that proved not enough, the company went on TV, putting up slickly produced commercials that sold the Farm Bank dream to the masses.

Farm Bank's marketing hardly touched the computer-game side of the business. Instead, they targeted young Turkish city dwellers' dreams of reconnecting with the *real* Turkey—that is, rural Turkey. Idealized images of the Turkish countryside were the center of Farm Bank's pitch.

For one commercial, the company got Turkish movie legend Mehmet Çevik as a pitchman. The rotund Çevik plays a good, honest, salt-of-the-earth Anatolian farmer gravely advising his son, a round-faced but serious-looking child who very much resembled the way Aydın must have looked at ten or eleven.

"Listen to me, son," the wise old farmer says, amid a verdant field against a dazzling blue sky, "if you care about the country and the nation, your goal must be clear, your horizons wide, your heart as vast as the blue sky, and you must stand tall!"

The camera zooms in on the earnest farmer as he puts his hand on his child's shoulder and cinematic music soars. "You will face obstacles. They will try to trip you up, but don't fall, don't you fall down and don't ever give in."[4]

If Aydın was a mountebank, these TV commercials were his soapbox. He'd put his finger on something important: a prior belief he could exploit. Millions of urban people in Turkey were nostalgic for the rural lives they had known as children or heard about from their parents. They had an idealized vision of life on the farm. *That*, they felt, was the real Turkey. They *believed* that to be a real Turk, you needed a connection with that old-fashioned world of hard toil on the land. Messages that affirmed that belief felt true to them before they had even thought about them. Their intuition filter was primed to accept the message Aydın was peddling, which meant he could just let confirmation bias do all the heavy lifting.

To hear many of his victims tell it, it was the commercial featuring that beloved movie star Mehmet Çevik that really launched Farm Bank into the consciousness of everyday Turks. Folks could no more imagine that something promoted by such a familiar, reassuring figure could be anything but honest than you could doubt Nespresso after seeing George Clooney selling it. (Çevik himself was not accused of wrongdoing in relation to the scandal.)

All Farm Bank's TV ads leaned hard into Turkey's tradition of agrarian nationalism. One featured archival clips of Kemal Atatürk, the almost mythical founder of the modern Turkish state, speaking to supporters in the 1920s. "The Turkish nation is hardworking!" Atatürk roars in the scratchy archival clip. "The Turkish nation is intelligent!"

Then a modern-day announcer declares in ponderous tones, "Turkey's proud brand Çiftlik Bank is taking firm steps toward becoming a global brand, transforming its gains in the gaming industry into real investments in the agriculture and livestock sector," he says, as the screen is festooned with images of state-of-the-art farming facilities.

"As we compete with global giants in the online gaming industry," the ad continues, "we are making new investments every day into the lands that brought us into existence. We will continue to be a source of confidence and stability for the Turkish economy as we share the excitement of producing together."

People loved it, and Farm Bank grew and grew, raking in cash as it looked to expand internationally.

By mid-2017, Aydın had launched versions of the app in Germany and Azerbaijan. He traveled to Argentina and Uruguay and discussed setting up a team to develop a Spanish-language version of the app. Farm Bank had been born digital, viral, and scalable: he now seemed determined to make it global too, an unstoppable juggernaut. At its head, the twenty-six-year-old Aydın was becoming a poster boy for a vision of a peculiarly Turkish take on the successful tech CEO: innovative, daring, but still rooted in the country's rural heartland and its conservative values.

All the while, Aydın was doing what Charles Ponzi had done almost a hundred years earlier: paying earlier investors directly from the cash put in by new ones. Farm Bank's word-of-mouth reputation was, consequently, excellent. Who wouldn't want to be involved with a fun, patriotic game that made you rich on the side? It was win-win.

To insiders, it all looked very different. Cudi Cumhur Yurdakul, Farm Bank's then twenty-seven-year-old lead software developer, began to think something was off as he noticed Aydın's spending was out of control. He spotted an internal report that said Aydın had paid $162,000 to charter a private jet to fly him and three others from Montevideo, Uruguay, back to Istanbul, including a $10,000 surcharge to allow his wife to smoke cigarettes on board.[5] Aydın seemed to be buying mansions, yachts, and luxury cars left and right, a lifestyle that just didn't seem to square with his public persona as a serious-minded son of Turkey's farming stock.

Nothing matters more for a Ponzi scheme than to keep more and more new people investing for as long as possible: so long as there's a steady stream of new investors, there's always more money around to satisfy earlier investors. This dependence is what makes them so damn sensitive to any negative press that might scare off newcomers. And that's precisely what happened in November 2017, when the government-aligned newspaper *Sabah* started asking hard questions about Farm Bank's finances.

Sabah noted that the company's accounts were registered to shell companies and based in banks in Turkish-controlled Northern Cyprus. Turks know very well that Northern Cyprus is a notorious money-laundering hub, the kind of place where you set up a company if you want to obscure its finances. At this, the Turkish authorities finally took notice. Inspectors from the Ministry of Customs and Trade began to look into the firm's finances. The minute that happened, Farm Bank's collapse was foretold.

Remarkably, Aydın was still "opening" new dairy farms as late as December 2017, inviting provincial officials to photo ops to cut ribbons—in reality, these were existing commercial farms his company was buying and leaving under preexisting management.

But trouble was in the air.

Payments to the branded delis where Farm Bank investors thought they were buying products of Farm Bank farms simply stopped without explanation. By February 2018, with the flow of new investors slowing to a trickle, Farm Bank had fallen far behind on payments to its early investors too. Consumer-complaint websites started to get floods of complaints from defrauded Farm Bank players.

By early March 2018, the Ministry of Customs and Trade inspectors had enough evidence to show that Farm Bank was a fraudulent enterprise. But they moved too slowly. By then, Mehmet Aydın had skipped town, allegedly taking $80 million worth of investor money with him.

It was at this point that the Turkish media went into an all-out frenzy of wall-to-wall Farm Bank coverage. Police raids on Farm Bank's few actually operating farms received blanket coverage, with live news feeds showing cops seizing Aydın's chickens.

Meanwhile, all kinds of rumors circulated as Aydın's whereabouts became an obsession for Turks. He'd been spotted in Ukraine! No, he's in Panama! No, Canada! Lies, we just spotted him in Honduras! All wrong, he'd jumped out of a high-rise window! Fake news exploded as the whole country seemed consumed with a new game even more addictive than Farm Bank: Where in the world is Mehmet Aydın?[6]

And the gossip in the papers about Aydın's lifestyle just kept getting more lurid. As reported by an investigation in the news site Rest of World, his bodyguard alleged Aydın engaged in cocaine-fueled gambling binges in Northern Cyprus, capped off by alleged trysts with prostitutes. The reports deepened people's certainty that he'd run off there. The same bodyguard alleged that he and his family had been ripped off by Farm Bank too, investing the equivalent of $47,000 and getting just $34,000 out before the firm collapsed.[7]

In reality, Aydın was where you might have expected him to be: in one of the places he'd been scoping out as sites for new Farm Bank franchises.

In March, a Turkish expat in Montevideo, Uruguay, spotted that unmistakable baby face recklessly driving a brand-new white Ferrari and caught him on a cell phone video: the first clear new evidence of where he was.[8]

So, Aydın skipped town again.

By the end of March 2018 Aydın seemed unsure whether to try to clear his name or lay low, vacillating between the two strategies. He put out long, rambling audio recordings where he protested his innocence, said he'd never meant to defraud anyone, blamed Farm Bank's troubles on his employees, and promised to stay and pay back everyone who'd invested in his company.

By then, Interpol had issued a Red Letter, putting police forces around the world on notice to arrest Aydın wherever he may be. Farm Bank's ripped-off investors banded together to hire an investigator to scour the world for their man. It took some time—Aydın seems to have taken the hint in Uruguay and toned down his spending—but soon after, he was located in a posh suburb of São Paulo, Brazil. Then the investors published his address.

Feeling the net tightening around him, Aydın surrendered to the Turkish consulate in São Paulo on July 1, 2020. He was quickly sent back to Turkey, where he told investigators that Uruguayan officials had seized his Ferrari and his yacht. All the money he had left, he said, was the thirteen dollars in cash in his wallet. In just two years Farm Bank had allegedly swindled some $250 million from 132,000 investors. Aydın had purportedly pocketed some $80 million of it . . . and seems to have burned through all of it in just three years.[9]

A true feat of charlatanry. But he did not get away with it in the end. In February 2025, he was sentenced to more than 45,370 years in prison.[10]

Zach Horwitz

Of course, there are as many types of business charlatans as there are dreams of getting rich quickly. Mehmet Aydın found his niche playing to high-minded ideas of patriotism of rural renewal, messages that hijacked the HumanOS his marks were running, letting him manipulate their brains to his benefit. But others begin with simpler dreams, like the basic, childlike wonder movie stars engender.

Take Zach Horwitz. As a teenager in Fort Wayne, Indiana, Zach turned heads with his movie-star looks. But why stop at turning heads? What Horwitz wanted more than anything in the world was to become an *actual* Hollywood movie star. He knew his chances were one in a million, and he soon turned that into his personal motto: "When your chances are one in a million, be the one."

In early 2011, after graduating from Indiana University with a degree in psychology, Zach moved to Chicago to open up a health-oriented juice-bar-and-sandwich-shop chain, serving things like grilled eggplant, roasted red pepper, arugula, fresh mozzarella, and grated Parmesan sandwiches (just 474 calories!). He named it FÜL, opened up a first location on Chicago's North Broadway, and brought in a nutritionist to give customers consultations (and sell them supplements). From the outside, it may have looked just like another struggling little sandwich shop, but Horwitz dreamed of franchising it and taking it national.[11]

Sooner than anyone would have dreamed, his business genius began to be recognized. One day toward the end of 2011, Horwitz came home excited to show his girlfriend Mallory the email that would change their lives forever. It was from Maveron, the billion-dollar venture capital fund run by Howard Schultz. Yes, *the* Howard Schultz—the fabulously wealthy and hyperconnected visionary behind the success of Starbucks.

It was an odd email. Maveron seemed interested not so much in FÜL but in its founder. They wanted to invest in *his* future. In fact, what they were offering him was a job: lucrative, glamorous, and . . . based in Los Angeles. It was a dream opportunity; he couldn't imagine passing it up. So, FÜL folded just six months after it opened, and Horwitz and his girlfriend went off to Los Angeles.

Horwitz had always dreamed of being in the movies, so in LA he found a way to juggle his demanding new job at Maveron with classes at a "Business of Acting" boot camp, marketed to LA newcomers as a way of jump-starting their Hollywood dreams. Now, if the idea that you can juggle both a highly lucrative, highly demanding venture capital job while simultaneously pursuing an intensive actor's training program seems far-fetched, that's because it is.

In fact—and this would become clear only much later—there was no Maveron job. There never had been. The emails from Howard Schultz's company were just the first of what would become a long string of fabricated emails and documents in Horwitz's path. He faked it, it seems, because he needed a ploy to get his girlfriend, Mallory, to agree to move to LA with him.

But it would be okay, he told himself, because he'd make it big in Hollywood soon enough. The plan was simple: he'd have to fake it 'til he made it.

Step one was to get himself a screen name. Professionally, Zach Horwitz would be Zach Avery. Step two would be to get himself some partners—in this case, Mexican director brothers Julio and Diego Hallivis—and launch a production company.

In their mission statement, they made it official company policy: "We believe that when odds are one in a million, we must be that one." The company's name? 1inMM Productions.

Hollywood trade publications covered their plans: "We created 1inMM Productions to produce high concept genre films with an edgy and unique approach to storytelling," the Hallivis brothers were quoted as telling *Deadline* in a statement.[12] Horwitz, for his part, told *Variety* they were "particularly interested in commercially viable horror, action, sci-fi and thriller titles."

In 2013, they teamed up with a Miami-based firm run by a former Fox executive to launch a partnership "aimed at acquiring English-language feature films to distribute throughout all Latin American countries via theatrical and other release platforms."[13] They talked the talk, and they walked the walk.

But Zach Avery wasn't about to take his eye off the ball. Licensing dubbed movies for the Latin American market was all well and good as a way to raise cash, but the purpose of raising the cash was to make Zach Avery a massive international movie star. And 1inMM got to work. In 2014, the company financed its first production very much starring Zach Avery. It was a sci-fi short called *Shifter*, directed by Diego Hallivis. Zach plays James Striker, who transfers his consciousness into a clone to bring down the oppressive government that has crushed all freedom in the United States.[14]

It was terrible. Nobody saw it.

There's some good evidence that Zach and the Hallivis brothers did their level best to turn 1inMM into the real deal in the early years. The company produced six low-budget features in its first two years, mostly horror and sci-fi titles aiming at a broad audience. All of them flopped.

Then, something seems to have shifted. Maybe Zach concluded that his films were flopping because they weren't big enough. Those small budgets made for films that looked small on the screen. If you wanted to be a big-time star, you needed big-time production values. Films that *look* expensive *are* expensive, though. So, Zach would need more money. And to get it, he'd have to lie on a whole new scale.

Zach had been eyeing the licensing market for Latin America for a while. To be clear, this is a legitimate business model: plenty of real companies do it. They scout the land for inexpensively produced movies, buy the rights, bundle them, and then sell licensing deals to TV channels or movie-theater chains abroad to show them in markets worldwide. If you've ever watched a low-budget American film in a hotel room in Mexico or Algeria or Sri Lanka, chances are this is how it got there: somebody bought the rights and sold them on to a local broadcaster.

But it's a brutally competitive market, and margins tend to be skinny. There's plenty of content out there to choose from, and buyers are sophisticated: they're not going to overspend on some crappy film for no reason. So, the business turned out to be a lot less profitable than Zach had dreamed. But the *illusion* of the business, well . . . that's something else altogether.

Soon Zach reached out to his old pal Jake Wunderlin. They were college friends from back in the day at the leafy Indiana University campus in Bloomington. Jake was by then working for the wealth-management division at J.P. Morgan in Chicago; he seemed to have done pretty well for himself.[15] Zach could smell the money there. He pitched Jake the licensing deals he said he was working on. Not the real licensing deals, you see, but fully fake ones, with the likes of HBO and Netflix, to license content to Spanish-speaking markets in Latin America. He said the deals were already in place. He said he could share the paperwork on demand.

Then he moved in for the kill, promising Wunderlin a stunning 35 percent return on his investment in just one quarter. He said he would personally guarantee the investment: if anything went wrong, he'd pay him back from his own account.

Zach knew Jake well enough to zero in on his dream: wealth, big-time wealth. But more than that, the kind of glamorous wealth that comes from the box office, through connections with a bona fide Hollywood star!

Now, how a sophisticated financial professional could have been snookered by a pitch like this is hard to say: 35 percent in three months is not the kind of return any one can reasonably expect to make outside the cocaine industry. But Horwitz showed him the licensing agreements—fully fake, but credible-enough looking. Plus, they were old friends. They'd known each other for ages. Jake figured he'd stumbled onto an amazing opportunity. Zach played on Jake's fear of missing out and spun a tale in which Zach was the hero for spotting a killer deal before anyone else had. So, Jake ponied up $37,000. And sure enough, three months later, he got his first $13,000 payment.

It's here that confirmation bias kicks in: Zach had given Jake solid evidence that this deal was as juicy as he'd said, in the form of that first $13,000 check. People *love* to have their dreams confirmed, and that payment was all the evidence Jake Wunderlin would need. Soon, another licensing deal followed, and it was bigger, for $300,000. Wunderlin had to tap some of his friends and family to raise a sum that size. But that one paid off too, and big.

It's the pattern we see so often in these kinds of scams: a commitment ladder. Guys like Horwitz "test the waters" first with a smaller commitment, a chance to demonstrate they are the real deal. Then they gradually ratchet it up. Commitment ladders proceed one small step at a time, with each step creating proof to confirm the mark had been "right" in trusting the charlatan. After a few cycles of this, as previously discussed, confirmation bias does all the heavy lifting. In this way, starting off with a smallish bet, charlatans build trust and solidarity with their marks by showing early results. If the bet comes up good, confirmation bias takes care of the rest. The mark will make a bigger bet, and if that one comes up good too, they will go even bigger. By the third or fourth rung on the escalation ladder, they have become a *believer*. By this point, they are all in. Admitting they've been snookered from day one is so unpleasant that people go to great lengths to avoid it. Charlatans know to rely on that mechanism.

It works on rubes. It works on finance executives. It just works.

And Jake Wunderlin, well, he was *all* in. From early 2015, Wunderlin would become the first of a series of "bundlers" looking out for upstream investors to pump money into Horwitz's production scheme. With his Chicago finance background, Wunderlin knew how to tap capital. He quit his day job to work full time on a partnership whose only goal was to funnel money to 1inMM. Over the course of Zach's Ponzi scheme, Jake Wunderlin's fundraising network would pour a staggering $485 *million* into 1inMM.

It didn't take Zach very long to figure out that he didn't have to be a movie star to live like one. With 1inMM attracting unprecedented amounts of cash, it behooved him to look the part of the massively successful Hollywood insider. By now, you won't be surprised to hear that high up on the list of priorities were the private jet flights—there's *always* a private jet! Those set him back $137,000. He spent another $125,000 on trips to Vegas. Then there were the luxury cars ($165,000); the six-bedroom, eight-bathroom Beverlywood mansion with a screening room, a gym, and a one-thousand-bottle wine cellar ($5.7 million); the luxury-watch subscription service ($55,000); the courtside seats for Lakers games ($5,000); and the bottle service he once tried to tip a waitress for . . . the works (another $5,000).[16]

You might think this was just Horwitz living it up, but it's not quite like that. Zach needed to project success. It was an imperative. Who's going to invest millions of dollars on a guy driving a seven-year-old Honda Civic? Lavish spending isn't just a perk of Ponzi scheming; it's a requirement.

Throughout, Zach Avery had been landing small parts in increasingly credible commercial films. He played a small part in *The White Crow*, a Ralph Fiennes biopic about Russian ballet legend Rudolf Nureyev. And, of course, he kept starring in terrible horror films that 1inMM paid for and nobody wanted to see.

Horwitz still seemed to be banking on movie stardom as the ticket out of the huge financial hole he was quickly digging himself into. Small parts in big films weren't doing the trick, but big parts in small films weren't working either. What he needed, he thought, was a *lead* role in a movie alongside some proper Hollywood stars.

The only problem, it soon became clear, was that Zach Avery is a *terrible* actor. In an interview with the *New Yorker*'s Evan Osnos, whose reporting we follow closely on this account, one colleague described sharing a scene with Zach Avery as being like interacting with a banana.[17]

He seemed to have calculated he could get around that little inconvenience with money—1inMM investor money, of course.

Zach had a movie-business friend, Andrew Levitas, who wanted to launch a production company but needed some cash for it. He came up with $21 million (from his investors, of course) at the ready. They cofounded Rogue Black, and when it came time to cast Rogue Black's first big movie in 2018 . . . well, guess who got the lead role?[18]

Last Moment of Clarity was billed as a neo-noir thriller lavishly shot on location in Paris and LA.[19] The plot surrounded a mafia hit on Sam's (Zach Avery) beautiful young fiancée . . . except, is she really dead? A brooding Avery is shown broodingly brooding in chic Parisian locales, working at a café run by Gilles, played by Brian Cox. Yes, *the* Brian Cox, the acclaimed actor who would play Logan Roy on the HBO megahit *Succession*.

The murdered-but-possibly-not-quite-dead fiancée was played by the stunning Australian A-lister Samara Weaving. Udo Kier played one of the bad guys. These were proper, bankable Hollywood celebrities, all playing roles supporting . . . Zach Avery.

Looking back, this was the make-or-break moment for 1inMM. Zach needed *Last Moment of Clarity* to be a runaway Hollywood blockbuster if he was going to have any hope of freeing himself from the layers of lies he had told. He seemed to have done everything right: the budget was ample, the costars were big, the locations were stunning, the plot was a proven moneymaker. He'd worked so hard for his breakout role. Here it was.

It had better have worked, because Zach's finances were by now on the brink.

By the end of 2019 Zach could boast of having raised $358 million that year alone.[20] Yet Horwitz was facing the fate that awaits every Ponzi scheme: the well of new investors inevitably runs dry, and the company has no real income-generating assets, or not nearly enough, so payments stop. And boy, did they stop.

By Thanksgiving 2019 he was having trouble paying early investors. Amazingly—and this detail is a real testament to his grift—Horwitz managed to keep the wheels turning on his scheme for another *six months* after that. He parried, lied, and deflected, telling his investors *his* clients—Netflix and HBO—were the ones who were late paying him. Then the pandemic hit in March 2020, giving Horwitz another rich vein of excuses to mine. The following month Mallory gave birth to their second child.

More excuses! More stringing along!

Zach just needed a *little* more time: *Last Moment of Clarity* was just about to be released. When it went megahuge at the box office, new money would flow. New roles would flow. Success begets success and cash begets cash, and this film was going to turn everything around for them.

The only problem was *the* problem with every 1inMM production: the movie was, once again, awful. Separate critics landed on the same line to pan it: Hitchschlockian. Rather than taking inspiration from old Hitchcock masterpieces like *Rear Window*, *Last Moment of Clarity* seemed to straight-up copy them. The plot twists were so obviously telegraphed that critics rolled their eyes. And Zach's performance . . . well, the less said about it, the better.

The review in the *Guardian* was unsparing:

> Zach Avery must be either very well financed or ridiculously persuasive because they've managed to pull together a supporting cast and budget for this debut thriller that far exceeds what the script seems to warrant. At heart, *Last Moment of Clarity* is a slight, imaginatively thin B-movie which doesn't so much as allude to Alfred Hitchcock's *Rear Window* and *Vertigo* as outright steal from them brazenly, ending up with a limp neo-noir that unfolds in the streets of Paris and classy apartments in Los Angeles.[21]

In his last moment of clarity, Zachary Joseph Horwitz should have realized *Last Moment of Clarity* was not going to get him out of the impossible situation he'd gotten himself into. But he was out of options. When the movie flopped, there seemed to be no plan B of any sort.

By March 2020 Zach's investors were lawyering up and trying to figure out what exactly was going on with 1inMM's deals. You'd think they would've done that *before* they pumped all that money into a no-name actor's licensing company, but the returns on capital were too good to check. It was only *after* lawyers for one of 1inMM's defaulted deals reached out directly to Netflix's legal department to ask questions about the delay in payments that they were told Netflix had never heard of 1inMM.

Remarkably, it wasn't until April 6, 2021—nine months later—that the FBI finally raided Horwitz's Beverlywood mansion. Even more remarkably, his wife, Mallory, hadn't realized her husband was running a Ponzi scheme until the moment the feds came barging, guns drawn, into her house. (Mallory has not been accused of any wrongdoing.)

By the end of that week, she had filed for divorce. By then the only thing she owned in the world was one hundred dollars and seventy-five cents in a single checking account.[22]

By the time prosecutors were done with his file, they'd charge Horwitz with five counts of securities fraud, six counts of wire fraud, and two counts of aggravated identity theft.[23] Charging documents claimed that, between 2014 and 2019, some 250 separate investors had pumped a total of $650 million into 1inMM. They lost at least $227 million of that. The victims included not only his college buddy Jake Wunderlin but also Zach's siblings, parents, and grandparents, as well as Andrew Levitas and Rogue Black—none of whom were accused of wrongdoing. In February 2022 Horwitz was ordered to pay his investors back $230 million and was sentenced to twenty years in federal prison for his role masterminding the scam.[24] He started a prison blog and called it *Be That 1*.[25]

The sheer bravado people like Mehmet Aydın and Zach Horwitz display is an endless source of fascination, and the scale their schemes reached is almost awe-inspiring. Both of them deployed social proof masterfully, convincing their marks that putting money into their schemes is just what people "like them" did. Both engineered commitment ladders that made it easier to draw marks deeper and deeper into their world.

But here's the thing: compared to the charlatan we're about to meet, Aydın and Horwitz were rank amateurs. They couldn't hold a candle to the true maestro of the twenty-first-century Ponzi scheme: Arif Naqvi.

Arif Naqvi

In April 2010, when President Barack Obama convened a Presidential Summit on Entrepreneurship, it surprised no one to see Arif Naqvi among the marquee names for the event.[26] Not yet fifty years old, the Pakistani financier had come out of nowhere to become one of the most consequential business figures in the developing world. The company he led, Abraaj Capital, was on its way to becoming the biggest venture capital firm in the Middle East, with $14 billion under management, which it used to buy out and reorganize businesses everywhere from Peru to Pakistan.

But Abraaj wasn't just a massive money machine. By then the company had also become one of the key partners of the Obama administration in a vast drive to transform the Middle East through the power of entrepreneurship. The Overseas Private Investment Corporation, the US government's development finance institution, was on the verge of investing $150 million of US taxpayer money in Abraaj: the ultimate imprimatur of official recognition from Uncle Sam.[27] People in the know quietly whispered Naqvi's name as a future reformist prime minister of Pakistan. Surrounded by other titans of development finance, Naqvi lectured high US government officials during panel discussions at the presidential summit on what they needed to do to bring prosperity to the Middle East.

Naqvi didn't quite come from nothing, but, by the standards of the people he was hobnobbing with, he'd come from very little. His father owned a small plastics manufacturing firm in Karachi, Pakistan. He was no captain of industry, but he did make enough to afford the steep tuition fees for Karachi Grammar School, the elite, British-founded institution that status-conscious Pakistanis competed to send their children to.

The young Arif was smart, charismatic: anyone could see that. The family was eager to give him the very best education on offer in post-Raj Pakistan. He was also immensely ambitious. And *everyone* could see that.

For university, he went off to the prestigious London School of Economics, trained as an accountant, and set off to build his name in Middle East business circles. He started off working for Arthur Andersen in London and American Express in Karachi, before he got his first big break, joining the Olayan Group in the early 1990s.

Olayan was a large and enormously profitable diversified conglomerate owned by Suliman Olayan, a captain of Saudi industry who, at the time, was the wealthiest man in Saudi Arabia. Naqvi caught the boss's eye for his sharp smarts and limitless ambition. Suliman Olayan, desperate to keep him under his wing, reportedly once told Naqvi he could have any job he wanted in the company.

"But you cannot offer me the job I want," Naqvi later recalled replying.

"Oh," the surprised Saudi plutocrat reportedly answered, "and what is that?"

"I want your job," Naqvi said.

According to *The Key Man*, the gripping 2021 book chronicling the Naqvi saga by the *Wall Street Journal*'s Simon Clark and Will Louch, the two journalists who eventually brought down Naqvi's empire, this quip about lusting for Olayan's power and wealth was classic Naqvi: a story he *loved* to repeat.[28]

But that would come later. Back in 1994, before he'd turned thirty-five, he had left Olayan and set himself up in offices in Dubai, organizing a deal to buy Inchcape, a trading firm that imported cars and other goods into parts of Africa.

By 2001 Naqvi's sights were set on bigger game. He organized the first ever takeover of a US-listed firm by Middle East investors. The target was a profitable parcel-delivery firm based in Amman, Jordan, which modeled itself on the early years of American Express, styling itself Arab American Express, or Aramex for short. With thousands of employees and a logistics operation that spanned the region, Aramex was a unique success story.

Arif Naqvi decided he would buy it.

Nothing like it had been tried before, but Naqvi was convinced that he could reorganize Aramex to make it worth many times what it was worth at the time.

Then disaster struck, and with it, opportunity.

The September 11, 2001, attacks on Washington and New York sent investors scurrying out of the Middle East, and Aramex's share price collapsed. Sensing his chance, Naqvi organized a group of investors to swoop in and complete the takeover. Naqvi paid $65 million for a majority stake in Aramex. He took the company private, delisted it from the NASDAQ, reorganized it, and then listed it again, four years later, on the Dubai stock exchange. That sale netted him $270 million and capped Naqvi's reputation as a major force in Middle Eastern finance.[29]

The Aramex deal left Arif Naqvi a millionaire many times over. He bought himself a Gulfstream private jet for his frequent trips between Dubai, London, Oxfordshire, Northern Pakistan, and Karachi, all places where he owned luxurious homes.

But it's not great wealth that made him unique: there are plenty of millionaires out there, especially in the Middle East, and most of them don't end up lecturing US government officials on how to do their jobs from the lectern of a US Presidential Investment Summit.

No, to take that one step further into the ranks of capitalism's true global chiefs, Naqvi would need to differentiate himself once more. Naqvi kept getting invited to global gatherings of the world's most powerful people: CEOs of huge companies, top political leaders, and the financiers behind the world's biggest deals where hand-wringing about the state of the world's poor was the order of the day.

This mostly came in the form of empty platitudes, but Naqvi sensed an opening. The torrent of empty platitudes signaled a trove of uneasy consciences. The world's most powerful people longed to square the circle between their wealth and the well-being of the world's poorest people. Many were frustrated to be constantly pilloried as agents of extreme inequality. The world's elite wanted to *feel good* about their wealth, to convince themselves that their wealth was good not just for them but also for the world. They dreamed of being seen to use their wealth to make the world's poorest people better off.

Naqvi sensed that dream and saw it at once as a vulnerability.

Convince these rich, powerful people that they could *do well by doing good*, and you could squeeze any amount of money out of them.

He got to work. At elite meetings from Davos to Sun Valley, Naqvi pitched Abraaj not just as a good investment, but primarily as a force *against* global poverty and inequality. It was a strategy to turn the insecurities of the world's rich into a stream of income for him. Over time, Arif Naqvi became an expert at prying the world's biggest wallets open on the basis of what amounted to a masterfully delivered guilt trip.

It was inspired.

At the time, "impact investing" was becoming a hot new trend. The phrase, coined at a Rockefeller Foundation conference in 2007, suggested that investors didn't need to choose between making big returns and helping the world's poor: they could do both, by redirecting their capital toward companies working in what finance types called "emerging markets"—basically, the developing world.

Abraaj was ideally positioned to cash in on this trend. Its early deal-making was fully focused on these kinds of markets. By 2008 Naqvi was all in, repositioning Abraaj to profit from the coming impact-investment boom. This meant transforming his firm's image. Far from negative associations with greedy 1980s Wall Street corporate raiders, Abraaj promised to become a different kind of private-equity firm, one that took its impact on the poor just as seriously in its decision-making as its impact on the bottom line.

It was a genius move, helping Abraaj move quickly into the highest tier of global capitalism. Soon, Abraaj was raising billions of dollars for its investment funds, and no longer only from rich Middle Easterners. Blue chip international investors like Deutsche Bank came on board, and money poured in from all over.

Riding the impact-investing wave, Naqvi became the subject of glowing business press profiles in *Forbes* and the *New York Times* hailing him as the visionary behind a new brand of Middle Eastern capitalism: sharp, aggressive, but socially inclusive.[30] A small mythology began to grow around him, as high-profile intellectuals held Abraaj up as a model of high-impact investment for the region. His next big deal—a high-risk leveraged buyout of Karachi Electric, an ailing utility company in Pakistan's business capital—was the subject of a fawning 2012 Harvard case study that praised Abraaj for making "great strides in turning around the company" in just two years.[31]

Naqvi had made it. The firm had become a strategic partner to both the American government and the Gates Foundation. Graduates of top business schools were foregoing job offers from the giants of Wall Street to work for him. And Naqvi's contact book had become as massive as his reputation was squeaky clean. Everyone flocked to Abraaj's conferences.

According to *The Key Man*, whose account we follow closely here, in this period Naqvi went on a hiring frenzy, poaching top talent from across Dubai's financial sector, seeking dealmakers ready to go into the world's most challenging markets and buy up companies.[32] Soon Abraaj executives were flying all over the world doing deals. Among many, many others, they bought a mattress maker in Nigeria; a company selling herbs and spices in South Africa; a payments-processing firm in the United Arab Emirates; the largest private oncology clinic in Casablanca, Morocco; a Panamanian ecotourism hotel chain; and a dairy-farming group in Turkey (not, alas, Farm Bank).[33]

On any given day Abraaj might be closing a deal to take over an ice-cream maker in Ghana for $300 million or moving to take over a hospital chain in Pakistan for $254 million.[34]

Naqvi next turned to nepotism, hiring the sons and relations of the top decision-makers he did business with. In *The Key Man*, Clark and Louch report that he hired the son of a Malaysian prime minister, the daughter of a Sri Lankan hedge fund capo, a nephew of the King of Jordan, and a relative of John Kerry, then US secretary of state.[35] In 2013 he held a charity match at the cricket ground on his Oxfordshire estate featuring former Pakistan captain Imran Khan, who happened to be running for prime minister of Pakistan at the time. The nebulous "charity" the match funded later turned out to be Khan's political party.[36]

Naqvi worked relentlessly to associate Abraaj with some of the biggest names in global business and finance. He paid a massive fee to bring Sir David Nicholson, fresh from a stint as chief executive of Britain's sprawling National Health Service, in as a consultant to his health-care funds. He met King Charles, then Prince of Wales, and was active in one of his charities, the British Asian Trust.[37] In September 2017 he hired Kito de Boer, who had founded Middle East operations for the legendary McKinsey management consultancy and had just left a prestigious job as head of mission of the Office of the Quartet (which consists of the United Nations, the United States, the European Union, and Russia), a role in which his immediate predecessor had been Tony Blair.[38] Hires don't come any more prestigious than that, unless you count recently out-of-work US secretaries of state, such as John Kerry, whom Naqvi also tried to bring on board, but without success.[39]

According to Clark and Louch's reporting, Naqvi ran the empire he built with an iron fist. Employees describe a company culture that bordered on a cult of personality, with Arif Naqvi personally making all key decisions, not only on which deals the company did but also on the minutiae of employee compensation and promotion. He put in famously long hours, sending employees into the office late at night to see which of his underlings was working like the boss, long into the night. He showered lavish bonuses on his favorite executives, including perks like stays at his palatial London apartments or his Oxfordshire estate and junkets on his $50 million superyacht or at his sprawling luxury complex in the mountains in the north of Pakistan.[40]

In 2013 Naqvi set his sights on, arguably, the world's most prestigious investor.

Since the early 1990s Bill Gates led what has become the world's biggest philanthropic organization. The Bill & Melinda Gates Foundation grew into a hundred-billion-dollar juggernaut, a force in the international development world to rival that of many donor governments. Nothing screamed "seriousness" in the impact-investing world like buy-in from the Gates Foundation. And for Naqvi, who was barnstorming the world's billionaire hangouts with harangues about ethical capitalism, the Gates imprimatur would be a signal of respectability that other big funders would hear loud and clear. Social proof doesn't come any fancier than this.

Naqvi knew that bringing health care to the world's poorest people was the central focus of Bill Gates's philanthropy, so he set out to create a fund custom-made to attract the Gates Foundation. Launching the Abraaj Growth Markets Health Fund, Naqvi set out to employ ten thousand health professionals in the world's poorest large cities to care for upward of two million patients. The fund would end up owning "26 hospitals, 18 clinics and 40 diagnostics centers, as well as brownfield and greenfield assets across India, Pakistan, Kenya and Nigeria."[41]

Naqvi pitched Bill Gates in person on the fund at his massive Oxfordshire estate. And Gates agreed to back him. The Gates Foundation soon pledged $100 million to Abraaj's Health Fund. The Gates imprimatur opened up the floodgates for other partners: the World Bank came onboard; so did the US, British, and French governments. Altogether, the fund raised $1 billion, making it the largest health-care-focused private-equity fund the developing world had ever seen.

By then Abraaj was expanding at breakneck speed, sucking in piles of cash from all over the world. It was inevitable that, as the company grew, not every investment it made would turn to gold in the same way the Inchcape and Aramex investments had.

Clark and Louch report that in 2013, several Abraaj deals were already giving signs of less-than-stellar profitability. By January 2014, they say, more and more Abraaj deals were failing to bring in the revenue projected, and the company found itself in money trouble for the first time, leaving Naqvi scrambling to make good on promised payments.[42]

This, US investigators would later charge, was the moment Naqvi tipped over the edge from ambitious upstart to financial criminal; to be clear, he could have come clean, playing it straight with his investors by disclosing unwelcome news that some investments had not gone as planned and the firm would need new capital to shore them up. But that would've projected weakness. And Arif Naqvi never *ever* wanted to do that. Indeed, to this day Naqvi maintains his innocence and strongly denies all charges against him.[43]

By early 2014 the company, and Arif personally, was allegedly running through money at such a prodigious rate that shortfalls soon arose in some of its funds, while others had piles of cash sitting around waiting to be invested. Without a fresh cash infusion, the firm would not be able to meet its next set of payment obligations, including payroll for May 2014. Payments due to fund investors and debt service due to banks would go into default unless the firm somehow conjured up these millions.

It's here that Naqvi allegedly crossed the financial-crimes Rubicon. Prosecutors allege he ordered associates to raid one specific fund that still had cash on hand to cover the shortfall in others.[44]

Naqvi apparently hoped he could cover his losses quickly with a win somewhere else. If so, he'd recoup his losses, pay back the fund he'd illegally raided, and nobody would ever need to know. But it never works out like that, does it? Like a gambler caught in an escalating series of double-or-nothing bets, Naqvi found himself getting deeper and deeper into trouble.

Having crossed the Rubicon, Naqvi soon found himself caught in an ever-thickening mess of lies.

The journalists who broke the story, Simon Clark and Will Louch, report that Abraaj soon found itself running two separate sets of books.[45] One set, kept by the company's accounting department to be shown to outside authorities, kept up the fiction that the company's funds were carefully segregated; a second set of books, closely guarded by Abraaj and just a handful of his most trusted aides, contained the awful truth of a company increasingly happy to shift money between funds to try to keep them all above water, however temporarily.

This mad juggling act could be kept up for only so long. The underlying issue was that, for all his assurances that the company was sound, Naqvi had blown too many calls. He'd overpaid for companies in troubled countries, loaded them with US dollar debts, then seen their balance sheets tank when the country's currency took a dive in international markets. Naqvi tried to console himself with the thought that some of his funds just had liquidity problems now and again. But the truth was much worse: Abraaj as a whole was nearing insolvency, with the value of its debts outpacing the value of its assets by more and more with each passing day.

Which is why just like Mehmet Aydın and Zach Horwitz, Arif Naqvi found himself locked inside the house of lies he'd built. He kept jetting around between his luxury properties, going to glittering conferences, and schmoozing investors. And he kept collecting honors and awards and basking in the glow of dazzled journalistic pieces about him.

Even as Abraaj's financial problems multiplied, Naqvi's list of honors kept getting longer. With a reputation as a luminary as well as a Croesus, he was made chairman of the British Asian Trust Advisory Committee and inducted into the Middle East Centre Advisory Board of the London School of Economics and Political Science. He served on the boards of the Institute for Management Development Foundation and of Endeavor Global, he helped lead the Pakistan Human Development Fund, and he sat on the advisory board of the Columbia University Middle East Research Center.

Naqvi won the 2013 Oslo Business for Peace Award, chosen by a selection committee made up entirely of Nobel Peace and Economics laureates, receiving the honor at a white-tie gala held in the same room where Nobel prizes are awarded. After that he was appointed to the United Nations Global Compact, a glittering group of the world's most respected business leaders tasked with advising the United Nations Secretary General on development strategy.

The glory spilled over to his wife, Fayeeza, who cofounded a charitable foundation with him and received the 2017 BNP Paribas Grand Prix award for Individual Philanthropy for her troubles. "You cannot think of a forum that [Naqvi] or his people were not there, and you cannot think of a prize that wasn't awarded to them," is how Unilever CEO Paul Polman put it.[46] Fayeeza has not been accused of wrongdoing.

As the Naqvis blew their carbon budgets many times over on private jet rides from one capital to another to collect these prizes and honors, Abraaj's finances were going from bad to hopeless. That original sin from back in 2014—when Naqvi allegedly began raiding one fund to pay for Abraaj's routine expenses—allegedly spun out of control, yet no one outside Naqvi's tightest circle of advisers seems to have known about it.

In one especially rich twist, Clark and Louch report that Naqvi was appointed to the board of the Interpol Foundation, the fundraising arm for the global consortium of police forces. This gave him access to a coveted "Interpol passport"—a special international travel document that ensured easy travel anywhere on Earth. Naqvi, employees later reported, loved to brag about his Interpol links, broadly hinting that he had a special line in to global cops as a way of intimidating people in negotiations. And to add one more layer of irony, he was asked to serve on the Interpol Foundation's special committee advising the foundation on the fight against global financial crime.

One struggles to imagine how Naqvi kept his sanity amid the cross-cutting pressures of being both allegedly a world-leading fraudster and a global leader of police efforts to curb financial crime. Perhaps he didn't. Abraaj executives told Clark and Louch that his long-standing penchant for humiliating underlings got worse in this period, as a harried Naqvi struggled to keep up the façade.[47]

Yet for four more long, excruciating years, Arif Naqvi kept up this impossible juggling act—bringing in more and more fresh investor money and then allegedly siphoning millions off to cover up the financial holes left behind by previous cash grabs.

All the while, Arif kept up an aggressively opulent lifestyle, which included a culture of decadent partying at company events. Clark and Louch report the social pressure to drink to excess at Abraaj corporate shindigs as intense, and sources reported to them that the sexual exploitation of the firm's secretaries was commonplace.[48]

It couldn't last. In the end, it was Arif Naqvi's biggest scalp that did him in. In 2017, Andrew Farnum, an executive at the Gates Foundation tasked with overseeing its $100 million investment in Abraaj's Growth Markets Health Fund, noticed that the accounting on the investment seemed off—as though Abraaj had simply been sitting on $200 million worth of investor money, instead of using it to buy health-care companies and build hospitals in South Asia and Africa, as the prospectus had promised.

His questions met with equivocation, which only made him more suspicious. Soon, Farnum was reaching out to other investors in the fund, including the development corporations of the US, British, and French governments. Abraaj struggled to explain the discrepancy to them. At one point, Farnum recounts with astonishment that Abraaj gave him conflicting information about the whereabouts of large sums of investor money: "You *cannot* forget where you put $240 million!," he said.

Smelling a rat, Farnum had the Gates Foundation and three other investors hire Ankura, a firm of forensic accountants, to look into the matter. When word of this was reported by the *Wall Street Journal* on February 2, 2018, things began to move very fast indeed.[49]

Naqvi was just then fundraising for his biggest fund yet, the Abraaj Private Equity Fund VI or APEF6. He had already signed up investors for $3 billion, half of the mammoth $6 billion fund he wanted to create to invest in companies serving the middle classes of the developing world's biggest megacities.

Abraaj's standard 2 percent management fee for the APEF6 would have earned it a cool $120 million a year. Perhaps Naqvi thought that would be enough to paper over the firm's troubles. His reach for this new pot of gold, alas, only got him into more trouble: US investigators would end up charging him with fraud for inflating valuations of Abraaj's previous investments to make the company look more attractive to potential investors in APEF6.

In any case, it was already too late—the moment news of the Gates Foundation's suspicions was published, investors began scrutinizing Abraaj's statements with a new level of rigor. Too often, reasonable questions could be answered only in ways that surfaced yet more questions.

In 2018, with dozens of Abraaj investors pursuing Naqvi for their share in funds gone wrong, the company entered a death spiral from which it would never recover. Abraaj executives scurried away in droves, seeking to patch up their reputations on the way out. In reality, Naqvi appears to have shielded even many of his most senior executives from knowledge about the firm's real financial picture. Many of them, like Kito de Boer, the former head of consulting company McKinsey, seemed genuinely bewildered to learn the truth behind the company they had joined the year before.

Abraaj—which at its height had managed $14 billion in investor money and been the world's leading emerging-market private-equity firm—was first split in two and later forced into bankruptcy by its creditors. Its longtime finance chief, Mustafa Abdel-Wadood, ended up in the high-security wing of the Metropolitan Correction Center, the same Manhattan jail where Jeffrey Epstein committed suicide, before pleading guilty to federal fraud and conspiracy charges that could mean 125 years in prison. Another top lieutenant, Sivendran Vettivetpillai, also pleaded guilty in US federal court on charges that could carry sentences of up to 115 years in prison. Both were still awaiting sentencing three years after their plea deals—their sentencing hearings are unlikely to be held before Naqvi's trial concludes.

Arif Naqvi, for his part, was banned for life from Dubai's financial markets and fined $135 million there for his role in Abraaj's collapse.[50] He remains under house arrest in London as he faces extradition to the United States on charges that could carry a prison sentence of up to 290 years. When British cops arrested him at Heathrow Airport, they found Naqvi was still traveling with the Interpol passport he so treasured as a token of his untouchability.[51]

Arif Naqvi's story is unique. He didn't fake it 'til he made it; he inverted the old cliché. First he made it, *big*, and only later did he allegedly start faking it when his investments ran into trouble. Perhaps Arif's ego couldn't handle the loss of status that would have come from accepting that Abraaj's finances were not as good as they seemed. Owning up to his problems would have meant giving up on the façade of perfect success he'd carefully built over decades. He would never do that. Now he faces up to 290 years in prison to mull over his decision.

Arif Naqvi was no ordinary charlatan. He climbed higher than almost any other figure we explore in this book. He didn't take in mom-and-pop investors; he took in some of the richest, most powerful, most sophisticated people in the world. He wasn't in it for millions or even tens of millions; he was playing for hundreds of millions and billions. His scam was big time.

And yet what's extraordinary is that, in certain ways, his story isn't really very different from the likes of Mehmet Aydın and Zach Horwitz. Just like them, he identified a dream many people shared, then sold it to them in glowing terms. Just like them, he leveraged social proof to give people confidence in his promises.

The more you look at it, the more you realize Arif Naqvi wasn't doing anything so different from what many other Ponzi schemers have done: he was just doing it on a global stage.

That, in itself, is interesting. It's always tempting to blame the victims of charlatans, to imagine they get swindled because they're not good enough, not smart enough, not sophisticated enough—that if only they were smart—like we're smart—they'd have been safe.

But these three stories show how wrongheaded that belief is. The same techniques that get a Turkish housewife to part with her life savings can work on the career investment experts at the US government's Overseas Private Investment Corporation. The same strategies that work on your old college roommate from Indiana University can work on the Gates Foundation.

It's a sobering thought, but here's a happier one: if all three of these charlatans went up in the world in the same sorts of ways, it's just as true that all three came down in pretty similar ways. However big the gulf in wealth and sophistication between two-bit hucksters like Aydın and Horwitz and a globetrotting fixture of the capitalist elite like Arif Naqvi, all three of them found themselves caught in similar webs of lies, trying to obscure the financial dark holes at the centers of their empires.

The most sophisticated marks aren't all that much more sophisticated than the simplest. But then, the most sophisticated charlatans aren't that much more sophisticated than the simplest either.

3

Star Power

The World's Oldest Grift

A CHILD OF EIGHT WALKS INTO A LUSH TROPICAL FOREST DEEP IN A verdant Caribbean isle. He spots a small bird. The bird is wounded, hurting, whimpering along the jungle floor. Is his wing broken? The child is deeply moved; he feels the tiny bird's pain.

He reaches out and holds the small, frightened animal in his hand. Just then he feels a jolt; some mysterious energy flowing through him.

The bird is healed, and it flies away with ease.

To hear Walter Mercado tell it, this was the moment he knew he was different. It was the early 1940s, and young Walter was struggling to fit in the provincial, conservative Puerto Rico of his childhood.[1]

Even then, everyone could tell that Walter was different. While most kids his age rode horses and played cowboys and Indians with toy guns, Walter wanted to dress up, and not always as a boy. Anything shiny attracted his attention, and when he found out there was such a thing as the theater, he wanted to do little else.

Walter spent his youth chasing the spotlight. He trained as a ballet dancer, later as an actor, launching a moderately successful career on the stage and on Puerto Rican television. The thirst for glamour seemed to run through his veins. He was handsome, his flowing blond mane arresting, but he seemed uninterested in the traditional macho style of Puerto Rican masculinity that was ruthlessly enforced at that time. And he never forgot that bird rescued as a child, and the promise of magic in his touch that the memory seemed to embody.

The ballet, the flamboyance, the deliberate androgyny invited inevitable speculation about his sexuality. Throughout his life, Walter Mercado refused to be drawn. Simultaneously somehow both in and out of the closet, he seemed to transcend the closet altogether. Nonbinary before there was any such label, he luxuriated in his feminine side without ever questioning himself as a man.

And it might never have gone beyond that. Walter Mercado might never have been anything more than a charismatic, gender-fluid small-time actor in Puerto Rico. Except, one day, he found himself on the air on Puerto Rican television with ten minutes of dead air to fill and, on a whim, he decided to read out a horoscope.

To be clear, there's no signal that Walter Mercado had ever devoted much time to astrology before that fateful afternoon in 1970, when a guest who had been booked for a section in the afternoon variety show canceled at the last minute, leaving the station scrambling for a way to fill the time. To hear Walter tell it, he improvised a horoscope right then and there, just to fill dead air.

Viewers were mesmerized. As retold in *Mucho Mucho Amor*, the hagiographic Netflix documentary starring Mercado and featuring a starstruck Lin-Manuel Miranda, calls began coming in to the station asking when Mercado would do it again. And he did, the next week, and then again the week after that. He would keep doing it again and again for four decades, until he had become one of the most recognizable figures in Latin America: a beloved pop idol who would literally stop traffic wherever he went.

It's not without a little trepidation that we're going to go ahead and call Walter Mercado a charlatan. We do so with eyes wide open, fully aware that compared with many of the predatory monsters who fill these pages, Mercado comes across as a bit of a choir boy. His relentlessly upbeat, positive horoscopes and his signature catchphrase—*¡mucho, mucho amor!*—paint a picture of a largely benign figure in his followers' lives: just some light entertainment beamed out on daytime TV to a mass audience of stay-at-home Latin American women hungry for a little bit of magic to liven up their humdrum lives.

That is true, to a certain extent but no further. A charlatan, after all, is one who talks as though he knows things he cannot know, and as though he can do things he cannot do, earning his marks' trust and then using that trust to his advantage. By that standard, Walter Mercado was undoubtedly a charlatan: conjuring deeply personal advice out of thin air, slinging certainties where honesty would impose uncertainty, making his audience feel better—and his audience certainly *did* feel better after hearing from him—and profiting from them by lying to them.

An Ancient Grift

Eight hundred years ago, people believed that insects spontaneously generated from rotting leaves, that diseases were usually caused by a mysterious unseen substance in the air called "miasma" and could be cured by bleeding a patient with leeches (except for syphilis, which required mercury to be placed directly on the sores), that criminal confessions were unreliable if obtained without the aid of torture, and that a person's fate was somehow determined by the positions of the stars and the planets in the heavens at the moment of their birth.

Fast-forward to the twenty-first century, and each of these barbaric beliefs has been jettisoned after a devastating collision with science.

All, that is, except that last one.

A 2022 YouGov poll found that 27 percent of Americans believe in astrology, while another 22 percent are on the fence about it.[2] Remarkably, younger Americans are more likely to believe in astrology than their elders: 37 percent of 18- to 29-year-olds believe that the positions of the stars and planets influence people's lives, versus just 16 percent of people over 65. A 2020 study found 36 percent of Canadians aged 18 to 36 said they "definitely" or "probably" believe in astrology.[3] A 2001 European Commission study found that more people in Europe believe astrology is scientific (53 percent) than is economics (42 percent)—a finding that may be attributable, in part, to people confusing the word with "astronomy."[4] In 2019 33 percent of Argentines believed in astrology, up from 26 percent in 2008.[5] In a 2015 survey 20 percent of Britons said you can learn something about yourself or another person from their star sign.[6] In 2020 41 percent of French people agreed that star signs explain a person's character.[7]

Out of all the subcategories of charlatanry, astrology doubtlessly has the longest lineage. Human beings have been staring up at the heavens and wondering what they mean for as long as we have existed. The first organized system of astrological belief archeologists have identified dates back to the Babylonians, around four thousand years ago. They identified celestial objects with particular gods and looked to the heavens for clues as to how this or that god might be inclined to act. When a dire omen, such as a lunar eclipse, was seen, they would implement elaborate rituals to appease the gods in the heavens before they lashed out.

China's own astrological era followed a few hundred years later, based on the same sixty-year cycle of the zodiac still celebrated by Chinese people today on the Lunar New Year. Egyptian pharaohs, Japanese emperors, Hindu rajas, and Catholic popes all employed a retinue of astrologers, both to work out the calendar and to foretell the future from the stars. No Greek or Roman general would dream of making a decision of State without consulting his astrologer first—but then, neither would Nancy Reagan, first lady to America's fortieth president.

All felt it imperative to consult the sages to learn how this or that star might influence the course of human events. In fact, "influence" was originally an astrological term: it comes from the ancient Roman belief that an emanation from the stars—a so-called ethereal fluid—would *flow-in* to people from the stars.

Nobody any longer believes in the existence of such a thing as "ethereal fluid," for the very simple reason that there's not a shred of evidence for it. Nor is your zodiac sign what you think it is: due to the impact of precession (the "wobble" the earth experiences in response to lunar gravitation as it spins on its own axis), the traditional, two-thousand-year-old mapping of birth dates onto constellations is now almost a month off, meaning most people's "real" zodiac isn't what they think it is.[8]

The "real" in that sentence has richly earned its scare quotes, because there is no detectable connection between when a person was born and their personality.

When, rarely, astrologers have agreed to put their insights up to scientific test, they've failed spectacularly. In one landmark 1985 study published in the journal *Nature*, researchers identified 30 highly reputed American and European astrologers and asked them to review the birth charts for 116 people without meeting them in person. They then provided three personality descriptions for each of the 116 people, only one of which actually described the subject, while the other two were real personality descriptions of other people. The researchers then asked the astrologers to match each birth chart to the correct personality description and found they were able to do so about a third of the time . . . which is about the same success rate as just by chance.[9] More recent research shows that astrologers not only fail to match people's real personalities to their birth charts but also seldom agree with one another about what a given birth chart is supposed to show about a person.[10]

There's a shooting-fish-in-a-barrel quality to trying to scientifically disprove a belief as knowingly unscientific as astrology, which is perhaps why it is seldom done.

But it *is* worth pausing to consider just how crazy it is to believe that where we see a star in the sky can have an influence over us, because the stars aren't even where we see them in the night sky. What hits our retinas are the photons that emanated from a given star many years ago: the time it took the light to travel from a star's point of origin to its earthly destination. By the time we see it, it's certainly not there anymore!

Einstein's theory of relativity does indeed show that stars exert a calculable gravitational pull on us, but as the force of that pull is given by the square of the (enormous) distance separating us from them, the actual effect is so infinitesimally small it amounts to zero—and certainly much less than the gravitational pull of a nearby ant. Somehow, though, nobody foretells your future based on the positions of the ants near you the moment you were born.

What is peculiar about contemporary astrology is that practitioners like Walter Mercado never see any need to come up with a new explanation to replace the debunked pseudoscience about the influence of an ethereal fluid. Rather than settling on some other, more plausible-seeming mechanism to explain the link between far-off stars and someone's life, today's astrologers usually just sidestep the entire messy subject of cause and effect, acting as though the link between distant astral phenomena and a person's life were so obvious it is in no particular need of explanation.

Of course, to discuss the relationship between people and the stars in the language of science is to miss the point rather spectacularly. The millions of adoring fans who hung on Walter Mercado's every word did so not despite the absence of a scientific basis, but because of it. Astrology exploits an extremely widespread dream: that you personally are enmeshed in a *meaningful* order of the universe, an order that is perhaps magical, certainly mystical, and blessedly beyond the grasp of modern science. If astrology could be confirmed scientifically, it would lose much of its appeal.

This is why never in a million years would Walter Mercado try to explain how, exactly, the stars influence someone's life. Walter spoke to his legions of followers at the level of raw emotion. With him, with astrologers generally, the style is the substance.

And boy, did he have style! From the start, Walter Mercado, who died in 2019, nurtured an unmistakable look: part late-stage Elvis, part amusement park psychic, Mercado was all sparkle all the time. His never-ending stream of garish, over-the-top capes studded with sequins and stones made for can't-look-away television. With set designs that spanned the Age of Aquarius, Walter wallowed in a kind of happy syncretism that put sitting Buddhas next to baby Jesus figures next to Santería ritual statuettes next to Lord Ganesha: a hodgepodge spirituality that hinted vaguely at an all-inclusive enlightenment freed from the shackles of any specific doctrine.

Then there was the makeup, and the hair, and the knowingly androgynous body language, all adding up to a complete package of unconstrained fabulousness. When a man who looks like that and dresses like that speaks with seemingly complete certainty about what the future will bring, people listen. Intently. And Latin Americans did listen, intently, for years, and years, and years. At the peak of his fame, in the early 2000s, Mercado commanded a daily audience tallied above one hundred million. That is raw power: star power, in more ways than one.

But where is the harm, one is tempted to ask? It's just light entertainment, right?

The theory put forward in the fawning *Mucho Mucho Amor* is that Walter wasn't really in it for the money. He was, instead, desperate for audience adulation, for the affirmation of a huge following and the lifestyle that came with it. The giant limos, the fabulous hotel suites, the celebrity interviews and throngs of admirers: this was the payoff Walter Mercado was after, and gradually, over the years, he carefully re-created himself into the character most likely to attract them.

But one cannot attract an audience on that scale without attracting hangers-on determined to make money on the back of it, and this, in time, proved to be Walter Mercado's undoing.

The name of the savior that would become Walter Mercado's tormentor was Guillermo (Bill) Bakula. A concert promoter by trade, Bakula realized the enormous potential to monetize Mercado's supersized audience before anyone else did. Becoming Mercado's manager in the mid-1990s, Bakula wove the web of commercial and licensing deals that saw Mercado break out of the Puerto Rican market and become a worldwide celebrity, with licensing deals from Alaska to Patagonia and as far afield as Britain and the Netherlands.

But Bakula wanted more. More viewers, more fame, and especially more money. He leveraged Mercado's brand into a multimillion-dollar empire in the scammy world of 1-900 number astrology hotlines, where people would pay up to eight dollars a minute to hear call center operators read them their birth charts and provide "customized" astrological advice.

The centers operated throughout Latin America, including a massively profitable operation in Brazil. Customers were often drawn from among the poorest people in society: desperate folk willing to pay prices they couldn't afford for solace that would prove illusory.

Even if Mercado had somehow convinced himself of his own mystical powers, he must have known that the 1-900 numbers were little more than a scam designed to part vulnerable people from money that ought to have gone to feeding their families. Yet he threw himself heart and soul into an aggressive marketing campaign that pitched his psychic-friends hotline to vulnerable people all around the region.

For social proof, testimonials came in from the street about the amazing results people who had bought readings were experiencing. "In just a week, I found a full-time job," said one satisfied customer in a commercial where Mercado spills rocks from a velvet bag and declares, "The stones tell the truth!"[11]

"My clairvoyants," Mercado affirms, "are illuminated souls and they *will* help you."

"He is the greatest and most powerful astrologer in the world," a Mercado commercial in Brazil plastered over his psychic-hotline number.[12] These were ubiquitous on TV for years, each stressing testimonials of people who claimed their lives had been transformed after calling the hotline.

For Mercado, the very fact of his popularity served as social proof—*every* woman in Latin America seemed to like his show. For years, the psychic hotlines became the profit engines that drove the Mercado empire, with his televised horoscopes becoming something like a loss-leader: a highly visible teaser meant to bring paying customers in through the 1-900 doors.

But the hotlines weren't the whole of it. In 1995 Mercado began to appear on TV stations up and down the Americas promoting kits for magical bead necklaces that, he said, could cure migraines, sexual dysfunction, even poverty. It seemed like plain nonsense; in fact, it was complicated nonsense. The magical necklaces were part of a complex multilevel marketing scheme that eventually defrauded around 16,000 people of $90 million. The promoter behind the scheme was ultimately sentenced to 14 years in prison. The scheme, which could never have worked without Mercado's imprimatur, earned him a $25,000 endorsement fee plus 12 percent of retail sales. Some of the "investors" in the scheme filed a class-action suit against Mercado after losing their life savings, alleging it was Mercado's influence that duped them.[13]

So much for Walter Mercado's charlatanry as some sort of victimless crime. He may not have been an actual scammer, but for decades he was, so to speak, scam adjacent—time and again he rented out his name to scammers who rented his charisma for profit. And real people suffered. Including him.

In time, Bill Bakula seems to have overreached. According to court documents, in 2006 he obtained Mercado's signature on a contract that Mercado claims to have signed without adequate legal advice, and without having read the paperwork.[14] The contract signed over complete control of Mercado's entire operation in perpetuity to Bakula. This included not only the entire back catalog of Mercado's TV appearances but also his image and likeness, and his very name. The contract led to a dramatic, protracted court battle between the two, during which Mercado was taken off the air. By 2012, when a court finally restored Mercado's control over his own name, his health was failing. He never returned to the airwaves, until his memory was rescued by Lin-Manuel Miranda's participation in the documentary. Months later, he died of renal failure in a Puerto Rico hospital.

It is a testament to the timelessness of Mercado's grift that his reputation has only improved since his death. His image graces a thousand T-shirts and keychains, his iconic blond hair as much a part of the Latin American zeitgeist now as ever it was when he was alive. Walter Mercado spent four decades spinning BS about the stars in front of the television cameras, bilked millions of followers for an unknowable number of dollars through scammy psychic 1-900 numbers, and was rewarded for it with immortality.

Grifts like Mercado's succeed because they speak to deeply held needs that people can't be reasoned out of, because they didn't reason themselves into them in the first place. Belief in astrology *begins* with a rejection of scientific reasoning and an attachment to magical thinking.

Now, if you yourself tend to think there might be something in astrology after all, you're likely feeling quite annoyed by now, and it's doubtful there's anything we can do to change your opinion.

But maybe, just maybe, you will think again if you look at a system of belief that has the same structure as astrology's, but in a completely different context.

Japanese Blood Types

Yoshi is earnest and neat; Masahiro is passionate and creative. To their friends, that's no surprise: Yoshi's blood is type A, whereas Masahiro is a type B. For her part, easygoing Yoriko is a type O—so of course she makes an excellent leader. And Yukio, who is talented but a little unruly, is an odd amalgam of the earnest and the passionate: a typical AB.

These composite sketches are drawn from the more-than-dubious science of "blood type humanics," the Japanese pseudoscience of blood types and how they relate to human personalities. With roots that stretch back to 1920s Nazi race science, and popularized for the tabloid crowd in a series of 1970s paperback bestsellers, beliefs about blood types in Japan and, more recently, South Korea show a startling similarity to the kinds of beliefs that proliferate in the West about the zodiac.[15]

For years, popular magazines and newspapers brimmed with columns on how to prepare your type-O son for college entrance exams, with tips for getting along with your difficult type-B boss or hints on catching the eye of your type-AB crush. Books with titles like *The Owner's Manual for Your Type A Boyfriend* have topped Japan's best-seller list, while folk wisdom about which types were compatible with which other types for marriage seeped into popular wisdom to the point where they just seemed like common sense for people.[16]

Needless to say, there isn't any evidence that the presence or absence of certain antigens on the surface of red blood cells has any influence on your personality, much less on how you relate to others. The glycoproteins that determine your blood type play an important role in the human immune system and certainly determine who can donate blood to whom, but they have nothing to do with your personality. To a scientist, the claim is plain old gobbledygook, no more defensible than the idea that a mysterious substance flows from stars into our bodies. Again, though, that doesn't seem to really matter.

Popular writers like Toshitaka Nomi made fortunes from a string of bestselling books with titles like *You Are Your Blood Type*, until so many had heard about them the theory had become impossible to debunk.[17] Nintendo game consoles in the 1990s asked users what their blood type was during setup.[18] It became an industry.

And it had a dark side. In 2004 Japan's Broadcasting Ethics & Programming Improvement Organization (BPO)—an industry self-regulatory body—warned broadcasters to dial down human-interest stories centered on blood type stereotypes, after counting more than seventy national broadcasts on the subject that year.[19] As BPO noted, incidents of blood type discrimination were on the rise, with type-B people especially prone to harassment. According to a survey by Professor Shigeyuki Yamaoka, of Seitoku University, three out of four type Bs report having been subjected to verbal harassment as a result of their blood type.[20] Many Japanese people, it turns out, just wouldn't date a type B.

And if you think that sounds outlandish, consider this: 42 percent of Americans who are interested in astrology say they avoid dating a Gemini.[21]

The temptation is always to think this kind of bigotry reaches only rubes: uneducated people with little social or cultural capital, desperate for solace and willing to take it from whoever is willing to dish it out with the greatest air of certainty.

If only. Astrology has as many followers among the highly educated as anywhere else. Indeed, for much of the 1980s, the US president's travel schedules could not be solidified without consulting a lady in California with no security clearance, no intelligence connections, no government experience of any kind.[22] Joan Quigley, one of the era's most charismatic astrologers, befriended the first lady, Nancy Reagan, shortly after the assassination attempt on her husband on May 30, 1981.

Quigley assured the first lady of the United States that she had known Reagan would be targeted on that day, and she only regretted she had not had a direct line to the White House to sound the alert. Now that she did, the first lady consulted her constantly. Elaborate ruses had to be devised to ensure Quigley's crackpot advice could be implemented without being traced to its source. At one point, her star chart convinced the first lady that to avoid a calamity on a foreign trip, Air Force One would have to take off at precisely 2:11 a.m. on the appointed date. Bizarrely, she got her way: a curious case of global diplomacy being run to a schedule determined by centuries-old nonsense.[23]

Quigley was an exception, of course. For years, most astrologers were just charisma-based small-time grifters, taking in clients one by one for chart readings that could begin by costing twenty dollars and then balloon to many times that sum, if the client were judged sufficiently promising to invest real time and effort on.

Such sidewalk astrology scams continue to flourish to this day. But costless connectivity has opened up space to target victims on a much wider scale, applying the powerful marketing techniques of the internet age to the business of bringing in new marks. Which is why astrology makes for a useful first place to look at how the deception space is evolving in the twenty-first century.

Sylvia Mitchell

You've certainly seen them. Walk down the street of any major city worldwide, and you will see astrologers and clairvoyants advertising "readings" promising to reveal your future. You likely pay little attention to them—why should you?—and to the extent you do think about them, you imagine they peddle entertaining and theatrical short sessions that need not cost more than the twenty dollars posted on the wall.

And that is, in fact, how it usually goes. Some storefront astrologers limit themselves purely to this sort of reading, perhaps offering ongoing readings to a few loyal customers that come to serve as a kind of stand-in for therapy for people who, for whatever reason, are indisposed to consult a mental health professional.

But a darker side lurks.

For a good number of astrologers, that first "reading" is a filter: the first chance to gauge the susceptibility of a mark. The very fact that you've chosen to walk in to a storefront astrologer already transmits useful information to them—and from that moment on, everything you say, every gesture you make, everything you do will be carefully scrutinized for signs of vulnerability.

Walk-ins who seem skeptical, at ease with their lives, or well supported by networks of friends and family hardly make for promising prospects. They tend to get a cursory reading, after which they are sent on their merry way. But if, in the course of that first reading, you reveal your vulnerabilities, things often change. Maybe you are in a moment of acute psychological stress. Maybe your answers reveal that you're socially isolated or primed to believe in outlandish tales. If so, your risk of falling victim to a life-blighting scam rises precipitously.

Take the experience of Debra Saalfield, a competitive ballroom dancer and instructor.[24] In the span of one awful week in 2008 she lost both her job and her long-term relationship. In despair, she walked in to Zena, a psychic shop she'd walked past many times before, in part to spite her now ex-boyfriend, who had warned her not to. Ms. Saalfield ticked all the boxes for vulnerability just then, and the soothsayer who saw her, Sylvia Mitchell, knew exactly what to do.

After an initial reading (price tag, $75), Mitchell told Saalfield she would need a deeper reading to get to the root of her troubles. It was a lot, yes, but Mitchell told her that her problems had their roots in a past life she'd lived as an Egyptian princess, and deep spiritual repair work was needed to rid her of a curse she lived under. Her performance was compelling, and to a devastated Saalfield, in the state of mind she was in, the $1,000 asking price seemed almost reasonable.

With each subsequent visit, Mitchell's money demands escalated. It was a classic commitment ladder, and Mitchell deployed it masterfully. Each step in the ladder seemed almost reasonable, in light of what had come before. And remember, Saalfield had no one else to turn to with her troubles, plus Mitchell exuded empathy.

So, when the psychic told Saalfield she needed to work on detaching herself from her fixation to worldly goods and demonstrate her trust by writing Mitchell a check for $27,000—which Mitchell promised would certainly be refunded—Saalfield complied . . . only to regret her decision immediately afterward.

Little did she know that Sylvia Mitchell was an expert predator, with years of experience exploiting people in personal crisis. Others had fared even worse than Saalfield. At around the same time, Lee Choong, a Singaporean investment professional, turned up at Mitchell's door to discuss Choong's desperate disappointment in an unrequited love.

The problem, she learned, was that her family had hurt her intended lover in a past life. The curse this engendered could be cleared . . . but not quickly, and not cheaply. In successive sessions, Ms. Choong gave Mitchell some $120,000 in all, each time reassured by promises of refunds if the cures did not work. The refunds, of course, never came.

In their court testimony against Mitchell, Saalfield, Choong, and others who testified against her stressed that they had misgivings about what they were doing almost from the start.

So, why did they keep doubling down?

They seemed to struggle to explain it even to themselves. But one important hint surfaced again and again: they were lonely. They had no one else to talk to. And Mitchell, whatever else she might have done, at least listened with a sympathy that seemed profound. And that kept them coming back.

The only thing exceptional about Sylvia Mitchell's astrology scam is that it eventually led to a formal trial, with Ms. Mitchell sentenced to five to fifteen years in prison for her crimes.[25] In reality, few such cases are reported, and fewer still go to trial. Victims are ashamed to report their stories to the police, because they're embarrassed to have been taken in. They hardly need to be silenced—they silence themselves.

Worse still, when they do turn to law enforcement, they often meet with incomprehension and condescension at best, and mocking hostility at worst. Cops can't believe they were so dumb to be taken in that way. Cases are not taken seriously, so they're seldom investigated thoroughly.

Some astrology scams can balloon to genuinely shocking proportions. In 2018 an astrologer who variously went by the names of Sally Ann Johnson, Angela Johnson, Angelina Johnson, and Sally Reed was found to have taken a single vulnerable elderly victim for more than $3.5 million.[26] She was sentenced to twenty-six months in prison, ironically not for the grift as such, but Al Capone style, for failing to pay income tax on it (the judge ordered her to pay $725,000 in tax penalties to the IRS as well).

Sounds like a lot of money, right?

Except it isn't.

The biggest fortunes being made with astrology these days are many times that size. And they don't draw prosecutorial scrutiny; they draw venture capital millions.

Chani Nicholas

Meet Chani Nicholas. The young tech entrepreneur from British Columbia looks very much the part: she is sassy, strong, and quietly attractive in a rugged, Western kind of way. Growing up in a progressive West Coast hippie village, she's entirely at home in the kinds of alternative belief systems now at the center of her $50 million online empire.

Nicholas has set herself apart through her forthrightly political, left-wing views, putting forward a kind of social justice astrology that marries astrological advice with a brazenly left-wing agenda. She hawks her app as "the most empowering way to use astrology."

Here, the contrast with Walter Mercado is startling: Nicholas never had any time for the closet, speaks often and lovingly about her relationship with her wife, and describes herself as "basically an angry feminist who also happens to be into astrology."[27]

A self-described professional astrologer, she has been reading people's birth charts since she was a teenager. In her world, though, what counts as apostasy isn't making birth charts . . . it's doing it through a cell phone app.

After landing a gig as the resident astrologer for *Oprah* magazine, Nicholas found herself writing to a mass audience for the first time.[28] A million people were logging on to her blog each week before she decided to launch her app: a slickly designed platform available on both iOS and Android promising to tailor astrological insights to *you*.

In the shift from Walter Mercado to Chani Nicholas, we see a microcosm of how the world of charlatanry is being upended by new technologies. Whereas Mercado had to spend arduous decades building an audience one channel surfer at a time, Nicholas can apply all the power of Silicon Valley's algorithmic wizardry to the problem of identifying her marks. Type "horoscope" or "star chart" into a search engine, and the wheels of Chani's empire spring into motion, zeroing in on you as a seeker and bombarding you with solicitations until you download her "free" CHANI app.

In the CHANI app, a commitment ladder is mass customized to the individual user. Just like any number of apps, Chani's makes a few very basic features available for free. But the more advanced features, such as the automated personal birth chart and customized weekly horoscopes, come at a price—$11.99 per month, or $107.99 for the full year.[29]

In the interest of science—and so you don't have to—we signed up to see what pearls of wisdom the CHANI app might have in store for us.

A workshops section helpfully suggested we deck out a "New Moon in Leo" altar and decorate it with "bright yellow, orange or red flowers, alongside actual gold, ruby, garnet and citrine (for the Sun), saffron, frankincense or chamomile, and maybe ginger, oranges, lemons and/or turmeric." It instructed us to journal on the ways "we are modeling good faith and kindness in [our] friendships and/or wider community," and it prompted us to organize a ritual at the exact moment of the new moon (10:55 p.m. on July 28), where we'd light a candle and incense, sit in front of our altar, meditate, and "get clear on an intention that [we will] have for the next six months." We were then told to speak an affirmation three times into a glass of water before drinking it, "knowing that [we] are imbibing its message."

That was a lot, so we turned to the birth chart section, looking for some more clarity. After inputting an exact time and place of birth, we were treated to a deep dive on the position of the stars at the moment of our birth and how exactly they would influence our lives. One of us (Quico) was told that because his rising sign was Virgo, he is "known for [his] ability to make the information [he has] access to useful to others"—and was left to ponder that the information he had access to right then and there was that the CHANI app was a straight-up gobbledygook.

It went on. "Your Mercury is in Gemini," the app offered, meaning "you are the poet, the reporter, the neighborhood gossip who knows everything and is ready to catch everyone up."

Interesting.

Then again, since "your Venus is in Cancer," it means "every connection is precious and every friendship, romantic relationship and family bond worth engaging in deserves proactive tending and thoughtful loyalty."

Still unconvinced?

Well, that's probably because "your Saturn is in Cancer," so you are "deeply sensitive, and you have a keen radar for other people's needs and an intuitive sense for the correct conditions necessary to grow just about anything, from a person to a pet, to a family."[30]

If those pronouncements sound like they apply to you, it's because they're expressed just vaguely enough to apply to, well, pretty much anyone. That, of course, is the dirty little secret at the heart of the astrological charlatan's grift: it's not so much that they scam us, it's that they give us the tools we need to scam ourselves.

The basic mechanism has been well understood for many decades, ever since a series of groundbreaking (at the time) social psychology experiments conducted in the late 1940s. In a landmark 1948 study Dr. Bertram Forer, then a researcher fresh out of UCLA, brought together a number of students and gave them a detailed "personality test."[31] One week later, Dr. Forer sent a student enrolled in the study the following personality assessment:

1. You have a great need for other people to like and admire you.
2. You have a tendency to be critical of yourself.
3. You have a great deal of unused capacity which you have not turned to your advantage.
4. While you have some personality weaknesses, you are generally able to compensate for them.
5. Your sexual adjustment has presented problems for you.
6. Disciplined and self-controlled outside, you tend to be worrisome and insecure inside.
7. At times you have serious doubts as to whether you have made the right decision or done the right thing.
8. You prefer a certain amount of change and variety and become dissatisfied when hemmed in by restrictions and limitations.
9. You pride yourself as an independent thinker and do not accept others' statements without satisfactory proof.
10. You have found it unwise to be too frank in revealing yourself to others.

11. At times you are extroverted, affable, sociable, while at other times you are introverted, wary, reserved.
12. Some of your aspirations tend to be pretty unrealistic.
13. Security is one of your major goals in life.

Unbeknownst to them, all the students received the same vignette. The thirteen points were, in fact, cribbed from a bestselling astrology book of the time. When Dr. Forer asked students to assess how accurate the descriptions were, from 0 (for not at all accurate) to 5 (exactly on the nose), they gave the personality vignette an average score of 4.3.

What came to be known as the Forer Effect is at the heart of astrology's ongoing appeal. It amounts to confirmation bias on steroids: faced with vague but largely positive pronouncements that purport to be about us, our minds latch on to what seems to fit and ignore the rest. This is how astrologers convince us that vague pap that might apply to anyone and could mean anything or nothing reveals some deep truth about *us*.

The trick works even when we're well aware of what is going on. If, upon reading the personality vignette above, you caught yourself semiconsciously trying to see how at least some of these items apply to your own life, you saw the Forer Effect at work in real time.

Confirmation bias is a hell of a drug, isn't it?

The CHANI app leverages the Forer Effect through the magic algorithmic capitalism, where pitching yourself to a well-defined niche audience can prove wildly profitable.

We do not know how many paying subscribers CHANI has, only that her astrology business donates "5% of all company revenue and 100% of the proceeds from all CHANI x Gifted by FreeFrom products directly to queer, trans, Black, Indigenous, people of color, and/or disabled survivors of gender-based violence via freefrom.org."[32] We do know that 15,500 people have taken the time to leave a rating for the CHANI app on Apple's App Store. Assuming she has around that number of paying subscribers, that works out to more than $1.6 million a year.

We are irresistibly drawn to discourses that purport to reveal deep truths about ourselves. Astrologists know this. Chani Nicholas simply had the acumen to build the app for it. But the question lingers: Is Chani Nicholas a charlatan?

The longer we looked into the CHANI empire, the harder we found it to label her a charlatan in quite the same way as we applied it to the other people in this book.

As we saw, the "victimless crime" label couldn't really be applied to Walter Mercado, whose hotline clients were fairly obviously exploited for gain. Indeed, exploitation is at the heart of our definition of a charlatan. But what about Chani? Is what she's doing *exploitative*?

We can't say it is. Spend time reading the hundreds upon hundreds of reviews her fans have left on the App Store, and it's plain to see few of them feel deceived. Just the opposite. One fan raved, "I cannot tell you how much this app has meant to me. Every week the personalized readings bring me to tears of truth: either exactly what is happening or exactly what I need to move forward."

Another enthused, "The weekly readings are so informative and helpful, and they provide a well put together map of the week's potential unfoldings that allow us to step more boldly into the unknown and capture all of the tidbits of magic and abundance that is available for our consciousness to imbibe."[33]

Hundreds and hundreds of reviews pile on along the same lines. Whatever Dr. Bertram Forer might have found in his lab, the reality is that thousands of people willingly pay Chani Nicholas for a service whose characteristics they understand and feel well served by.

If ever that changes, canceling a subscription to CHANI is straightforward, as is speaking up about your displeasure with the service. Few followers seem to do so. Chani Nicholas probably has some disappointed users, but we could find no evidence that she had blighted anyone's life.

That Chani Nicholas dishes out junk advice on the basis of nonsense knowledge seems, to us at least, fairly obvious. That is why we do not subscribe to her services. Others, for their own reasons, plainly disagree, deriving obvious satisfaction from the experience of being told what seem to be pleasant lies. In a way, Chani Nicholas has cracked the code: she walks right up to the edge of charlatanry without ever crossing over the exploitation threshold.

Looked at in its most favorable light, what Nicholas does is something like mass customized therapy: giving clients a space to make themselves feel better through a series of positive messages that just happen to be couched in the language of the stars. At times, in her public pronouncements, Nicholas herself comes pretty close to admitting this is what her gig is about.

"Astrology," she once told an NPR interviewer, "comes out of scientific roots and because we are studying the movements of planetary bodies over time and coming up with facts about them, it's not to say that there is nothing scientific about astrology, but, and also, obviously it's speaking a symbolic language."[34]

Look past the nonsense about the transit of the stars, then, and we're squarely in self-help territory here. Charlatans leave a trail of broken lives in their wake. As far as we were able to tell, the CHANI app falls far below that threshold.

And, indeed, the CHANI app has plenty of room to grow: even only the most profoundly devoted of astro-heads in the United States would still amount to an audience of millions. Which may be why Chani is so very relaxed about her doubters: "I don't need you to approve of me, I don't need you to like anything I do," she recently told the *Los Angeles Times*. "I love skeptics, I think they're fantastic. I think we should all be skeptics."[35]

Astrology is charlatanry on "easy" mode—the people drawn to it more or less advertise their eagerness to be taken in, and charlatans hardly need you to ask twice. In the Forer Effect, we see confirmation bias run amok—out of an astrologers' many vague pronouncements, people seem to notice only the parts that appear to apply to them and disregard the rest.

Digital astrologers apply these techniques on a scale not possible in previous centuries. The first-generation digital technology of television was enough to turn Walter Mercado into a regional megastar. Second-generation digital technologies on the internet allow for a much more sophisticated targeting effort that could be vastly more profitable. As AI algorithms with their capacity to mass-produce simulated intimacy get folded into this mix, it's easy to see how the potential for harm will multiply. Chani Nicholas may be a scrupulous astrologer, but the CHANI app is proof of concept that will surely be emulated by other, less ethical players.

From the sequins and capes of Walter Mercado to the shoulder-padded splendor of the Reagan White House, and from the storefront readings that escalate into million-dollar shakedowns to the slick apps of algorithmic astrologers, the world of the zodiac is a rich hunting ground for charlatans. And with new generations increasingly disposed to believe the pronouncements of astrologers and information technology relentlessly refining its ability to match hucksters to their next victims, it's going to be a growth market out there.

It's written in the stars.

4

Megachurches and Megabucks

Turning God into Mammon

SAY YOU'RE A CHARLATAN AND YOU WANT TO MAKE MONEY. LIKE, A LOT of money. At first sight, Christianity seems like a bad way of going about it. After all, Jesus—the one in the gospels, at least—is pretty clear about money: it's bad news. Really bad news.

It's such bad news that it makes him fly into a violent rage. Now, it takes a *lot* to make Jesus angry. In fact, we see him fly off the handle only once in the gospel: at the sight of the money-changers in the temple cashing in on people's faith. He loses it and chases them off with a whip. Jesus Christ. With a whip.

In his calmer moods, his message isn't much different. In Matthew 6:24, he's as explicit as it gets in teaching us that you can devote your life either to serving God or to getting rich, but not both: No one can serve two masters, for either he will hate the one and love the other, or he will be devoted to the one and despise the other. You cannot serve God and money.[1]

There are plenty of points of doctrine on which Christians have to squint hard at the gospel to make out how Jesus might have felt. The treatment of gay people, say, or the practice of contraception are touched on obliquely, if at all. Somehow, that doesn't stop some Christian leaders from pontificating loudly on these issues.

When it comes to money, covetousness, and greed, though, no squinting of any sort is required. The Jesus of the gospels was loud, insistent, repetitive, almost obsessive in his message about money: devotion to wealth is ungodly. Those who fixate on money will have their rewards in this world, not the next. You'd think that settles it. Right?

Not a chance.

There's just too much money in Christianity for charlatans to give it a pass. And some of today's most iconic charlatans have made their fortunes precisely in this way.

We were spoiled for choice when it came to picking cases to study in this chapter. That's no coincidence: religion has always been a driver of the dreams that propel people through life, and where people dream, charlatans will always crop up to exploit them.

Sadly, it's also no coincidence that Protestantism has become a particular magnet for some of the most shamelessly exploitative charlatans of our age. With a theology that always stressed that God would show his favor by bestowing wealth on the elect, Protestantism was ripe for exploitation by the unscrupulous from the start.

Indeed, it's but a short hop from Martin Luther's sixteenth-century theology to the debased twenty-first-century incarnation that the charlatans in this chapter all explore: the prosperity gospel. In essence, the prosperity gospel is about taking the idea that money flows in the direction of God's preferences to its logical extreme and twisting it in the charlatans' favor.

Of course, more mainstream Protestant leaders have always denounced the prosperity gospel for the blasphemy it very obviously amounts to, with one calling it "a damning heresy that paves the road to Hell."[2]

Such critiques do nothing to prevent the unscrupulous from exploiting its moneymaking possibilities. We might have selected from any of dozens of pastors plying this trade, but in this chapter we confine ourselves to three of its most consummate practitioners: people who've taken the art of turning the gospel on its head further than you might ever think possible. Strap in.

Kenneth Copeland

Our first stop is in East Texas as it was some eighty years ago. A little boy named Kenneth was growing up in a strict evangelical Christian family in Lubbock in West Texas, just near a newly built Air Force base. Kenneth Copeland likes to describe in detail his wonder at all those glimmering planes taking off into the sky. It was 1942; the Second World War was raging.

When little Kenneth turned six, the US Marine Corps built an air base just off Eagle Mountain Lake, some twenty miles north of Fort Worth—a few hundred miles east of his home in Lubbock. The Marine Night Fighter Group used the new facility to train pilots to fly Grumman F6F Hellcats and F7F Tigercats to take the fight to the Nazis and the Japanese at night.[3] Kenneth didn't know it then, but this new airfield on Eagle Mountain Lake would become the stage on which much of his remarkable life would play out.

To hear Reverend Kenneth Copeland tell the story decades later, back then he was just a small-town West Texas boy who loved planes and music and struggled mightily to fight temptation. Not temptation in general, you see. Just one temptation.

Little Kenneth wanted to cuss. Yes, to use bad language: to swear.

In God-fearing, Bible-loving Texas back then, swearing was no small matter. Oh no. Swearing, Copeland learned, was how Satan got you into the habit of sin. And that was no laughing matter.

Decades later, Kenneth Copeland would regale his parishioners with folksy tales of his childhood struggles against the evils of swearing.[4] With his deep, singsong baritone and his West Texas drawl, he'd draw them in, showing them how that itch, that *wanting* to swear, was the very model of the way the devil works in the world, how he leads us to sin.

"The easy sins are the ones you don't want to get rid of, the easy stuff. Satan doesn't come up to you and just blare it out to you—'why don't you be a prostitute?'"

At this, the congregation gives out a smattering of nervous laughter, but Copeland is just getting warmed up.

"'Why don't you be a killer?' Nobody starts off a killer! It starts off little, and then it *growwws*," drawing out that last sound.[5]

It is a thrilling performance, a furious indictment of the evils of letting Satan plant seed in your mind by letting yourself cuss. Copeland's command of scripture and the cadences of Southern preaching are pitch perfect.

Born into an evangelical family, Copeland trained as a pilot and went to Oral Roberts University, then America's most important evangelical institution of higher learning. There, his love of flying stood him in good stead—he served as chauffeur and pilot to Oral Roberts himself, the most influential preacher of his day.[6]

With his pretty singing voice, Copeland dabbled in music, even recording a hit single ("Pledge of Love") that landed in the Top 40 in 1957.[7] He studied his scripture, and, in 1967, founded his own church just off the old, now decommissioned Eagle Mountain Marine Corps Air Station.

He called his church the Eagle Mountain International Church, after the huge Eagle Mountain Lake it adjoins. He turned the church into just one part of the now immodestly named Kenneth Copeland Ministries. There, he would spend decades warning his flock about the spiritual dangers of bad language, because the devil puts into you the urge to use bad words to prepare the ground for much worse to come.

The devil has to operate that way, because all things follow the law of God, that is, "plant seed; it will grow." That, he says, is the law of Genesis, that is the way it is, he has to start with seed, and he plants the seed right there, right in the mind. When you were a little boy he didn't start you off desiring to be a hit man for the mob; he started you off wondering what would happen if you cussed just a little bit.

It's the kind of riff that leaves his parishioners eating right out of the palm of his hand. And it's just as well, because what Kenneth Copeland calls "the principle of the seed," is at the center of his pitch: a biblical metaphor that, in the hands of the unprincipled, becomes a license to grift.

The seed metaphor comes up again and again within the prosperity gospel: a charlatan-infested branch of Christianity that teaches that God *wants* to reward the faithful with health, wealth, and happiness in this world, not the next.

Let's be clear: this isn't normal Christianity.

To traditional Christians, praying for earthly bliss is, well, heresy. Not in some metaphorical sense, but in the most literal, theological sense of the word: a belief contrary to orthodox religious doctrine. It's not hard to see why. The Jesus we meet in the gospels seems to spend half his time warning people not to seek the things of the world. He seems to spend the other half of his time warning about false prophets, by which he means the kinds of preachers who try to twist his words into meaning the opposite of what they say.

Those aren't the bits of the Bible Kenneth Copeland likes to dwell on, though. He has his own set of favorite verses, carefully culled from both the Old and New Testament, verses where God seems to shower earthly goods on those who are faithful to him, from Job on up. Painstakingly selected and presented with his golden tongue, those verses allow Copeland to build a kind of upside-down theology where Jesus's fondest hope is for you to live in a mansion and drive a hundred-thousand-dollar car in this world before going up to claim your celestial reward in heaven as well.

Plant seed; it will grow.

Five simple words of plain old horse sense.

The seed in this metaphor soon turns out to be money, and by "planting it," Kenneth Copeland means giving it to Kenneth Copeland Ministries.

Copeland's first televised speeches date back as far as 1971, but his big break came in the 1980s, when he managed to get in on the first big wave of televised evangelical preaching.[8] The growth of cable and satellite television was just starting to break the three TV networks' stranglehold on television programming, and an upstart series of Southern preachers was bursting straight into millions of Americans' living rooms and hitting them up for cash.

In the 1980s Copeland's televised ministry was relatively low profile. Then, in the early 1990s a string of high-profile sex scandals felled some of the biggest names in televangelism. As stars like Jimmy Swaggart and Jim and Tammy Faye Bakker vacated the evangelical airwaves, they left a giant gap in the market that younger preachers like Kenneth Copeland were only too happy to fill.

Copeland's show, *Believer's Voice of Victory*, found a large and profitable audience on Trinity Broadcast Network, the country's largest Christian broadcaster. Under a huge banner that reads "JESUS IS LORD," Copeland built a nationwide following of devout Christians entranced by his down-home style and silky-smooth delivery.

Did he ask for money on these shows? Of course he did, though in a muted sort of way. For the hard sell, well, you'd have to go see him in person.

For decades, Copeland's strategy was careful, measured, and quite smart. His on-screen persona is that of a charismatic, blow-dried evangelical preacher, quite orthodox in his teachings. The goal seems to have been to raise his profile, to build up the audiences for his in-person appearances. Flying all over America, he would hold spiritual "camp meetings" in sports stadiums and halls. And that's where he really let the crazy fly.

It's at these meetings that Copeland would lay his hands on the sick, promising their faith could cure them through his touch. And it was at these meetings where the dark side of the seed metaphor would become clear.

Plant seed; it will grow.

In person, the motto became an aggressively manipulative grab for the flock's cash. Quoting Bible verses about tithing, Copeland makes sure attendees understand that big blessings will come from big offerings, and nothing smaller will do. Huge portions of these in-person meetings amount to manipulative fundraising pitches promising miraculous cures for virtually any illness, at a price. The audience is bombarded with stories of people cured from any and every disease, from acne to cancer, after making a monetary donation to the church. This is all delivered in a revival-festival atmosphere of intense devotion that makes any doubt seem heretical.

These meetings—the real cash cows behind the Copeland empire—take place all across America. But the thing about the United States is that, well, it's a big country. To get to those meetings, Copeland needs to fly a lot. Which is no problem at all: Kenneth Copeland loves airplanes. He loves them so much that former members of his church say he had his church buy him three of them—a 1998 Cessna Citation II, taking him and five others on shorter flights; a bigger Cessna 750 Citation X, built in 2005, that could seat twelve for longer flights; and a passion project, a restored 1962 vintage twin-engine Beechcraft Model 18, which he promised his church would use to fly emergency supplies to disaster-stricken areas.[9]

But of course any old rich guy can buy an airplane—it takes a true megalomaniac to buy a whole airport, and that's exactly what Kenneth Copeland did. No shrinking violet, he called it—what else? Kenneth Copeland Airport.[10] Kenneth Copeland Ministries bought what had been an old Marine Corps air station along with thirty-three acres of prime lakefront land in one of the priciest suburbs of Fort Worth.

Just up the road, on the same compound, is Kenneth Copeland Bible College. It sits next door to the ten-thousand-seat Eagle Lake International Church and just down the road from the VICTORY Channel studios, which the church has claimed seventy-five thousand people watch regularly. The channel is a multimedia operation that also oversees Copeland's aggressive social media presence and publishes a magazine.[11] It even has its own news division broadcasting God-infused hard-right news and views straight into devotees' homes via satellite or, for the younger crowd, through the GO VICTORY app (available on both iOS and Android, of course).

Kenneth Copeland does not need to trouble himself with public infrastructure at all to navigate this little kingdom. He can go back and forth between his church, his Bible college, his TV station, his airport, and his house without ever setting foot on land he doesn't own.

Remarkably, it wasn't the sprawling megachurch or the TV station, the Bible college or the planes that got him in trouble. It wasn't even the airport and the three airplanes.

No, the thing that finally got him into the headlines was his parsonage.

If the word "parsonage" conjures up an image of a quaint little stone house back behind a bucolic English church, you're going to have to think bigger. Copeland's parsonage boasts "a sweeping spiral staircase and a bridge that spans across the living room and connects the two sides of the house," according to a report by the US Senate Finance Committee cited by the *Houston Chronicle*.[12]

That same investigation found that "it also has crystal chandeliers and, according to Gloria Copeland, doors that came from a castle." The bedroom has a "huge drop-down ceiling projector and screen," according to the same report. Altogether, the six-bedroom, six-bathroom monster has eighteen thousand square feet of living space—around four basketball courts' worth.

Perched right on the water, it has 270-degree views of Eagle Mountain Lake. Outside, there are tennis courts and two garages that are bigger than a normal-sized house. Down on the waterline, there's the covered boat dock with three slips.

The whole thing looks less like a parsonage than a gaudy millionaire's over-the-top showpiece mansion, which is exactly what it is.

On the open market, it would likely fetch north of $7 million. And yet for this Xanadu, Kenneth Copeland Ministries paid exactly no property tax at all because—remember!—it's a parsonage, and housing for clergy is tax-exempt in Texas.

Eagle Mountain International Church's sprawling properties across Texas—some 1,400 acres of often prime suburban Fort Worth real estate—squeezed tax rules in favor of churches to pay just $23,000 in property taxes in 2021. A normal property owner would've expected to pay around $1 million in property taxes for that much land.[13]

This outrage, brought to light by an investigation by the *Houston Chronicle*'s Jay Root, opened a fresh discussion in Texas on church tax exemptions. But Copeland isn't shy at all about his parsonage's grandeur. In the twisted logic of the prosperity gospel, the gaudy excess all around him only proves that God approves of his ministry and has blessed him in return.

That's one interpretation. The other one sees Kenneth Copeland as running one of the most successful and predatory faith-based grifts of our time.

On TV Copeland often pushes his viewers to send in "prayer requests" in cash-stuffed envelopes to his church, promising to include each request in his prayers. Back in 2007 a former employee alleged that Copeland in fact never reads the requests at all: the envelopes are picked over for cash, then the requests placed in one big pile, where junior ministers in the church pray over the unopened letters. According to the former employee, during his time there, literally thousands of such envelopes would pour into Copeland's church every week.[14]

Copeland declared himself a billionaire back in 2008; in fact, independent estimates peg his net worth in the hundreds of millions. That probably still makes him America's wealthiest pastor, and arguably one of the nation's most successful charlatans.[15]

The reckoning, such as it was, has been mild.

The COVID-19 pandemic disrupted Copeland's business model, reliant as it was on giving the hard sell during in-person prayer meetings. The pandemic seemed to reveal the worst in Copeland, bringing the most scandalous side of his faith-healing tactics to light. A video from April 2020 shows him blowing directly into the camera and declaring, in theatrical style, to the novel coronavirus, "I blow the wind of God on you!! You are destroyed forever, and you will never be back! Thank you, our lord!"[16]

Later, he cited COVID-19 vaccine mandates as the reason he had to fly private jets, describing the jab as "the mark of the beast," before infamously saying he could not be expected to fly commercial because such planes were full of "demons."[17] At one point, amid mass pandemic layoffs, he warned parishioners who lost their jobs to continue tithing, to not even think about reducing their donations amid hard times since the real source of their wealth was not their employment, but Jesus.[18]

One anonymous testimony from a former church member alleges there was an atmosphere of total control within the organization, where questioning the leader is not even thinkable.[19] It then describes in detail how Copeland encouraged people on limited incomes to put themselves at immense disadvantage by raiding scant nest eggs to donate to Copeland's church.

Often the most striking view of a charlatan is from the victims' family members. Maud Newton has written about her mother, in dubious health and far from financially comfortable, continuing to make proportionally large donations to Copeland and living in an information bubble where all her news comes from the VICTORY Channel.[20] Given the scale of Copeland's empire, similar stories are shared by thousands across the United States.

By the standards of American evangelicalism, Copeland is a mostly apolitical preacher. Still, it was no surprise to see him follow the evangelical crowd and file onto the Donald J. Trump bandwagon. Officially a "faith adviser" to President Trump, he held a 2,500-person fundraiser rally for Trump despite COVID lockdowns in August 2020—directly contravening local health officials' repeated pleas not to.[21]

Least surprising of all is Kenneth Copeland's reaction when Trump lost the 2020 election. Right after the vote, he led parishioners in a bizarre, maniacal ninety-second laughing fit at the idea that Joe Biden would be president: "Yah-huh he gonna be president and Mickey Mouse is gonna be king!" he guffawed.[22] The following month, in a more somber mood, he told his followers the devil had stolen the election so he could continue killing babies, an apparent reference to the abortion debate.[23]

The rapid accumulation of bad headlines seems to have led Trinity Broadcasting Network to finally cancel Copeland's TV show after four decades on its programming grid, replacing him with a younger, more Instagram-friendly pastor.[24] Of course, Kenneth Copeland still owns his own TV channel, so it's not like he's entirely off the air, but his reach is now much diminished.

He's still out there, still giving the hard sell, still flying his private jets out of his private airport, still pulling millions into his church's coffers tax free. There's no stopping Kenneth Copeland.

But for all his bombast and all his millions, Kenneth Copeland is far from the worst of the evangelical grifters. No, for that distinction we have to fly due south, all the way to Brazil.

Edir Macedo

Come with us now into the world of the Universal Church of the Kingdom of God. And be prepared for a crowd too. The church's gaudy, over-the-top headquarters—a supersized, Vegas-style re-creation of the Second Temple of Solomon—dwarfs the neighboring building in São Paulo, Brazil's biggest city. Built from stones brought from Jerusalem for this purpose, the hulking, eighteen-story behemoth is reported to have cost $249 million to build.[25]

The church claims that this gaudy monstrosity is now Brazil's single biggest tourist destination, attracting some two million visitors per year, more than the iconic statue of Cristo Redentor in Rio. Also, the church hastens to add, the temple is twice as tall.

Back in 2014 Dilma Rousseff, Brazil's first woman president, was on hand for its inauguration—even though she was a leftist and reported to be an atheist, she couldn't afford to snub the Universal Church's millions-strong flock. Once there, Madam President praised the Church's role in Brazilian society as she inspected the temple's imposing nave, which the church says is the size of sixteen soccer fields—everything in Brazil must be measured in terms of soccer—and seats ten thousand.[26]

Week after week, it's full. And hundreds of other Universal Church halls around the world are full too, for services that stretch the meaning of Christianity to the very edge of the imaginable.

Forget everything you think you know about what church is like. At the Universal Church, you're in for a wild ride. A service is at least two hours long, and parishioners spend most of that time on their feet, eyes closed, singing and praying fervently while assistant pastors in hokey, Jewish-style prayer shawls scour the aisles on the lookout for signs of demonic possession, because demons, demons are everywhere for the Universal Church. Fighting them is a full-time job.

Now and again, these junior pastors will spot a congregant with the telltale signs of the devil and step forward to exorcize them—a violent ritual in which pastors lay hands on him and entreat the demon out. The possessed writhes on the ground. The crowd thrills, the music swells: God is in the house.

They can feel it. Everyone can feel it.

The emotional intensity of Universal Church services staggers the uninitiated. Once a week, the church envelops its flock in a total-body experience—a spiritual journey designed to shake them to their core. It's not just the music; it's the theater: mini–morality plays are on display almost every week, followed by emotionally searing testimonials.

There are sermons too, of course. But up on the pulpit, the pastor has little time for traditional preaching. Actually, the sermons seldom mention Jesus at all.

The focus for the Universal Church—down to its globally prominent logo of a white dove silhouetted against a red heart—is on the Holy Spirit. In its theology, the church describes the Holy Spirit as an active force in the world, fluttering about in a constant fight with the demons that lurk all about and, more often than not, inside of you.

The demons explain it all: Everything that is wrong in your life. Your money problems. Your love problems. Your work problems. Your health problems. Any problem. Every problem. In fact, that you have a problem at all proves it: a demon must be to blame.[27]

And who can get rid of demons . . . ? You guessed it: the Universal Church of the Kingdom of God.

Only the church knows what to do.

But there's a catch: it won't come cheaply.

The entire final half hour or so of every Universal Service session is devoted to the collection. Here you really have to forget everything you think you know about how a church works. This isn't about a single plate being bashfully passed around in front of parishioners with an understated plea for support. In our minds, it feels more like a shakedown.

It goes almost without saying that parishioners are pressed hard to tithe, habitually donating 10 percent of their income to the church. But that's only the beginning: the very *least* you can do. As pastors will often remind you, if you really want the Holy Spirit to step in and help you, you should be prepared to make a significant donation.

The church's whole theatrical approach kicks into high gear when the time comes to collect. Fundraising drives are called "missions" and put at the center of the church's spiritual undertaking. Dramatizing the value of each gift is an obsession for the Universal Church: a small stone replica of the biblical Mount Carmel might be built on the altar, with parishioners pressed to make a pilgrimage up its slope to lay down their money donations on the summit.[28] At other times an open Bible is used almost like a fetish, with the faithful pressured to heap riches on top of it: cash, sure, but also checks, even jewelry and watches.[29]

The church isn't the least bit shy about making the deal explicit: if you have a big favor to ask of the Holy Spirit, your gift must be proportional to the request. Asking for a generous blessing in return for a stingy donation isn't just foolish; it risks offending God.

Scholars of religion classify all this as neo-Pentecostalism, an offshoot of a branch of an outgrowth of the sixteenth-century Protestant Reformation; you know, the one Martin Luther launched out of outrage that the Catholic Church was selling tickets to heaven to the highest bidder under the guise of "indulgences." Luther would be aghast at a Universal Church service, where miracles seem to be explicitly for sale at set prices.

The difference is that the Universal Church's promise isn't only of salvation in the next life but also of riches in this one: pay today, and great wealth will flow to you in this life as well as the next.

Universal Church services—both in person and in its ubiquitous televised presentation—bear a startling resemblance to a late-night infomercial.[30] A lot of the techniques are the same. Heartfelt testimonials are front and center: emotional stories of people fallen on hard times who nonetheless manage to cobble together a substantial sum of money for a donation they are convinced shall come back to them tenfold.

The special emphasis on first testimonials in church videos is a straightforward application of social proof: they set out to show the faithful that people just like them have benefited from making large donations. In socially ambiguous situations, these kinds of techniques have long been shown to influence decision-making. And the Universal Church is nothing if not aggressive about its marketing. As one former member of the church put it, "What we believe is that through your sacrifice of money you can please God, that is, that the more money you give, the more God will bless you."[31]

The brazenness with which the church pushes members to go for broke—sometimes literally—in handing over their cash is stunning. And, as a way of hacking HumanOS, few charlatans have marshaled social proof as aggressively as Edir Macedo.

In one video, a Brazilian woman describes how she sold all the furniture in her house so she could make a big enough donation to the church. When that turned out not to be enough, she says, she went out to collect aluminum cans on the street to sell for scrap metal.[32]

This isn't, mind you, the result of some shocking exposé by critics or investigative journalists looking to blow the whistle on the Universal Church. This is the Universal Church's own message on late-night TV. It was worth it, the can-scavenging woman says, smiling at the camera, because the miracle God granted her made it all worthwhile.

This theme of sacrifice is always stressed: the Universal Church has no time for a "give what you can; every little bit helps" style of Christianity. The Holy Ghost, parishioners are told, will come through big for you, but only if you come through big for him, in the form of a donation that represents a real sacrifice to you. After all, if you don't show your commitment is deep, why should you expect a life-changing miracle?

None of this is hinted at; all of it is shouted from the rooftops: big donations bring big, life-changing miracles. Donations that don't represent a real sacrifice to the giver mean nothing to God. The bigger the sacrifice, the better. The Universal Church doesn't want some of your money. It wants all of it, and then some.

To be sure, the gospel has to come in for some heavy editing to fit in with Macedo's message. All that nonsense Jesus spoke on the mount about how those who seek wealth and power in this life "have already had their reward" in this world and will not get it in the next has to be carefully elided.

But then, the Universal Church of the Kingdom of God is Christian in the same sort of way Kentucky Fried Chicken is Southern—notionally, vaguely, theoretically—but not in any way that stands the least bit of scrutiny.

You've already guessed that a system this cunning could only have come out of the imagination of a truly gifted, world-class charlatan. Let's meet him.

His followers know him as the Bishop, and his bishops know him as *o chefe*, the Chief, but his name—according to the Forbes Billionaires list he has found his way into—is Edir Macedo.[33]

Skinny, balding, with a long but thin beard, Macedo comes across as a frail, somewhat shy, and soft-spoken uncle. But listen to his sermons, and his spiritual intensity creeps up on you—building slowly through long sermons about the demonic influences afoot all around, but especially on the political left.

Macedo doesn't shout; he cajoles. Softly. And comes back again and again to the dangers in the demon-stuffed world of the unbelievers, of the doubters, the leftists, the Catholics, and the magical powers of financial sacrifice to God . . . by which he means to himself, of course.

Born in 1945 in São Paulo, Macedo was brought up Catholic but became a Pentecostal at the age of twenty. There were almost no

Protestants in Brazil back then; he was one of the very first. After a short career as a low-level lottery official, he founded his own church, basing its theology on a brazen, no-holds-barred version of the prosperity gospel that makes Kenneth Copeland look tame in comparison.

Like other prosperity gospel preachers, Macedo teaches that God expresses his favor of the faithful by showering material goods on them. But unlike other preachers, his approach is explicitly mercantile. For Macedo, money is good, and the only way to get more is to give however much you have now to his church.

Politically, Macedo is every bit as reactionary as you might expect, actively mobilizing his followers to vote for Jair Bolsonaro in 2018, when he was first elected, and 2022, when he lost his bid for reelection. But Macedo is too canny to fight openly with the party in power: he said that while he had prayed for Bolsonaro's victory, he had also prayed for God's will to be done, and as God's will had been for Lula to win, he welcomed him and "forgave him for old sins."

Mostly he rails against his competitors: other Protestant denominations siphoning off the parishioners he wants to exploit himself, yes, and Muslims, of course, but most of all the enormously hated Catholic Church.

Macedo's Jesus-lite Christianity is built mostly around an oddball version of Old Testament theology. Macedo's temples are built to look like the Old Testament Jewish temple, because his theology is heavily Torah-infused. Menorahs and replica arcs of the Testament are prominently displayed; as he explains in his book, "To be an Evangelical in Brazil is like being a foreigner in Egypt at the time of the Pharaohs."

"Moses' mission was to liberate the people of Israel, recover their citizenship, and guide them to possession of their own kingdom," he says in his book *Plan for Power: God, Christians and Politics*.[34] "This book is like the burning bush that revealed God and his great national project to Moses," he says.

So, you know, it's no biggie if you don't support him . . . as long as you don't mind ending up on the receiving end of a few biblical plagues, as the Egyptian pharaohs did.

Macedo is ruthless. What started in 1977 as a single church in São Paulo mushroomed into a multinational operation laser focused on parting the faithful from their cash. And his Universal Church has proven incredibly profitable, with billions flowing out of the pockets of some of the world's poorest people and directly into his own.

As early as the 1990s, the biggest problem Macedo had was what to do with all the money pouring into his fantastically profitable church. As a nonprofit, the Universal Church didn't have to pay taxes, but it also couldn't invest in moneymaking activities. So, redirecting money out of the church and into other business ventures was something he could do only at the outer edges of the law.

His first target? The media.

In 1989 Edir Macedo bought Rede Record, a long-standing Brazilian broadcaster of both radio and TV content that had fallen on hard times. He began investing, hard, with money prosecutors have always suspected—but have never proven—was laundered from his church.

Soon enough, Macedo found himself at the head of a massive media conglomerate. Rede Record owns some twenty-three TV stations and forty-two radio stations, by one count, and is Brazil's second biggest media conglomerate, now branded, simply, as Record.

In 2013 Macedo expanded into financial services, buying a 49 percent stake in Renner Bank, then expanding his stake to 89.9 percent in 2020. Banco Digimais, as Macedo restyled it, is not one of Brazil's major banks, but neither is it tiny: it had 213,889 clients in the second quarter of 2024, focusing mostly on car loans.[35]

Talk about God and mammon!

If that whole way of thinking and acting sounds more than just wildly exploitative to you, if it sounds outright criminal too, well, rest assured: it has sounded illegal to a wide variety of investigators around the world as well. Macedo has been denounced for illegalities by his own accountant. He was briefly jailed for charlatanry in Brazil all the way back in 1992. In a taste of things to come, he had to be freed when thousands of his followers began camping outside the police station where he was held.

The Universal Church has been officially designated a dangerous cult in Belgium and investigated for money laundering in the United States. In 2002 the Colombian representative of the Universal Church was found living in one of the properties belonging to a prominent Colombian drug cartel capo. São Paulo state prosecutors charged Macedo and other top church officials with embezzling some $2 billion from the church between 2003 and 2008, following an investigation into ten years of the church's finances that showed how Macedo used a tangled web of offshore shell corporations in places like the Channel Islands and the Cayman Islands to siphon off money intended for charity.[36] In 2019 Rio de Janeiro investigators presented evidence linking the church to over $1 billion worth of money laundering just over the previous twelve months.[37]

None of it has ever stuck. Macedo's never been convicted of anything. Just the opposite. Since 2006 Macedo and his wife have traveled on a Brazilian diplomatic passport, a privilege that used to be granted only to top government officials, members of the political and business elite, and high-ranking Catholic bishops but is also now held by Edir Macedo, who thereby enjoys diplomatic immunity abroad.[38]

Aside from those eleven days back in 1992, Macedo has never done a lick of prison time. Time after time, he's walked off scot-free, his army of lawyers always one step ahead of the law.

It is a truth universally acknowledged that a charlatan in possession of a good fortune must be in want of political clout. Edir Macedo is no exception. Back in 2005 he launched his own political party, the Partido Republicano Brasileiro, and church members began to run for elections all around Brazil. As of 2022 Brazil's Republicans account for 43 out of the 513 members of the Lower House of Congress; 212 mayors, including the Mayor of Rio de Janeiro; and 2 out of 27 state governors. The party president, Marcos Pereira, used to serve as a cabinet minister and is now deputy speaker of Brazil's House of Representatives. He moonlights as a bishop in the Universal Church.

It has been said that Edir Macedo is the only person in Brazil who can boast that he owns a church, a political party, a bank, and a broadcasting network.[39] He also has what amounts to a small army; the Universal Church's security operation is as oversized and well funded as the rest of his empire. People argue about what the biggest source of Macedo's power is. That honor should probably go to Record: it's his direct line into millions of Brazilian living rooms that makes Macedo an irreplaceable power broker in his country.

Charlatans in our time run grifts that are digital, viral, and scalable, but few have succeeded in taking their vision global like Macedo. His church now claims an active presence in Portugal, Spain, the United Kingdom, Germany, France, the Netherlands, Belgium, Luxembourg, Italy, Switzerland, Poland, Russia, Latvia, Sweden, Ukraine, Romania, Angola, South Africa, Mozambique, Cape Verde, Kenya, Lesotho, Gabon, Côte d'Ivoire, Malawi, Uganda, Botswana, India, Singapore, Malaysia, Hong Kong, the Philippines, Japan, Taiwan, Thailand, Macau, Timor-Leste, the United Arab Emirates, South Korea, Papua New Guinea, New Zealand, and Fiji.

Today, the Universal Church of the Kingdom of God must surely count as Brazil's most successful export. Macedo's church claims to have followers in 128 countries.[40] McDonald's operates in only 114 countries.

But Macedo never lost sight of where home turf lies: the church's power remains overwhelmingly concentrated in Brazil, where it claims eight million parishioners and where Macedo's wealth, media clout, and devoted following have turned him into one of the nation's most influential figures.

Few charlatans can boast success on the scale of Edir Macedo's. Wherever you live on Earth, there is likely to be a Universal Church of the Kingdom of God within easy distance. You can just drop by on any given Sunday and look inside. You'll see people singing. You'll see people praying. You'll see them tithing. Willingly.

As extraordinary as the stories of Kenneth Copeland and Edir Macedo are, they are in some ways the same: both are charismatic, profit-focused pastors squeezing the blood out of their parishioners. It's a popular format . . . there was no paucity of characters to choose from in this category of charlatan, and we might have gone with a dozen others.

But that format is far from the only way to use Christianity to cheat the gullible. There are plenty of others. And among the most creative was perfected by our next charlatan, who mastered the art of turning a nonprofit evangelical university into the petty cash box that financed his weird sexual kinks.

Jerry Falwell Jr.

Parents know it well: that jolt of worry at the thought of a preteen daughter going to a big concert for the first time. It's a rite of passage, sure, but it's hard not to ruminate on the idea that something terrible could happen to her. And, to be sure, sometimes terrible things do happen.

But putting Donald Trump in the White House?

Outlandish as it sounds, the train of events that got rolling when our next charlatan's preteen daughter told mom and dad she absolutely needed tickets to that upcoming Justin Bieber performance on *The Today Show* had world-changing consequences.[41]

It's hard to think back to those halcyon days of Biebermania, but it was 2014 and the Biebs was the hottest act in the world. Concert tickets were hard to come by, and for a live TV performance, all the more so. You needed connections. And the parents of our particular preteen, for one, had a lot of connections. Michael Cohen, Donald J. Trump's fixer, was just one of them. And Michael Cohen, well, that guy had nothing but connections.

So, when Cohen found out that the daughter of one of the most influential players in Republican politics was having a hard time getting tickets to see the Biebs, he knew exactly what to do. He swung into action, got her great tickets, and stashed the episode away in his thick web of reciprocity relationships. One favor had been done, and a slightly bigger one could be extracted for it down the line.[42]

The particular preteen in question wasn't just anyone: she was the daughter of Jerry Falwell Jr. and his wife, Becki. This made her an heiress to one of America's most powerful families, a third-generation descendent of the founder of the politicized evangelical right wing, among the most formidable voting blocs in the country. And that tiny favor, just some concert tickets, led to a friendship that, in due time, would blossom into one of the unlikeliest partnerships in American politics: the bizarre pairing of a twice-divorced, thrice-married libertine with the evangelical family values lobby.

Let's back up a little. Who exactly is Jerry Falwell Jr., and how did he end up in a position to swing millions of US votes behind anyone, let alone a figure as unchristian as Donald Trump?

Falwell Jr. was the president of Liberty University in Lynchburg, Virginia. Founded by his father, Jerry Falwell Sr., as Lynchburg Baptist College back in the 1960s, Liberty University had grown into the largest evangelical Christian institution of higher learning in the country and one of the most influential addresses in Republican politics.

With 15,500 students at its sprawling 7,000-acre campus and 95,000 more online, Liberty was the spiritual and academic home to the politicized sort of right-wing Christianity that Falwell Sr. preached into life in the 1970s and led until his death in 2007.

Jerry Falwell Sr. wasn't just another 1980s televangelist. He was, by any reckoning, one of the most consequential political leaders in the United States starting in the 1970s. The political organization he founded for conservative Christians, the Moral Majority, turned American politics upside down, mobilizing evangelical Christians and rallying them around a single political party in a way they had never been organized before.

These days in the United States, we're so used to thinking of evangelical Christians as reliably conservative Republican voters that it's hard to cast our mind to a time before that was automatically so. But before the 1970s, most evangelical Christians were proudly apolitical, believing things of this world were secondary to the real work of salvation. And those who did participate in politics were just as likely to be on the left as on the right: for example, a pious if little-known Sunday school teacher and peanut farmer from Georgia by the name of Jimmy Carter.

It took decades of tireless work to politicize this sleeping giant and align it solidly with the Right, and the man who did most of that work was Jerry Falwell Sr. An extraordinarily talented preacher, Falwell Sr. became the voice of a forgotten America of devout, old-fashioned Christians who believed that to affirm your faith in Jesus Christ as savior was tantamount to being "born again" on Earth.

Born-again Christians, as they came to be known, had always scorned the temptations of this world in favor of an austere, patriarchal order based on prayer and devotion to scripture. They lived by a code that held family sacred and divorce sinful, and they held that sex is permissible only in the context of marriage between one "natural-born man and one natural-born woman," as they would put it.

Implacably opposed to the new secular moral codes of open sexuality, LGBT rights, and, especially, legal abortion, the followers of Falwell's brand of Christianity set out to take over the Republican Party. They first put their mark on the electoral map in 1980, turning out in huge numbers in favor of Ronald Reagan (who, ironically, was not an evangelical Christian) in his race against the born-again incumbent, Jimmy Carter.

They rallied around Jerry Falwell Sr.'s televised ministry in huge numbers. By the 1990s they had become the largest voting bloc in the Republican Party.

Without substantial support from born-again Christians, no aspiring Republican had a serious hope for the party's presidential nomination, which, for a twice-divorced serial philanderer, was a bit of a problem. Donald Trump desperately needed a way into the insular little world of the evangelical Right. And it just so happened that, a couple of years earlier, his lawyer had helped the most important name in evangelical politics to score some Justin Bieber tickets for his daughter.

As he tells this story in his book, Michael Cohen and the Falwell family would become the best of friends in the months after he secured them those tickets. The Cohens and the Falwells would visit, drink together, and party together.[43]

Compared with Falwell's buttoned-up world of pious believers, the fast-living New York lawyer with Donald Trump as a client was a total blast. The Falwells soon realized that they could talk to him about things they couldn't talk to anyone else about.

And so, when a much bigger problem turned up in their lives, they knew whom to call.

Most of the charlatans in this book are talkers: guys who love to be the center of attention, spinning tales that leave their audiences spellbound and leveraging their charm into riches, power, or sex. Jerry Falwell Jr. isn't like that. He is, perhaps, that rarer type of charlatan: a quiet one, happier in half-shadow than in the spotlight.

Trained as a lawyer and with a professional background in real estate development and debt financing, Falwell Jr. isn't an evangelical preacher. He has never claimed to be a religious leader. In the never-ending contest between God and mammon, he's known all along which side he stood on.

Here's the beauty of it, though: he didn't have to preach, and he didn't have to claim religious authority, because of his name. His very name was trusted and beloved by millions of older evangelicals, for whom his father had been the most important spiritual and political figure in their lives. Jerry Falwell was such a well-positioned political brand that the mere addition of a "Jr." at the end hardly seemed to make a difference.

Since Falwell Sr.'s death in 2007, Jerry Falwell Jr. had served as the head of Liberty University. It had been one of his father's passion projects: a plan to give evangelical Christians the kind of world-class university that Mormons enjoyed in Brigham Young and Catholics had in Notre Dame.

Liberty University was conceived as an explicitly and militantly religious kind of school, a training academy for the professional cadres of political Evangelicalism, under the mission statement of training "champions for Christ in every important field of study."[44]

Like most universities, Liberty U is a nonprofit institution, and as such enjoys hugely valuable tax breaks as a result. Falwell Jr., ever the businessman, soon saw its vast moneymaking potential. Across America, evangelical parents were desperate to send their children to a good, God-fearing school free from the cultural liberalism that dominated so many mainstream campuses. Falwell Jr. saw they'd be willing to pay substantial premiums to send their kids to Liberty and would ask few questions about the quality of the education on offer.

But that was just the beginning. In its early days, back when it was just Lynchburg Baptist College and its mission centered on training new evangelical pastors, the school had begun experimenting with early forms of distance learning. This amounted to mailing out on VHS badly taped Bible-study sessions led by Falwell Sr., along with tests that could be mailed back in exchange for college credits. Falwell Jr. intuited this could be a growth market if brought up to technological snuff.

In 2008 and 2009, amid the fallout from the financial crisis that rocked the world, Falwell Jr. became keenly aware that hundreds of thousands of evangelical Christians around the country were losing their jobs and sitting at home at a loss for what to do next. Suddenly, those old VHS tapes became an inspiration for a daring new ploy to rake in millions for Liberty U.

Falwell Jr. grasped that for every student able to come together with Liberty's $20,000-per-year tuition bills, there would be many more aching for a Christian education: a chance to improve their earnings prospects while remaining true to their faith. That dream is powerful, and Jerry Falwell knew there was money to be made from exploiting it.

As established in a landmark investigation by Alec MacGillis in the *New York Times Magazine*, the result of this gap in the market was Liberty University Online: an internet-based distance-learning institution that would soon dwarf Liberty's brick-and-mortar operation. President Falwell pressed the faculty members to put as much of their teaching materials as possible into online-ready formats, to be served up to distance learners worldwide—for a fee, of course.[45]

The faculty initially revolted: Liberty's online offerings were obviously designed first and foremost to make money. Course materials were to be made as easy as possible, grading was to be automated, and expensive face-to-face time between teachers and students was to be cut down to the minimum manageable.

The result was a series of courses that made Liberty's best professors squirm: painting-by-numbers exercises dumbed down to be nearly impossible to fail. The courses cost little to produce and nothing to maintain, and they could be sold innumerable times to students who would hardly learn anything from them, but would often go into debt to finance them.[46]

Liberty seemed to be morphing into a diploma mill, pure and simple, though one shot through with the saintly aura of its president's name: Jerry Falwell . . . Jr.

The stories of the lives blighted by Liberty University Online make for some grim reading. It's not just that Liberty shoved off degrees of little value on vulnerable students; it's that it specialized in exploiting precisely the kinds of evangelical students the university had been founded to serve. Students trusted Liberty precisely *because* of its evangelical identity, and because of the Falwell name. Surely, a university founded to train champions for Christ wouldn't shake down its most vulnerable students, would it?

Except it would.

And it did.

The investigative piece by MacGillis found ample evidence that Liberty Online was run on a ruthlessly commercial basis. MacGillis reports that the university paid Google more than $16.8 million in 2016 for online advertising to rustle up fresh "admissions leads" for prospective online students. When they clicked on an online ad—an ad that invariably trumpeted Liberty's Christian credentials—they were prompted to enter their phone numbers. A Liberty "admissions representative"—in fact, nothing more than a sales rep—would often be on the phone within minutes, and their only priority would be to sell, sell, sell.[47]

At its height Liberty University Online had hundreds of these admissions reps working two shifts, from 8 a.m. to 8 p.m., out of a call center set up in an old, vacated Sears store in Lynchburg, Virginia.[48] Though federal rules ban explicit quotas, people on Liberty's sales floor allege it was an open secret that if they didn't enroll eight new students a day, their jobs were in peril. There was no place to hide: the previous day's new sign-up tallies were posted prominently on the sales floor, with the names of recruiters who signed up four or fewer students in red. Monthly tallies also went up, and they too shamed the laggards with red ink, while the best performers could expect a raise. A whole separate operation had some sixty admissions reps focused on veterans and military families. This was a particular focus because federal dollars for veterans' education are abundant. At one point, some thirty thousand Liberty Online students came through the military path.

The *New York Times Magazine* investigation found that, like the sleaziest of online scammers, the reps would push and prod during these calls to find out just how much the student could afford to pay. They'd max that out first, then push them to seek federal financial aid and take on student loans to finance the rest. Some Liberty Online students ended up with nearly $100,000 in student debt to obtain online degrees that cost the university almost nothing to deliver: dumbed-down courses in which students received little or no individual instruction, with assignments that were automatically graded, leading to degrees that few employers took seriously.[49]

And why didn't they take Liberty's online offering seriously? Because Liberty didn't either. In 2017 Liberty spent just $2,609 per student—averaged across both online and in-person learning. It doesn't disclose how much it spends per online student, but given that in-person learning typically costs tens of thousands of dollars per student, the online-only number must be tiny indeed. In some years, Liberty spent less than half the money it collected in tuition fees on actually instructing its students.

By 2016 net income from this operation topped $215 million per year, the *New York Times Magazine* investigation found.

And as a fully accredited nonprofit university, Liberty Online students qualified to receive government funding as well. Falwell Jr. was unrelenting when it came to seeking out these subsidies. Indeed, in 2017 Liberty received the sixth-largest sum of federal financial aid money out of all the universities in America: a staggering $772 million. On top of that, Liberty was raking in $42 million in benefits from the Department of Veterans Affairs alone. Indeed, the majority of Liberty's revenue was taxpayer funded.

Squeezing Uncle Sam for all he was worth, Liberty became a money machine, unsparing in cost cutting and enormously aggressive when it came to raising money. For a nonprofit, it was staggeringly profitable too. In Jerry Jr.'s first ten years in charge, Liberty's net assets ballooned from $150 million to $2.5 billion.

These figures were not revealed by a feat of investigative journalism. Jerry Falwell Jr. never hid them; he reveled in them. He bragged about Liberty's financial prowess at every opportunity. If anything, he said he was surprised that more universities weren't following his path of ruthless cost cutting, bare-bones online offerings, and relentless pursuit of revenue.[50]

On the receiving end of this bonanza, Jerry Jr. profited handsomely. His $1.1 million salary made him one of America's fifty best-paid university presidents, outearning the leaders of several Ivy League schools.[51] But that was not enough for him. When the time came to renegotiate his compensation package, he asked Liberty's board (which he'd naturally packed with cronies) for a jaw-dropping $2 million salary. That would have rocketed him into the top ten highest-paid university presidents in America, past the leaders of Harvard and Stanford.

He made a compelling case for himself. It wasn't just the way the endowment had grown; it was the way the campus had been transformed. Since taking over, Falwell Jr. had gone on a building spree on Liberty's leafy, seven-thousand-acre campus in Lynchburg, Virginia, tearing down the shoddy temporary buildings that anchored the university in its upstart days in the '70s and building a slew of stylish new state-of-the-art facilities for everything from tennis to the performing arts. Speaking to the Liberty board, he could confidently say that while his father had the vision for a world-leading Christian university, it was he, the son, who had really made it happen.

But it's not just about the fat salary that Falwell Jr. was after. It's that he seemed to treat the university's assets pretty much as his own. Liberty University Police Department officers kept watch over his home, which was nowhere near campus. Liberty custodial staff did odd jobs around the house too, though they weren't supposed to. Liberty's private jet became a particular plaything: Falwell Jr. would use it to fly to Miami for vacation, letting the university pick up the tab. Why? Because he'd get his yearly medical checkup in Miami, and since his contract with the university mandated an annual checkup, the whole junket would count as "university business."

Slowly but surely, Jerry Falwell Jr. had turned his father's passion project to create a world-class evangelical university into a private fund, jet included.

It was on one of these jet-setting trips to Miami that Jerry Falwell Jr. made the mistake that, years later, would help place Donald Trump in the White House. Jerry and his wife, Becki, were staying at Miami's famous Fontainebleau Hotel, where anything goes.

Lying on a daybed costing $150 per day, Becki noticed the chiseled nineteen-year-old pool boy and knew right away she wanted much more than a drink from him.[52]

His name was Giancarlo Granda. Tall and impossibly handsome, he looked exactly like what he was: a Miami Beach weightlifter. A few drinks in, Becki had little to hold her back. Soon she was flirting with him. Minutes later, she was inviting him to her room.

What comes next is disputed. The Falwells deny Granda's story, which is that when he got to Becki's room, he found her husband, Jerry, sitting in a corner. Startled, he began to leave, only for Jerry to put him at his ease. "Just go for it," is the message Granda says he got as Becki reassured him: Jerry just wanted to watch.[53]

The Falwells now admit that Becki had an affair with Giancarlo Granda, though they continue to deny that Jerry was in any way involved. It might just have been a case of he-said/they-said except for one detail, one scandalous detail that would change the course of history.

There were photos.

And those photos were taken very much from the angle where Giancarlo Granda says Jerry had been sitting.

To be clear, what happened between Giancarlo Granda and Becki Falwell was fully consensual. Indeed, had it involved anyone but the president of America's premiere born-again Christian university, it would hardly rate a mention. But Liberty University trumpeted its devotion to family values from the rooftops.

Just to enroll, students would have to agree to pay five-hundred-dollar fines if they were caught drinking, and they could face expulsion if discovered. Naturally, no sex of any kind could be countenanced between anyone other than the aforementioned "natural-born man and natural-born woman" joined in matrimony. Liberty's honor code, known as the Liberty Way, was binding not just on students but on employees too—employees including the university's president, of course.

How, exactly, those photos ended up in the possession of Giancarlo Granda and his business partner is still unknown. What is known is that the Falwells soon became business partners with Granda, bankrolling an investment in a Miami youth hostel that a partner ran. It was when that partnership went sour that Granda realized he had some killer leverage to use against Falwell Jr. And that's where Michael Cohen, Trump's attorney, comes back into our story.[54]

You can imagine the situation the Falwells were in, and why they'd turn to a guy like Cohen to fix it. Cohen knew how to handle situations like these; he'd done it plenty of times before for his good old boss, Donald Trump. In his memoir Cohen says he "went for the jugular," hinting at ruthless legal action against Granda's partner unless he handed in all his photos and deleted all copies of them.

Which he did . . . for a prize that's never been revealed.

Cohen, for his part, wasn't as reliable. He received the photos and deleted them all except one, which he'd keep for leverage against Falwell when the time came.

And the time came soon enough, in the summer of 2015, when Cohen's boss was revving up his long-shot campaign for the White House and wanted—no, needed—a high-profile evangelical endorsement to cement his standing with the Republican Party's most influential voting bloc.[55]

It's easy to forget now, but in early 2015 Donald Trump's presidential bid was widely assumed to be a publicity stunt for some upcoming TV show. The notion that a famously horny casino mogul could end up leading the straightlaced religious Right was outlandish—little more than a joke, really. Political pros took it for granted that the GOP's evangelical base would balk at the idea of voting for such a man. Surely, the family values crowd would coalesce around some challenger, and that would be the end of Trump, right?

That was certainly Senator Ted Cruz's strategy. A devout Christian and the son of a born-again preacher, Cruz spoke the language of Evangelicalism fluently. He'd grown up in that world; he was one of them, which is why Cruz went all out to land Jerry Falwell Jr.'s all-important endorsement, and why most people took it for granted he would get it.

What Cruz didn't know—what no one outside a tiny group of people knew—was that Trump had kompromat on Falwell Jr.; Cohen said so himself.[56]

And so, when Michael Cohen called in the favor on behalf of his boss, Falwell Jr. was in no position to push back. Jerry Falwell Jr.'s was the first high-profile evangelical endorsement Donald Trump received: a key milestone on his path to the presidency. From that moment on, the Trump juggernaut became unstoppable. Trump swept primary after primary on his way to the White House.

"After that, Steve Bannon called me and said, 'You won the election for us,'" Jerry Jr. told *Vanity Fair*.[57] And the compromising photo of Becki Falwell with Giancarlo Granda stayed safely stowed in Michael Cohen's hard drive all along.

The reckoning, when it did come, was fast and furious. On August 24, 2020, Granda went public with allegations that he'd had a seven-year affair with Becki Falwell while her husband got his kicks from watching.

First he spoke to Reuters, which had been on the trail of the story for years. Then he went on a tour of national media, speaking to ABC News, CNN, *Politico*, and the *Washington Post.* By the end of that day, Jerry's tenure at the head of Liberty University was over. Before another year had passed, Liberty had sued him for millions for concealing the affair from its board.

To hear Jerry Falwell Jr. tell it, Granda was little more than an extortionist, holding evidence of his affair with Becki ransom to try to extract as much as $2 million from him. Falwell continues to deny he was aware of the affair. Questions about who took the photos said to have ended up in Michael Cohen's care remain unanswered.

Liberty University's board would go on to sue Falwell for $10 million in compensatory damages for a long list of breaches of fiduciary duty. In a long and sordid seventy-four-page complaint, the suit alleges Falwell's habitual drunkenness impaired his judgment and led him to make a series of blunders that cost the university dearly. Falwell returned fire with a defamation suit. The saga was finally settled out of court in July 2024, with Falwell apologizing for "errors of judgment and mistakes" while Liberty University paid him an undisclosed sum in retirement and severance pay and retained the right to use his father's name and likeness under agreed conditions.[58]

One thing we're sure of after writing this book is that there are all kinds of different charlatans out there. Jerry Falwell Jr. is unique primarily for having inherited a cherished institution and turning it into a personal vehicle, and inheriting a powerful position within a religious-political movement and turning *that* into an occasion for making a fortune. Piggybacking on the dream his father spent decades turning into a reality, he mercilessly exploited the reserves of goodwill his name engendered.

Like the parishioners of the Eagle Mountain International Church and the Universal Church of the Kingdom of God, Liberty's students found themselves in the hands of charlatans not even a little bit shy about turning some of the central messages in the gospel on their heads.

How did they manage this? What was it that left their marks so vulnerable to the kind of manipulation Kenneth Copeland, Edir Macedo, and Jerry Falwell Jr. proved so adept at plying? Was it their marks' thirst for spiritual connection that left them vulnerable, or was it something else that moved their followers?

To answer this, it pays to step back and understand the role religion—in its traditional guise—plays in the lives of the faithful.

Religion has long been the scaffolding on which local communities build the sorts of ties that keep societies vibrant and help people flourish. At their best, Protestant churches can be drivers of community involvement: places where thick networks of face-to-face ties are created and sustained week by week.

These kinds of networks are fundamental to human well-being. Studies show that religiously observant people report higher levels of subjective well-being, and people who attend religious services not only report they're happier but also engage in fewer unhealthy behaviors like smoking or excessive drinking. More than one meta-analysis now shows statistically significant correlation between religious observance and measures of well-being. Other studies find results hold just as true for Jews and Muslims as they do for Christians: more observant people report higher life satisfaction. The relationship seems robust and can't easily be explained by outside factors.[59]

It makes sense, then, that people crave this positive influence in their lives. Where local religious communities break down, however, people become isolated and lose access to this life-enhancing experience. In 1994 just 38 percent of Americans told Gallup they seldom or never went to church; by 2023 that figure had shot up to 57 percent.[60] This decline in religious observance brings increasing social isolation, and that isolation leaves people exposed to the kind of exploitation we've been exploring.

Notice what the cases we've looked at have in common: all three mimic the community dimension of traditional churches, but in a debased and exploitative new form. All are mediated by new technologies, with the entry point into new forms of worship on a screen, rather than in the form of a face-to-face interaction.

The more we looked at these three cases, the more we came to see that the heart of their appeal wasn't really about the spiritual realm at all. Eagle Mountain International Church, the Universal Church of the Kingdom of God, and Liberty University Online appealed to people thirsty for community ties. But their promise was false: rather than satisfying their need for human connection, they enmeshed them into webs of exploitation relentlessly focused on separating them from their money.

This is a theme we'll return to again and again throughout this book. As social interaction increasingly moves from the real-life world of face-to-face interactions to the virtual world of disembodied pixels on a screen, people's unmet need for social interaction increasingly exposes them to exploitation.

If today's charlatans are increasingly digital, that's partly because the digital realm is becoming home to more socially isolated people, and isolation itself leaves people at increased risk of exploitation. This dynamic is pervasive and perverse, and nowhere is it more obvious than in the realm of the digital-first scam.

5

Born Digital

Dawn of the AI Grift

THERE WAS A TIME WHEN A CHARLATAN HAD TO *HUSTLE* TO FIND marks, or even potential marks. It may be that, as they say, a sucker is born every minute, but going out and *finding* those suckers used to take time, shoe leather, and effort. They'd have to identify marks one by one, woo them one by one, and even then, many might just walk away. It was exhausting, painstaking work.

That was the twentieth-century model, at least. These days, charlatans can skip all that aggravation.

What used to take months can now be done in minutes by anyone online.

The age of the artificial intelligence grift is upon us.

Borrowing the techniques developed by legitimate online businesses to identify new customers, today's charlatans are *born digital*. Rather than transferring old, pre-internet scams to the online world, they're launching them there, beginning with online personas that promise the world and deliver heartbreak.

It's easy to see why: artificial intelligence allows charlatans to target potential marks with unprecedented speed and ease. "By their searches thou shall know them" is the name of the game here. As long as people share the most intimate secrets of their lives online, their innermost fears and desires, they'll lay themselves open to victimization by AI-enabled charlatans.

The cases we look at here got their start in the soon-to-seem-quaint world of social media search algorithms: the kind of technology Facebook and Google first developed to try to figure out which ad to show to which web surfer. Soon, though, full-fledged AI models will be able to feed on YouTube histories and Facebook profiles, laying bare people's feelings about family and friends, their place in the world, their fears and desires. As digital technology improves, charlatans' ability to zero in on each individual user's intimate *dreams* will only grow. This is dangerous. Turning our dreams into leverage against us is the charlatan's stock-in-trade—putting more of our dreams in the hands of more budding charlatans can only lead to growing victimization.

But it's not just about finding marks. These sophisticated new technologies turn into powerful accelerators of every part of the charlatan's craft. But digital-first charlatans don't only find marks more quickly and efficiently than their offline predecessors; they can also dig much deeper into their marks' lives. This can act as an alternative to scalability: some charlatans find a profitable niche in going not wider, into more and more people's lives, but rather deeper into the lives of a few.

This came as a surprise to us. We did not set out to write a chapter about online cults, but as we looked deeper into the stories in this chapter, it dawned on us that this was exactly what we were doing. It turns out today's most successful online charlatans reliably find themselves as the heads of organizations that look very much like classic cults: organizations that take over every aspect of their followers' lives and are built around charismatic leaders who demand total fealty and absolute obedience.

These organizations are born in the online realm, but they don't stay there. Little by little, they take up more and more room in their followers' lives until they crowd out everything—and every*one*—else.

And what we've seen in this space is just a taste of things to come. As AI technology improves, and as more budding charlatans begin to experiment with creative new ways to deploy it to meet their goals, the cases we describe here could well come to look like the relatively tame forerunners of the more destructive cults to come.

As some charlatans find success, those who come after them will do what they've always done: learn from their tactics, refine them, and try to improve upon them. Many will fail, a few will succeed, and a smaller number still will win big, attracting their own wave of imitators and improvers. This is how charlatan tactics have always spread. But with newer, better tools at their disposal, the world will soon find that these digital and viral plays are born scalable too.

Bentinho Massaro

When you first run into Bentinho Massaro's Instagram feed, your initial reaction will be that he must be some sort of fashion influencer.[1] The dapper young Dutch guru wants very much to be seen as one. Shot in exotic locales and dwelling on his fondness for fine cigars, Bentinho's public image doesn't immediately scream spiritual enlightenment.

But that's only until you start to listen to him . . . because once you shift into his videos, you quickly realize that Bentinho Massaro has used his social media footprint to launch a remarkably successful group with worryingly cultlike aspects.

But the talk comes later.

What you see first is a vision of the life many young people aspire to. Mixed in with glamorous photos of Massaro frolicking on the obligatory private jet wearing three-piece suits, there are his videos, and at the end of many of them, an invitation to join courses promising to bring you into communion with "the absolute truth of the one infinite creator."[2]

Bentinho's business ventures—from the No Limits Society to his imaginatively named Trinfinity Academy—were born digital. He did not graft an online presence onto a preexisting following; he did it the other way around, growing a following out of a Facebook page, a YouTube channel, and an Instagram feed. On each platform, Massaro puts out content foregrounding his Hollywood good looks and expounding on themes from parallel realities in nonlinear time to mirror consciousness. Then he sits back, and he lets the algorithms do their thing.

Many of the videos on his YouTube feed look almost like therapy sessions, with Bentinho lending a sympathetic ear to one of his follower's problems and giving her—it's usually a "her," most often young and beautiful—spiritual advice on how to overcome them. One woman in obvious emotional distress tells him she scheduled a vacation from work to concentrate on her spiritual state but has just spent the first three days of it crying uncontrollably.[3] Bentinho, wearing a "Fuck Politics" T-shirt, never asks her questions to try to understand the source of her grief. Instead, he advises her to lean into her sadness and reflect that three days is really such a short time to achieve a higher level of consciousness.

Bentinho's spiritual teachings are a kind of Eastern spirituality mishmash, cobbled together from the lessons learned as a twenty-year-old on a gap year in the ashrams (spiritual schools) of India. At his spiritual retreats, he expounds at length on his view of the oneness of creation, and your role in it.

Here's a taste, from a retreat held in Hawai'i in April 2018. A relaxed but focused Bentinho wearing a backward baseball cap held forth for over an hour, with gems such as these:

> Your direct connection to the source is already here. It's the "I" from where you see, the "I" from where you hear, the "I" from where you think. But it is before the thinker, prior to, more original than, more already here. Thoughts you have to add every single day. It's a job. You have to continue to add thoughts to what is, to what is, to what "you" is. That "isness," that "I am" is your gateway to the direct recognition, the realization, the deepening, the

> purification into source, becoming transparent as an individuated entity to that source that transcends individuation, just the oneness beneath all things. But if you cannot cut through the bullshit of mind at any given moment with great intensity and joy and surrender, then how will you really be successful at anything else?[4]

The technical term for this kind of pitch is *word salad*. Massaro has mastered the art of the meaningless but profound-sounding pronouncements. His lectures are filled with ideas that stay just below the level of intelligibility yet are filled with buzzwords designed to make them seem transcendentally meaningful.

With a charlatan's uncanny knack for making the commonplace seem extraordinary, Massaro has built an online following of tens of thousands on the back of these teachings. And why shouldn't he? After all, Massaro "vibrates at a higher frequency" than run-of-the-mill human beings, or so he says. And he can show you how to do it yourself . . . just following his meditation tutorials on YouTube can help to "activate your pineal gland."[5] After all, who wouldn't want to be trained as a free agent for the ignition of a global awakening?

So, are you in? Then an in-person retreat might be just the thing for you.

If this stuff gets your bullshit-o-meter ringing loudly, it's likely you've never come across Bentinho online. Why would you? Bentinho Massaro is too smart to waste his marketing dollars on you.

Chances are, if you're skeptical about this kind of pitch, the algorithm's already figured out you're not a promising prospect and is targeting his ads elsewhere.

But if you show the machine that you're interested in Eastern mysticism, if you watch meditation videos on YouTube or follow yoga groups on Facebook, if you give the artificial brains the data to peg you as a good match for the spiritual solace Bentinho is selling, then chances are that sooner or later an ad for one of his videos will turn up on a screen in front of you.

You don't actually have to punch his name into the search bar: it is enough to engage with similar content from other creators, and the algorithm will do the rest.

Sooner or later, YouTube will queue a Bentinho Massaro video for you, and Instagram will start populating your feed with his posts. Artificial intelligence will make sure that its spiritual pitches feel as real and human as the sentiments they cunningly evoke.

You may not click on it. You probably won't click on it. And Bentinho is cool with that too. It's not necessary for him that everyone who sees one of his ads clicks through to one of his feeds.

He needs only a tiny percentage of the people served his content to click through. And then he needs only a tiny percentage of *them* to stick around long enough to get seriously interested in his teachings. And then he needs only a tiny percentage of *them* to eventually buy one of those expensive courses.

That's enough.

Enough for him to make bank. Enough to bankroll a lavish lifestyle. And enough to keep his days and nights full of beautiful women who feel it is a glorious spiritual privilege to be a part of Bentinho's world.

It's the same business model every online business follows. It's just that instead of selling you scented candles, he's selling you enlightenment.

His goal is for you to make his spiritual lectures part of your everyday routine, which is why video is so central to Bentinho's appeal. YouTube has beamed out hundreds of Bentinho videos to his 111,000 followers.[6] They feature a mix of guided meditations, spiritual teachings, and pitches to attend those pricey in-person seminars.

What's terrifying is not how big those numbers are, but how small. By YouTube influencer standards, Bentinho is a minnow: thousands of content creators have bigger follower counts. He's okay with that too: his business model prizes depth over breadth. Bentinho doesn't need tens of millions of followers. He needs only a few thousand truly committed followers, willing to turn their lives over to him.

Bentinho's spiel amounts to standard New Age gobbledygook. If he just put it into books and sold them, his business would be indistinguishable from that of any number of spiritual charlatans out there. The difference is that Massaro has a marketing mind as well, and the No Limits Society has mastered that sleek, contemporary aesthetic—a kind of Eastern twist on the prosperity gospel, where you attract abundance to yourself by devoting yourself to his word.

The nonsense doesn't stay online, though. For his wealthier marks, Bentinho offers a variety of "spiritual retreat" options in exotic locales from Sedona, Arizona, and Ecuador to Egypt and Costa Rica, with price tags to match. In 2018 a *Vice* videography team managed to access one such retreat at a stunning neoclassical castle in Bentinho's native Netherlands.[7] We see a parade of gorgeous people of all ages streaming in, yoga mats in tow, earnestly looking forward to a weekend of enlightenment.

People walk in through the door *wanting* to believe and immediately find themselves surrounded by others also desperate to believe. An atmosphere of mutually reinforcing certainty soon takes over, with confirmation bias, motivated reasoning, and social proof all working together to allow Bentinho to hack into the HumanOS his followers are running and turn their brains into his instruments.

We see them sitting in silence for extended meditation periods, then dancing ecstatically with one another. In one lighthearted break, they don swimsuits and have a joyous water fight with each other, dousing one another amid shrieks of laughter. It looks like the most amazing party, the fun punctuated only by earnest spiritual lectures from Bentinho Massaro.

It's perfect. A little too perfect? During a sit-down interview, the *Vice* reporter confronts Bentinho directly, asking for his reaction to allegations that his group amounts to a cult.[8] Bentinho takes it in stride, saying, "We *are* a cult! We are a curious, understanding, loving tribe," with a laugh.

"When they label it a 'cult,'" he explains, "it's because they haven't really experienced the benefits. They see it from the outside in, and it reminds them of things that they fear, or they've been taught to fear."

Yet former members paint a far darker picture, one in which these joyful, ecstatic retreats work as a recruitment mechanism and a filter for initiates into Bentinho's inner circle. Only once there, they alleged, do the stranger aspects of his belief system come to the fore: the preoccupation with readying your soul for contact with extraterrestrial superbeings, for one. But it's not just the more bizarre doctrines that he reserves for these in-person gatherings; it's also the full spectrum of cultlike control techniques that come into play.

Unquestioning commitment to Bentinho's teachings is a given. Some of those who've left the group describe a stultifying atmosphere, with members subjected to grueling "distortion" sessions where Massaro leads the group in a viciously prying examination of each member's shortcomings.

These are the "distortions" that are keeping them from attaining complete enlightenment of the type Massaro claims to embody. Hour after hour, members pick apart any foible in one another's character, ostensibly for the purpose of "helping" the victim to overcome his or her distortions.

Several women in Massaro's orbit have alleged Massaro subjected them to a terrible pattern of exploitation. Speaking on the cult whistleblower podcast *A Little Bit Culty*, one former member, Jacqueline Graham, alleges that soon after joining his group, Bentinho told her they formed a "divine union" that would accelerate one another's path toward enlightenment . . . if only she would merge her (considerable) bank account with his.[9] Over the course of a monthslong relationship, she alleges, a pattern of emotional, financial, and sexual abuse arose in which Bentinho would switch between showering admiration on and coldly withholding attention from her to obtain complete compliance. Graham told interviewers that though Bentinho claims to have lost much of the money she gave him through investments that went bust, she suspects he instead ferreted it away beyond her reach.

The allegations are echoed by Jade Alectra, another former follower who describes her brutally emotionally and sexually exploitative relationship with Massaro. She alleged that Bentinho would openly sleep with several of his young followers at the same time yet forbid each of them from sleeping with anyone else.[10] She alleged that he liked to establish psychological dominance over the women around him by demanding they strip naked during group discussions, supposedly to "help them" shed the illusion of individuality and fulfill the "law of one"—oneness with the universe itself. These intensely traumatizing episodes would, she alleges, sometimes culminate in a demand that the woman do a handstand, naked, in front of the group. Alectra says fear of reproach, of getting "in trouble" with Bentinho or being shunned by him, cowed her into compliance.

Bentinho's original business venture, the No Limits Society, turns out to have quite a few limits, all of them relating to any criticism, real or perceived, of its founder. In the group's cosmic teachings, spiritual entities are divided into two groups: service-to-self entities, which are evil, self-centered bodies that suck the spiritual energy from others, and service-to-others spirits, saintly entities beyond ego. Service-to-self entities are seen as demonic spirits that wrestle for control of people and drive them away from enlightenment.

You can see how this sets up a watertight closed loop system of logic to protect Massaro from criticism. Talking to *A Little Bit Culty*, Keilan McNeil, another former follower of Massaro's spiritual enterprise, recalls how any and every perceived criticism of the leader or the way he runs the group was instantly met with claims of possession by service-to-self demons.[11] After all, Massaro is a "clear mirror," flawless and without distortions, in perfect resonance with the universe. Naturally, service-to-self entities feel threatened by him and want to cut him down to size. It follows that if you find fault with anything he does—his allegedly chaotic finances, the way he allegedly emotionally abuses the women he sleeps with, the entire system of guru worship he has allegedly built around himself, or anything else—you are more likely than not demonically possessed.

McNeil reports a repeating pattern of abuse, where Bentinho would pick out followers—usually wealthy and attractive young women—for emotional and financial abuse. If they push back in any way, if they even try to speak out for themselves, they are instantly accused of demonic possession and discarded in favor of the next victim. Other followers would rally around Bentinho, turning against any member newly discovered to be in the grips of a "service-to-self" demon. Alectra—the follower who accused Massaro of sexual exploitation above—verifies his allegations, describing the panic she felt during a retreat in Costa Rica when she herself became convinced that a service-to-self entity, acting through her, was attacking Massaro.[12]

"I'm sitting in my room, *shaking*," Alectra says, recalling the episode. "Like, 'what the fuck do I do?' I don't even know how to get it out. Like, how did it get in me!?" It's a remarkable testament to Massaro's power: when he accuses a follower of being demonically possessed, the follower *believes* him.

Not, of course, that you'll see anyone being accused of demonic possession on Bentinho's social media feeds. There, the beautiful fantasy of an influencer lifestyle gets pumped out 24/7, bringing in new recruits even as, within the group, episodes of gaslighting and abuse become routine. The algorithms don't know that; they couldn't know that. Instead, they keep doing what they were programmed to do: recruiting the next batch of victims.

Stung by the damaging stories survivors of his group have been telling in the media, Bentinho's tried to protect himself by getting his followers to sign increasingly restrictive contracts limiting their ability to tell the stories of what they see during their time with him. In May 2024 journalist Matt Bruenig filed an unfair labor practices complaint with the National Labor Relations Board alleging the highly restrictive agreements, which include confidentiality rules, a media-contact rule, a nondisparagement rule, a no-recording/no-camera rule, and a mandatory-arbitration rule, violate US labor law by potentially silencing victims of abuse. No decision has been made in that case.[13]

But Bentinho Massaro is far from the only charlatan to have discovered the digital world's infinite potential as a recruitment device for his schemes.

Teal Swan

Drive a few minutes north of the small town of Atenas, in Costa Rica, then off on a little dirt road to the left for a few hundred yards more, and you'll find it. Nestled within a lush, tropical forest, the Philia Center bills itself as "a sacred space where healing occurs first and foremost through connection."[14]

Turn up for one of the center's retreats—$5,000 a week, not including airfare—and at first you could be forgiven for thinking you'd reached just another New Age wellness spa: a place for yoga, vegan cuisine, and lots of talk about aligning chakras. And Philia certainly is that, but it's also so much more.

"It is our intention that at Philia," the website says, "each person will experience new depths of interpersonal connection, emotional intimacy and relationship."

At the center, retreat participants meet each other and quickly settle into a series of emotionally intense workshops, each aimed at revealing deeper and deeper layers of childhood trauma.

To begin, they're guided through an intensely personal meditation on their own death: how it happens, how they are grieved, what they leave behind. The experience seems to shake participants deeply, with many weeping softly to themselves by the end.[15]

Then comes the curveball.

What you've just experienced, they're told, is no mere imagination. You've just had an actual, first-person experience of your actual departure from this life.

Not a version of it.

Not a symbol of it.

Your death thing itself.

How do a few dozen perfectly normal-seeming people from North America and Europe end up paying thousands of dollars to preexperience their own deaths in a Central American jungle?

Welcome to the very strange, very dangerous world of Teal Swan.

With her deep blue-green eyes, waist-long chestnut hair, and stunning figure, Swan leans into her sex appeal as part of her recruiting pitch. Divorced multiple times by the age of thirty-seven, Swan comes across as whip-smart, fast-talking, and no-nonsense: her charisma grabs you at once.

Born Mary Teal Bosworth in 1984 and raised in the small town of Logan, Utah, Teal Swan says she could tell she was different from a very early age. She claims to have synesthesia, a rare neurological condition that gives rise to the sensation of senses blending into one another, leading people to report "hearing" colors or "seeing" music, both in quite a literal way.[16]

But that was just the start. From the beginning Swan could sense realms of consciousness closed off to most people: dead relatives, strange spirits, and past lives. Not just one, but many, including some, she says, who lived before the earth was formed.

Her extrasensory experiences led to what she recounts as a horrendous childhood and adolescence, including a harrowing history of psychological and sexual abuse. Swan describes the abuse she suffered as ritualistic and satanic, aimed at snuffing out her special powers, the entire thing leading to a first suicide attempt at the age of seventeen.[17]

Swan puts her experience of abuse at the center of her pitch. If she can help you cope with trauma, it's because she herself has been through some of the worst trauma imaginable. As she tells it, no one had a way for her to heal from the profound trauma of her childhood. So, she came up with a system.

Swan's *Completion Process*, published in book form in 2016, set out a step-by-step process for victims of profound childhood trauma to put their lives back together again.[18] It was an enormous hit.

Swan has no mental health training of any kind, nor does she think she needs it.[19] A scathing critique of conventional mental health provision is at the center of her appeal. Swan pours scorn on the milquetoast, swaddling approach of conventional mental health professionals, their timid avoidance of the hardest feelings and the hardest topics. She preaches facing trauma head-on and counsels her followers to run toward their pain rather than away from it. Only by forthrightly confronting the episodes in our past that bring us pain, she says, can we hope to heal.[20]

Teal Swan's followers seem mostly to be emotionally fragile people disappointed with the care on offer from conventional mental health practitioners: people struggling with bereavement, with financial crises, with lost love. They've been through therapy, and it hasn't helped. Virtually all describe themselves as desperate, clutching at straws, looking frantically for someone, anyone with answers to their deep pain. Many struggle with suicidal ideation.[21]

These are the people Teal Swan targets, quite consciously, quite strategically, with a sophisticated online marketing strategy proven to bring paying customers through the door.

This isn't a supposition.

We know it's true, because she told us. In a remarkable 2018 podcast series produced by *Gizmodo*, Swan is disarmingly blunt about her approach.

"Most people were going through a fucking huge crisis, like a gun-to-your-head kind of crisis, and then they typed something like 'how do I not kill myself,' and my videos popped up," she tells journalist Jennings Brown.[22] "I specifically try to go for tags [. . .] that capture audiences, because when you're in a desperate state, it's not sophisticated. People when they're in that state they type things like 'I just lost my mother what the fuck do I do?'—literally, that will be the Google tagline," she explained.

"So," she concludes, "even when we're doing videos we'll add things like that so that if someone's suicidal or somebody's had a breakup or whatever, that's the video that comes up."[23]

Swan's search-engine-optimization game is on point. It's no coincidence that people with suicidal ideation flock to her. She has quite consciously set the algorithm to go search out the suicidal and bring them to her.

Teal Swan soon built a flywheel on the backs of these emotionally volatile, deeply vulnerable people. Her fantastically popular YouTube channel drives sales of her books, her books drive people to her retreats, her retreats create a never-ending pipeline of unpaid volunteers for her business ventures, which put out her YouTube feed, and then it's lather, rinse, repeat.

Mainstream practitioners are deeply troubled by the types of messages Swan brings to the vulnerable people she targets. Swan's Completion Process, with her emphasis on facing sources of trauma head-on, seems to help some people, as her legions of devoted fans attest. But for some acutely suicidal viewers, Swan's techniques could be dangerous, or even fatal.

One particular concern surrounds that death meditation, in which she encourages people to imagine, in detail, what their deaths will be like. Plenty of her devotees love the experience for the way it allows them to reconceive their current lives in a transcendent framework. They feel they benefit from it, and perhaps some do.

But encouraging an acutely suicidal person to luxuriate in this kind of ideation is risky. For a subset of the suicidal, imagining the act itself could tip one over the edge.

And it all gets much worse when you layer in esoteric ideas about reincarnation. She believes people are mostly reincarnated aliens from different planets, the worst being a class of evil reincarnated reptilians.[24] Swan claims to remember many past lives, so she naturally downplays the importance of any one death: in the cosmic scheme of things, it's not really such a big deal. At some point, her multiple-lives perspective can bleed into almost an apology for suicide. In one now infamous 2012 video, since taken down from her YouTube feed, Swan likened suicide to a "reset button"—just a way to start all over again if your current life isn't going great: "What suicide is, is pushing the reset button. It's not a good or bad decision in and of itself. It's not something that source either condones or condemns. You cannot say that suicide is wrong without also saying that death is wrong. Death is always a choice. You choose not to participate in the same way as you chose to participate in the first place because you are two points of perspective."[25]

You can see why this kind of messaging sets mental health professionals' hair on end. And while Swan retracted that video, she replaced it with another (titled "What to Do If You Are Suicidal," which has over 151,000 views on YouTube) that is slightly subtler, but amounts to the same idea: "Death is nothing more than a halting of forward momentum, and from that place we find we desire momentum, and so after death, the only place to go from there is towards life once more. So, here is the dominant question: Why leave? Why not do the most with the life you have already built, the things you've acquired, the stuff you've learned, the stuff you've learned as opposed to starting over, from scratch."[26]

Swan does then lay out a way people can "recommit to life" (by, of course, watching more of her YouTube videos). And, to be clear, many of them do. At every in-person event she does, Swan hears a familiar refrain: "You saved my life," or "You saved my sister's life." There's nothing figurative about it: people right on the verge of taking their own lives find solace in Swan's teachings, and they step back from the brink.

And the numbers we're dealing with here are not small. The so-called Teal Tribe is massive. Her Instagram feed is followed by more than six hundred thousand people; her official Facebook community has more than 2.4 million members.[27] Her YouTube videos have been watched a cumulative 150 *million* times.[28] That's what happens when your grift is digital, global, and scalable.

The dream Teal Swan targets is primal: relief from a life of psychic torment. For many, many emotionally fragile people who have felt ill-served by conventional mental health approaches, Swan becomes a guide, a champion, a voice of companionship amid a life of pain.

It's just that, as happens with so many of these groups, a positive, life-affirming, self-help-oriented outer ring of followers seems to have built up around a far sketchier inner core: at Philia, her Costa Rican retreat center, not everyone goes home at the end of the retreat. A committed core of Teal Tribers live there full time in what they describe as an "intentional community," but which many would describe as a cult.

To be clear, Swan is well aware of the accusation, and she strenuously denies it. So much so that in 2020 her company hired a private investigator, Molly Monahan, to produce a report investigating the allegations. So confident was Swan that a careful assessment of the facts would clear her that she willingly put a team of documentary filmmakers led by director Jon Kasbe with her.

"Teal's organization," Monahan says, "requested that I fully cooperate."[29]

What followed is the very definition of being hoisted by your own petard. As Monahan dug into Swan's group, she found it satisfied more and more items on her cult checklist. As she looked into the treatment of the people who have left Swan's inner circle for signs of ostracism, she met Jared, who describes his brutal exit from the group: "The last thing, I think the last thing, that she told me as I'm, like, leaving and everyone's, like, ganged up on me, she said, 'If I were you, I would just go kill myself, cuz there's no hope for you.'"[30]

And it gets worse. Later in her research, Monahan is shocked that Swan's business chief, Mathias, has willingly shared a wildly incriminating document with her: "The Non-Negotiables." The file lists the things people need to agree to if they want to join Swan's inner circle.

It reads like a manual for cultic abuse. Here is Monahan's summary of what it says:

- You can't put your own family first.
- Teal has to come first: if she wants you there, she gets you.
- The priority of the entire community is whatever is in the best interest of Teal; everything else is second to that.
- You can't have personal boundaries that have in any way an effect on Teal.[31]

And that's not all, as the expectations of absolute subservience to Teal were made ever more explicit in the document:

> You will now be in the world of fame, this makes relationships very, very complicated and often painful. Your associations are in fact your potential biggest liability. Anyone you introduce to the community could turn on Teal,

> blackmail her, rip the community apart, put extra pressure on Teal or other members of the community. When fame and money are involved, people simply cannot be trusted. Your life is not going to even remotely resemble normal. If you want to have a normal life, do not choose to be part of the inner circle.

Monahan was left with little doubt that Teal's inner circle meets the classic criteria for cult groups, which is awkward given that she was specifically hired to reach the opposite conclusion. Teal predictably blew her top when she received her final report, blamed Mathias for it, and declared herself very disappointed, her narcissistic rage on full display.

It barely needs saying that she never published the report.

What's remarkable isn't Monahan's findings—anyone moderately equipped with bullshit sensors looking at the revealingly named "Teal Tribe" can tell it has strong cultlike aspects in the first five minutes of the first Google search.

What's remarkable is the naivete with which Teal's followers share with investigators and documentarians all the information that definitely establishes them as a cult, and the genuine surprise they express when those same people then turn around and tell them, "Yup, it's a cult."

It's as though something about proximity to a charismatic charlatan just blinds people to what's plainly obvious to anyone looking on from outside.

Twin Flames Universe

To really get some traction in the age of the AI charlatan, you need two things: First, you need a great search term that corresponds with your marks' dream. Second, you need enough charisma to convince people that you can solve their problems: not necessarily a lot of people, or even a lot of charisma, but *enough* people and *enough* charisma.

And Jeff and Shaleia Ayan, well, they certainly found a killer search term: love.

These days millions of young people turn to the internet looking for love. Most of them will end up on dating sites, of course, but when disappointment strikes, many of them go on to look for advice online. There's a thriving marketplace out there for dating and relationship advice, and you can find a guru catering to just about any question you might have. But few get their claws into their marks quite as deeply as Jeff and Shaleia do.

According to *Twin Flames*, the compelling Wondery podcast series that picked through their story, the young couple seems to have met online sometime around 2015, and they hit it off.[32] Big. Jeff was the skinny, working-class kid of a Greek immigrant, fresh out of Western Michigan University, where he majored in business.

Shaleia was from Ontario, and for years she'd been dabbling in mysticism: everything from astrology and tarot to more esoteric ideas about mystical communion with nature. Neither of them had a lot of money, or connections, or even a place to live, really, when they first met.

For a time, they ate nothing but hot dogs for breakfast, lunch, and dinner—convincing themselves that Mother Earth wanted it so.[33] What they had was . . . each other, together with a growing belief that their link was special.

Jeff and Shaleia became convinced they were twin flames: perfect, mystical lovers able to complete one another through total and perfect personal, sexual, emotional, and spiritual union. They called it harmonious union, a state of uninterrupted bliss that could be explained only by reference to the divine. Rather than two beings, they reasoned they were a single being, whose separation would run counter to the laws of the universe.

Then they launched a YouTube channel.

The Twin Flames Universe that Jeff and Shaleia launched wasn't exactly a new idea. The concept that men and women are half beings made whole only by union with their mystical other half dates back twenty-four hundred years to Plato, and even the phrase *twin flames* dates back to nineteenth-century esoteric writings. But Jeff and Shaleia took these old ideas and packaged them in a whole new way as a system for giving dating advice that would morph into what seems like a mystical cult, bringing a community of followers to genuinely bizarre extremes.

Jeff and Shaleia say the group they created is not a cult, but a community founded on love and mutual respect. Yet the YouTube following they built promises not only to fix your love life but also to align you with fundamental mystical forces at the wellspring of the universe. Togetherness with your twin flame isn't just a lifestyle goal; it's a spiritual imperative. God demands that you achieve your harmonious union, because the world's ills—*all* the world's ills—arise from the destructiveness that follows when twin flames are kept apart.

Click onto their YouTube page, and the disconnect between the message and the look and feel of their productions strikes you at once. We're far here from Teal Swan's slickly produced videos or even Bentinho Massaro's three-piece suits: production values are basic. Usually you just see the couple sharing a couch and talking straight to the camera. The backdrops are ratty; there are no lush tropical gardens or exotic anythings. Nor is their delivery spellbinding and sleek the way Bentinho or Teal can manage. Jeff peppers his sentences with the word *like.*

Their videos have view counts in the thousands, not the hundreds of thousands. Their outer ring is small, because Jeff and Shaleia concentrate most of their energy on their inner circle: a select group of perhaps one or two hundred people who are all in, devoting more or less *all* their time to participating in the Twin Flames Universe.

Their doctrine is simple: Jeff and Shaleia have a direct line to God. They know how you should live because God told them. God's plan is simple: to get first you and then everyone into harmonious union with your twin flame. Your job is to learn, with Jeff and Shaleia's help, who your twin flame is and then go get them. No matter what.

It sounds outlandish, and certainly it *is* outlandish, but for some lonely, love-starved people, the confidence with which Jeff and Shaleia put out this message can be intoxicating. There's no need to second-guess yourself, to figure it out laboriously over time. You just need to do what they say, and perfect harmonious union will be your reward.

In practice, the people who fall into the Twin Flames Universe orbit seem to have a lot in common: they're mostly isolated middle-aged women desperately in love with a man who won't give them the time of day. Jeff and Shaleia affirm their feelings—*yes*, the fact that they're so deeply in love does prove that they've found their twin flame.

Then they give them terrible, terrible advice.

Twin flames are permanent, eternal, and unalterable, they say, but your twin flame may not realize that that's what he is for some time. To give up on him simply because he refuses to take your phone calls isn't just wrong: twin flame separation is actually a sin, an offense against God's way.

The resistance your twin flame feels is quite natural, they'll say, and it will certainly be overcome in due time. Your job, as a seeker, is simply to work harder at it: make yourself more attractive, slimmer, fitter, more feminine, more appealing, and then just refuse to take no for an answer, no matter what.

If that sounds like a recipe for stalking and harassment to you, well, at least a few judges agree. At least two Twin Flames followers have found themselves in jail for following Jeff and Shaleia's advice. One, let's call her Katie, was charged with stalking and harassment after violating a restraining order her supposed twin flame had sought after she stalked him for more than a year, following a brief affair at the Burning Man festival in 2012.

The court heard how Katie had followed the object of her affection around the world, flying off to Germany when she learned he was there, then following him back to the United States when he returned, and continuing to stalk him even after being served with the restraining order, whose authority she refused to acknowledge. She deluged him with calls and voicemails, which of course wound up as evidence. In one she tells him, "The cops are not God, they're not going to protect you; only God can." Remarkably, on the night in August 2018 when she followed him into his usual San Francisco nightclub and he called the cops to have her arrested, she seems to have used her one jailhouse phone call to call . . . him. She was charged with seventeen counts of stalking, harassment, and violating her restraining order.[34]

Within the small, tight-knit Twin Flames Universe world, Katie's antics weren't frowned upon: just the opposite. Katie became a kind of folk hero in the group. Audio of her call with Jeff after she was freed on bail ended up on the internet, and it was featured on the *Twin Flames* podcast. In it, he urges Katie to embrace her martyrdom at the hands of the police as a case of bravery and courage. "You are courageous," he tells her. He urges her to think of herself as a spiritual master and tells her that her stint in jail gives him "enormous trust" in her, "where before [he] had none."

Katie now faces charges that could carry up to four years in prison as a penalty.

The power even a threadbare group like Twin Flames Universe has over marks like Katie is remarkable. But, amazingly, getting people to feel good about committing crimes that could land them in jail for years isn't these charlatans' most destructive coup. No, for that you need to look at what happened next, when Jeff and Shaleia began to take even more invasive steps into their followers' lives.

As the online following they led matured into its third and then fourth year, the situation for some of its most devoted members threatened to become untenable. As one of the group's most influential (now former) members put it, "There were multiple people in the community who had been in the community for a long time, very dedicated, watching all the classes, doing coaching sessions every week, doing discussion groups, doing it all, but no results, no union, no twin flame, no one around."

Some of these people had even cut off contact with friends and family members outside the community—which is one of the classic signs of cultic abuse. And *still* they weren't together with their twin flames.

One straightforward solution would be for Jeff and Shaleia to just declare various group members to be one another's twin flame and send them on their merry way. But there was a problem with that: Jeff and Shaleia taught that twin-flame unions were always between a divine masculine and a divine feminine, yet there weren't enough masculines in the group, divine or otherwise. The community was dominated by women, by *straight* women: there weren't enough guys to go around. But a solution was at hand.

First, Jeff needed to bolster his credibility with the group. This he did by declaring himself divine.

You read that right: Jeff Ayan, the kid who used to eat hot dogs three times a day, announced to his group that he was the second coming of the Christ. The literal messiah.

By then he'd grown his hair long, had grown a beard, and looked pretty much like a Sunday school–book picture of Jesus. He told the group this was no coincidence, that the traditional image of Christ was in fact a prophecy . . . of him.

Now, this revelation was so outlandish some group members do seem to have drifted away following its disclosure. But for those who stayed behind, this new, explicitly religious stage redoubled their commitment to the group. And they would need to be thoroughly convinced they were facing Jesus Christ in the flesh (or, well, on the Zoom screen). Otherwise, they would never accept what came next.

At the start of 2020 Jesus, that is, Jeff, explained that twin-flame unions were always between a divine masculine and divine feminine . . . *but*. There was more to it than that. Not every divine masculine was born in a male body. Sometimes a divine masculine was born in a female body. And Jesus-Jeff, channeling the divine mind, was now ready to reveal to group members who their *true* twin flames were. In many cases, as a matter of mathematical necessity, these turned out to be pairings of two women. The detail was that, in each case, one of the women was not a true woman, but a divine masculine trapped in a female body. To make their twin-flame unions come true, they would have to *switch genders*.

To be clear, these were women who had no gender dysphoria diagnosis. In most cases, this message was going out to middle-aged straight cisgender women who'd never expressed any kind of conflict about their gender identity. Jeff could claim to be the messiah all day and all night, but this was going to be a problem.

Group members resisted, obviously. But Jeff and Shaleia would have none of it. Through their coaches, they instructed their followers to fall in line. One who expressed unease about being declared a divine masculine was harshly reprimanded: "To receive such information from your gurus is a high honor, this message was brought to you directly from God through Jeff and Shaleia, and delivered to you through your former coaches. To deny Jeff and Shaleia's word is to deny the word of God. You must choose to move through any and all upsets and completely surrender to God's way."

Some members actually began to transition: switching to masculine pronouns, cutting their hair short, changing their names, working hard to inhabit their new masculine identities and make a future with their new twin flames. Jeff and Shaleia insisted that only they had a direct line to God. If they said you were a man, you were a man—that was all there was to it. According to deep dive reporting about this period by Alice Hines for *Vanity Fair*, not everyone in the group went along. At least five women resisted their new genders and ended up leaving the group.[35]

That *Vanity Fair* article took a serious toll on the group. Business suffered, and Jeff had to do live classes again to bring money in the door. It's not clear how many followers have actually accepted to live with a newly assigned gender on a lasting basis.

What's remarkable is that the Twin Flames Universe may not have expanded, but it did not collapse either. Even though the group exists only online, it continues to exert cultlike control over many of its members, and core members have stuck by Jeff and Shaleia even through the revelation of these damaging secrets. Cults close ranks around their leaders; they always have. And that's precisely what they've done, what they're doing now: pumping out videos, selling courses and seminars, and waiting for the curious to find them. Where?

Online. Where else?

Bentinho Massaro, Teal Swan, and the Twin Flames Universe point to a startling feature of digital-first charlatanry. When your grift is digital, it becomes surprisingly easy for garden-variety charlatans to find themselves at the head of something that seems like a full-blown cult. With artificial intelligence left in charge of identifying marks, serving them pitches, and bringing them in the door, charlatans find it vastly easier to zero in on the people most ready to hand over control of their bank accounts, their brains, and their bodies. They are not doing anything different from what cult leaders have been doing for generations, but being digital first accelerates every part of the process. With AI doing the heavy lifting, their followings grow bigger, faster than has ever been possible before.

One thing we know for certain is that success spreads on the internet. In this chapter we've reviewed three varieties of this business model, but we might have spoken about any of dozens of others. The most appealing will spread. They will be emulated, adapted, tweaked. In this artificial game of natural selection, the algorithms themselves act as the selection mechanism.

And what will happen in the future when someone adds a layer of simulated, mass-produced AI intimacy to a scheme like this one?

While law enforcement naps, the algorithms themselves do the hard work of matching dreamers with charlatans. With millions of isolated seekers looking for spiritual, emotional, and financial guidance, algorithmic gurus can only continue to proliferate. At very little cost, they can fill up the wide end of their recruitment funnel: a steady stream of new prospects keeping them permanently supplied with sources of funding, power, and sexual gratification.

They don't even have to get out of their pajamas.

6

Trust Me, I'm a Charlatan

THE DEATH PENALTY.

That's the punishment that Paolo Zacchia, the renaissance father of medicolegal scholarship, proposed, "for any doctor or quack who sold medicaments without first having ascertained the nature and causes of the disease, or having laid eyes on the invalid."[1] The year was 1621, and already the problem of medical fraud was rampant enough to merit discussion of such measures.

The early history of charlatanry is strewn with tales of peddlers of panaceas—the magical cure-all substances that promised relief for, well, pretty much anything. This makes sense: the longing the afflicted have for health is intense, unreasoning, and all-consuming. Before the advent of modern medicine, few diseases could be treated successfully. The sick and suffering had nowhere to deposit their dreams of health but in the hands of the quacks who hawked pills and potions on the backs of promises of miraculous recoveries.

The practice was widespread enough to demand an official response. In 1638 the Republic of Venice issued a decree to suppress the "peddlers of elixirs, powders and oils that were operating without a license or permit from the college of physicians," noting that they were "active everywhere, in the city of Venice, on the mainland and country estates."[2] More than a century later, in 1760, the quacks were still preying on unsuspecting Venetians, and another decree imposed fines and prison terms to those who sold secret remedies in public or private. Eight years later, in 1768, little had changed, with the Senate acknowledging that "forbidden goods were still being hawked, damaging the health of rural workers."

In fact, as Grete De Francesco shows in her 1939 book, *The Power of the Charlatan*, as far back as legal records go, stories of medical quacks go with them. At a time when medical science took *miasma*—or bad air—as a cause of disease and practiced bleeding for almost any ailment, the distinction between true physician and ruthless quack was not as clear as it would later become. It's little wonder people had a hard time recognizing the difference between one and the other.

You might have thought these concerns would abate as medical science advanced. After all, modern medicine is one of humanity's crowning achievements. In the span of a few short centuries, we as a species have gone from the brutality of surgery without anesthesia to the everyday medical miracles on offer in any of today's hospitals. Diseases that have blighted humanity since the dawn of time—from the bubonic plague to tuberculosis—now have simple, routine cures, with more on the way all the time. Of all the marvels of our age, few are more marvelous.

It is, at first glance, unimaginable that people would turn their backs on this monumental human achievement. And yet, they do. A small but persistent minority of people express to pollsters little to no trust in the medical profession. Day to day, we've all had the experience of meeting people who just don't trust doctors and avoid seeing them as much as they can.

There are reasons for this. Modern medical systems can be intimidating, even to those who recognize their benefits. They are large, impersonal bureaucracies run by fallible people tasked with handling an almost infinite variety of ways human bodies can break down. Naturally, patients' experiences vary. Plenty of people suffer grievously from diseases for which medical science still has no treatment. Others are misdiagnosed, mistreated, or just plain put off by the antiseptic look and feel of modern medical care. Not everyone has a good experience. And those who have had a bad experience quickly become inviting targets for all kinds of charlatans.

It's a problem worldwide, but it seems particularly bad in the United States, where a culture of rugged individualism collides with a ruinously expensive, notoriously complicated health-care system. It's a recipe for generating skeptics and malcontents, people burned by a visit to the doctor that left their finances in turmoil and their health just as bad as it was before.

You don't need a lot of these malcontents to find yourself in front of a massive market opportunity. Even if 9 out of 10 Americans were fully on board with mainstream medical science, the remaining 1 in 10 still adds up to some 26 million US adults. The real number is likely much higher than that—a 2014 study reported in the *New England Journal of Medicine* found just 58 percent of Americans agreed with the statement that "overall, the doctors in [my] country can be trusted."[3] That leaves the other 42 percent of Americans—more than 100 million adults—vulnerable to pitches from charlatans: a huge market just waiting to be exploited.

And *boy* does it get exploited.

Spurious supplements, dodgy medical devices, superhyped vitamins, bizarre diets, breathlessly aggrandized detox regimens, nutritional tall tales, healing crystals—a whole, unending cottage industry of medical quackery thrives in the United States, connecting today's charlatans to their earliest forerunners. As a reminder, the word *charlatan* hearkens back to the *ciarlatani*, or market-square hawkers of miracle cures in seventeenth-century Italy, and comes down to us through the storied snake oil salesmen who dot the history of the Wild West. For as long as people have been sick, others have been peddling iffy miracle cures to them.

It's just that today's communications technology makes it possible to reach many more people much more quickly and cheaply than you could manage standing on a soapbox on a medieval market square. And so the damage today's medical charlatans inflict is far, far greater than what their forerunners in previous centuries could do.

Joseph Mercola

Meet Joseph Mercola. The prep school–educated son of a solidly middle-class Chicago family, Mercola was interested in alternative healing practices from an early age. After studying chemistry at the University of Illinois, he trained as an osteopathic physician in Chicago.

His choice was telling: osteopathic medicine had begun as a type of alternative medicine, favored by practitioners put off by the cold rationalism of the medical mainstream and looking for a more holistic approach to health.

In the 1980s, when Mercola studied the discipline, osteopathy was in the process of ditching its pseudoscientific roots and adopting scientific medical practices. Mercola, for his part, was traveling that same road in the opposite direction.

He did qualify as an osteopathic physician in 1985 and began using the title he had legally earned: doctor.

From that point on, Joseph Mercola was legally entitled to put "Dr." in front of his name. This became the lynchpin to a wildly profitable marketing campaign—the respect due to a doctor becoming integral to his brand.

Mercola positioned himself as a critic of mainstream medicine from the very start, echoing many of the themes already established in opposition to medical science. In the early '90s, a few years into his practice, he wrote a letter to his patients announcing a radical departure in his practice. "I said, 'Listen, if you're not interested in getting off your medications,'" Mercola later recalled, "'you're going to need to find a new doctor.' I lost 75 percent of my patients."[4]

Mercola later described the mass departure of his clientele as the best thing that ever happened to him, because it allowed him to work only with patients willing to go all the way with him in exploring alternative therapies. Growing familiarity with that clientele helped him build the basis of the massive supplement business that he would market under the Dr. Mercola brand.

As is so often the case, it's hard to know to what point Mercola believes what he peddles, and to what extent he's just exploiting the beliefs of others to make money. In Mercola's case, there is better reason than usual to think he's a true believer. His classmates from osteopathic school remember him as someone determined to push the alternative paradigm as far as it would go.[5] Whether his bunk was heartfelt or not, there's no questioning its commercial success.

Perhaps because he shares their beliefs, Mercola knows his customers. Well. Extremely well.

His core followers are united by one thing: they've been to the doctor, and it hasn't gone well. The experience has shaken their belief in the medical establishment, leaving them mistrustful of the claims of knowledge it makes. They see the Food and Drug Administration (FDA), the pharmaceutical companies, and the government as little more than players in a vast conspiracy to defraud sick people, and as a result, they leave themselves badly exposed to . . . a blatant charlatan who targets sick people.

Because Mercola knows this audience inside and out, he knows how suspicious they are of "chemicals" or anything that looks and feels like it was produced by the vast, impersonal machinery of modern medical science. He mirrors back to them their longing to reconnect with nature and their determination to seek remedies that affirm that connection. He knows that, to people primed to believe the worst about the medical establishment, even simply portraying yourself as a critic of that establishment helps you to gain their trust. To his audience, just attacking Big Pharma helps cement his bona fides; it establishes his credibility as one of the good guys, one of the guys who get it. Best of all, he attacks medical science while wearing a white medical coat and with that "Dr." title affixed proudly before his name.

And so attack Big Pharma he does, often and to great effect. And, crucially, *online.*

Mercola took to the internet early and perfected the craft of selling to this audience online long before his competitors did. In video after video, he talks directly to the camera, crafting a calm, affable online persona as the doctor willing to tell you the truths the medical establishment wants to hide from you. The pitch begins with a wholesale rejection of modern medication and builds out that rejection on a series of increasingly ludicrous conspiracy theories, from a panicked denunciation of water fluoridation to regurgitating old, repeatedly disproven bunk about the health dangers of cell phones.

So, what's the answer?

There are plenty: from fasting fourteen to sixteen hours a day, to sleeping in a Faraday cage—you know, lined with actual tinfoil to stay safe from electromagnetic radiation—to consuming three-quarters of a pound of butter each day, to bingeing on red meat but also refusing to eat chicken.[6]

And then, of course, there are supplements; lots of supplements. Every imaginable type of supplement—from zinc liquid drops to magnesium L-threonate to organic ashwagandha liquid drops ("regarded as the go-to herb in India's traditional Ayurvedic practice . . . experts believe the potential benefits of the root come from a synergistic effect of all naturally occurring root compounds including phytosterols, flavonoids, coumarins and essential oils").[7] All of them, of course, are branded with Dr. Mercola's logo front and center on the label.

Worried about Teflon? He knows you are, because he just spent an hour making you paranoid about it. No problem—go on his website and get yourself some Mercola Healthy Bakeware—(described as metals-free and "a relative bargain" at $197 per set).

As the self-proclaimed number-one most-visited natural-health site on the internet, Mercola.com does a roaring business and has for many years. People who come to Mercola for the pseudoscience tend to work up a healthy rage against the pharmaceutical industry, and then stick around to do a bit of shopping. It's a proven business model: the direct, twenty-first-century heir to the *ciarlatani* of Italy and the snake oil peddlers of the old West.

Naturally, if Mercola sells a product, it's because he believes in it, and if he believes in a product, he'll not be shy about writing about it on his website and talking about it on his podcast. It's a perfect marketing circle, with pseudoscience posing as dissident science, giving rise to breathless talk about the health wonders of this or that pill ("that *they* don't want you to know about!") that, conveniently enough, you can buy from the very same source.

Joseph Mercola had perfected this marketing strategy long before the COVID-19 pandemic struck. Much of the pitch was based on anti-vaccine disinformation, repackaged in the guise of brave truth telling. In fact, anti-vax rhetoric has always played an important part in his sales pitch: once you've convinced your audience that the *entire* medical establishment is complicit in a vast conspiracy to harm children, you've got them exactly where you want them.

Anti-vaxxers will never listen to the mainstream doctors denouncing Mercola as a quack, precisely because the thing that brings Mercola's marks together is a visceral distrust of mainstream doctors. If the entire system is corrupt—corrupt enough to pull off a conspiracy as vast and nefarious as childhood immunization—then you can believe nothing they say about anything. You can trust Mercola and *only* Mercola.

And if you buy his message, it's a good bet you'll buy his pills.

Mercola was far ahead of the game in repackaging pandemics as manufactured crises, ginned up out of thin air by an evil cabal of corporations and government officials to take away your freedom. All the way back in 2009, when a novel avian flu virus briefly threatened to grow to pandemic scale, he published *The Great Bird Flu Hoax: The Truth They Don't Want You to Know About the "Next Big Pandemic."*

Most of the ingredients of Mercola's COVID-era malarkey are already there in this book, published eleven years before the real pandemic. Mercola's signature move is to treat public health officials' efforts to *prepare* to respond to a possible future pandemic as evidence that those same officials were planning to *stage* that pandemic, to blow it out of all proportion . . . and to use the panic they would generate as a way to enrich themselves and control you by giving you dangerous, unproven drugs labeled as "vaccines."

Bird flu petered out, but Mercola already had his business strategy in place. He'd recycle all the same talking points when SARS-CoV-2 arose. Using his own logic, you could then argue that if Mercola had known such a hoax pandemic was possible beforehand and had actively practiced his response to it, then he likely orchestrated the 2020 pandemic.

One thing's for sure: Mercola sold a *lot* of products during the COVID-19 pandemic.

It was only the COVID crisis that brought Mercola to national attention, where he was soon labeled a COVID "superspreader" for the impact his disinformation was having. Calling the COVID vaccine drive "the most effective brainwashing propaganda campaign in the history of mankind," he relentlessly pushed people away from vaccines proven to save lives and toward quack cures that made him millions of dollars while leaving his customers exposed to a deadly virus.[8]

Amid the public health emergency COVID-19 had set off, Mercola's anti-vaccine message came under intense pressure. Professional bodies pleaded with him to cease and desist. The FDA admonished him repeatedly for making unbacked claims, demanding he stop.[9]

Eventually, Joseph Mercola was included in "the disinformation dozen"—a list of just twelve social media users found to be responsible for two-thirds of the vaccine disinformation spreading online.[10] That was the breaking point. Web giants from Facebook to YouTube deplatformed him, but of course this only played into his hands.[11]

In Mercola's narrative, the pressure he came under was proof positive of the scale and power of the conspiracy he had uncovered. He alone stood as the brave voice willing to blow the whistle on their whole rotten scheme. The bad guys were out to stop him. It was up to a few brave, enlightened souls to stand firm against them.

Partly as a result of repeated warnings from the FDA, in August 2021 Mercola agreed to take down his website's entire old archive, depriving the internet of the texts of such gems as "Could hydrogen peroxide treat coronavirus?," which was shared some five thousand times on Facebook before it was taken down.[12]

Amazingly, Mercola managed to turn even *this* into a way of trying to bring in new marks. Search any term on his website now, and you're met with this message:

> *Dr. Mercola's Censored Library*
>
> In August 2021, all content from our site was removed due to threatening censorship pressures. The good news is that with our new free-speech Substack site, you're now able to access many of those deleted articles. So far, we've transferred the past three years of the over 25 years of content to our Substack site. To help share in the cost of this protection, the monthly subscription is only $5, or $50 annually, which is donated to non-profit health partners.

So, you can still *get* access to Joseph Mercola's dangerous nonsense; it's just that now you have to pay for the privilege!

The chutzpah behind so much of Mercola's operation makes it natural to assume that he's just a cynical huckster out for a quick buck. There is certainly a lot of evidence that Joseph Mercola loves a quick buck as much as the next guy. So, as we waded into the man's long podcast archive to research this book, we expected it to serve as little more than an infomercial for his online store: marketing all the way down.

But here, well, we found a surprise. Mixed in with the screwball diet advice and dark conspiracy theorizing, we found a man obsessed with ideas that seemed unlikely to make him any money.

Key among them is a fixation with iron and the way it can, Mercola believes, build up to toxic levels in your blood. That is, not in your blood serum, but inside your blood cells. And in the mitochondria within each cell that cells use to power themselves.

To say that there is little science to support this interpretation is to be kind. Mainstream doctors have long known about hemochromatosis, a rare blood disease affecting about 0.5 percent of the adult population that can lead to damaging blood-iron levels.[13] Mercola's contention is that many or even most adults suffer from excess iron toxicity.

This is outlandish. There's just no evidence for it.

But here's where it gets interesting. You might have expected that Mercola would pivot from scaring the daylights out of you about hemochromatosis to selling you some kind of pill to solve the problem. That's certainly his modus operandi on most other things. But not this time.

Mercola swears that dietary copper is helpful in regulating blood-iron levels—another screwball theory mainstream doctors just shrug at. Mercola is happy to talk in great detail about why he believes this, in discussions shrouded in a haze of molecular biochemistry terminology that few of his listeners are at any risk of understanding. And, yes, Mercola's website does sell some supplements that contain copper. But he doesn't hard sell them. What he pushes, hard, is blood donation.

To hear Mercola tell it, the problem with blood iron is about us having too much damn blood, and the way to deal with it is to donate blood, *often*. How often? "The minimum is twice a year; better, it's four," he says in one podcast, before adding that some people could consider doing it more often at home and simply dumping their blood in their yard as fertilizer.[14]

Mercola would've been an excellent eighteenth-century doctor: like them, he is *obsessed* with removing excess blood. He makes sure to ask his podcast guests if they're in the habit of doing so. He especially enjoys going into detailed explanations of the absence of a natural discharge mechanism for blood iron, and of the miraculous, sometimes near-instant positive health effects of donating blood.

To be clear, there is good scientific evidence that people who donate blood *do* have a lower risk of death than those who don't. The magnitude of the effect is small, and the observation "cannot be interpreted as conclusive evidence of a beneficial health effect [of donating blood]."[15] The reasons why blood donors live longer are not well understood, but few researchers think it has anything to do with iron. The leading hypothesis seems to relate to the way donation changes the lipid composition of the donor's blood.[16]

Few doctors would cite this arcane probabilistic correlation as the best reason to donate blood. The reason to donate blood is to save the lives of the people who receive it. Benefits to the donor are negligible in comparison.

So, Mercola certainly isn't wrong to encourage you to give blood, and he isn't even wrong, exactly, when he says it's good for you. And Mercola has no obvious financial stake in people donating blood. He doesn't profit from it or involve himself in it in any obvious way. But boy, does he put his back into marketing it!

And he's good! After listening to a few of his podcasts, we ourselves started thinking we should probably go and get an appointment to donate blood, which we hadn't done in quite a long time.

"It couldn't hurt," we found ourselves thinking, against our better judgment, "and who knows, what if there *is* something to this excess iron thing after all!?"

That Mercola managed to sell even *us*, people listening to his podcast for the purpose of denouncing it, tells you all you need to know about his talents as a salesman. But that part had never been in dispute. What was in dispute was whether Joseph Mercola was just a cynical opportunist or believed his own nonsense. And his obsession with hemochromatosis argues strongly in favor of the latter.

Mercola appears to be passionately convinced that donating blood is so good for you that he spends a considerable portion of his most valuable resources—his voice, his credibility with his audience—to persuade people to do so.

That's not how a grifter behaves. That's how a true believer behaves.

The result is a peculiar bundle of nested ethical paradoxes: a quack doctor using pseudoscience to convince his listeners to do a safe, legal thing that will save lives, though not for the reasons he thinks, and doing it all despite the fact that it won't benefit him personally.

Iron overload is one of Mercola's abiding obsessions. The theme crops up again and again in *Take Control of Your Health*, Mercola's blockbuster podcast, and Mercola returns often to the theme of blood donation as perhaps the single most useful lifestyle change you can make to improve your state of health.[17]

Is this a case of a stopped clock being right twice a day? Perhaps. In between advocating for a variety of discredited therapies, unproven treatments, and dark fantasies about Bill Gates and Klaus Schwab (the founder of the World Economic Forum) conspiring to unleash the pandemic, Joseph Mercola does sometimes offer advice that sane people would do well to follow.[18] It hardly makes him a medical hero.

It just makes him a quack of a different kind: one who cares about money, but not *only* about money. In that regard, let's be clear: the man has done well. His company is privately held and so discloses virtually nothing about its own finances, but in a 2017 affidavit Mercola declared himself worth somewhere north of $100 million.[19] How far north, we don't know. By any measure, his obsessions have been fabulously profitable to Dr. Mercola.

How did Joseph Mercola become famous enough to make that kind of money? A big part of it was the jump-start he got early in his career, when he was booked to give advice to an audience of millions on a show run by one of the world's most talented heart surgeons: Dr. Mehmet Oz.

Mehmet Oz

There is plenty of room to wonder if the title "Dr." belongs in front of the name of Joseph Mercola, but nobody in their right mind would question the medical credentials of Dr. Mehmet Oz.

A young medical superstar in the 1990s, Dr. Oz both performed and taught surgery at one of the most prestigious institutions in the world: Columbia University in New York City. There, Dr. Oz wasn't just a celebrated practitioner but a leading-edge researcher, who published or copublished seventy-five studies on heart and thoracic surgery between 1989 and 2010 and ended up with his name on nine patents. This fact would come back to haunt him decades later—but we'll come to that. He was the object of a fawning 1995 profile in that most establishment of publications, the *New York Times Magazine*, which described him matter-of-factly as "probably the most accomplished 35-year-old cardiothoracic surgeon in the country."[20]

Already then, even as he sat at the apex of America's academic medical establishment, Mehmet Oz was starting to dabble in the kinds of not-exactly-standard therapies that got *New York Times Magazine* reporters all abuzz. The profile recounts how, with the consent of his patient, Joyce Donadio, Dr. Oz operated while two trained Reiki practitioners manipulated the invisible energy flows around her feet.

Reiki is one of these New Age fads that touts its own ancient heritage, even though it was made up pretty recently: the practice was invented in the 1920s by an eccentric Japanese healer, Mikao Usui, who made it his life's work to personally train up to two thousand practitioners. Literally, *Reiki* (霊気) means "mysterious energy"—though the word sounds suspiciously like *rieki*: the Japanese word for "profit."

The *ki* in Reiki comes from the Chinese spiritual notion of chi: an essential, mystical life force notable in a number of Far Eastern spiritual traditions. Reiki masters describe chi as an invisible force "impossible for science to detect." By placing their hands near the subject—without actually touching her—they believed they could redirect the flow of chi to speed her recovery from major chest surgery. Now, one of the nation's hottest young surgeons was going to scientifically test whether it worked or not. You can see why journalists were eating this stuff up.

Dr. Oz had performed the procedure enough times to gather data about its effectiveness, and early results seemed to suggest the presence of these energy healers helped. Patients who received Reiki during surgery seemed to recover faster than those who hadn't received this benefit. It was blockbuster stuff.

Or was it?

Dr. Oz's early forays into alternative medicine seem to coincide with his encounter with Lisa Lemole, herself a devoted Reiki master, whom

Oz married in 1985. Lemole's mother was herself a devotee of alternative health approaches, while her grandfather was a leading surgeon. She graduated from Bryn Mawr College in 1985, where she had served as captain of the tennis team, and married Oz in June of that same year.

Oz's father, Mustafa, saw his son's turn to alternative medicine as career suicide and tried to warn him off. Himself a highly regarded surgeon, Dr. Mustafa Oz had immigrated to the United States from Turkey in the 1950s and pushed his talented son hard to follow in his footsteps. But the younger Dr. Oz had ideas of his own . . . or rather, of his wife's own. He followed up his undergraduate degree from Harvard—where he played on both the football and water polo teams—with twin medical and business professional degrees from the University of Pennsylvania. Mehmet Oz was the ultimate overachiever.

As a medical researcher in the '90s, Dr. Oz made fundamental discoveries for improving the practice of heart surgery. His name features on multiple patents for heart surgery inventions, including for MitraClip, a device designed to "repair your leaking heart valve" that went on to be widely adopted and has saved thousands of lives.[21] Under his leadership, Columbia University's already famous medical center rose even further in prominence, coming to be seen as one of the world's top research institutes for heart and chest surgery. This wasn't hype; it was real.

By the turn of the century, though, Mehmet Oz faced a fork in the road. He might have chosen to deepen his medical and research practice, which was already wildly successful. He was still young, barely forty, and had already fundamentally altered the way heart disease was treated in the world's top medical centers. Another twenty-five years of that, and he could have cemented his place in history as a truly consequential medical innovator. Among the world's top doctors, his name was often murmured as a contender for the Nobel Prize in Medicine.

Instead, he ended up in this book. What happened?

In 2003 the media buzz around the hotshot surgeon using energy healing in the operating theater soon landed Mehmet Oz his very first

TV show. *Second Opinion with Dr. Oz* was a five-episode series on the Discovery Channel on which Oz would treat celebrities for health problems—celebrities from Charlie Sheen to Magic Johnson to . . . and this would change everything, Oprah Winfrey.[22]

Oprah liked that experience so much she soon invited him to appear on *The Oprah Winfrey Show*, the undisputed reigning champion of daytime-television ratings. It's easy to see why Oprah's audience loved him: charismatic, handsome, extravagantly credentialed, Oz spoke approachable, jargon-free English with a tone brimming with reassuring authority. He would be back on *The Oprah Winfrey Show* a total of sixty-two times, picking up the Oprah-bestowed honorary title "America's Doctor" in the process, and edging toward his definitive status as a household name in the United States.[23]

Oprah's enormous reach vastly expanded Dr. Oz's visibility, depositing him at the doors of celebrity. But he wouldn't cross that threshold until 2009, when Oprah's production company, Harpo Studios, agreed to produce Oz's very own daytime-television talk show. Over the course of its eleven seasons spread between 2009 and 2022, *The Dr. Oz Show* was a huge ratings hit, consistently ranking in the top-five most-watched daytime-television shows in the United States. Throughout that time, Oz straddled the border between traditional and alternative medicine, dispensing plenty of sensible, middle-of-the-road advice about diet and exercise but mixing it up with increasingly breathless claims about alternative therapies that slowly eroded the show's credibility.

The central conundrum Oz faced is easy to fathom: filling up five hour-long celebrity specials with credible, scientific health advice, as he had done in his 2003 series, was straightforward enough. But filling an hour-long slot with content every single weekday for years on end is an entirely different kind of challenge.

Dr. Adam S. Cifu, a biomedical researcher at the University of Chicago, explains it well in a scathing post on the National Institutes of Health's website tellingly entitled "Why Dr. Oz Makes Us Crazy." He writes,

> The day-to-day practice of medicine is about caring for the individual. While we physicians fill our days providing sound advice to our patients, there are, by comparison, remarkably few recommendations that we can make to the population as [a] whole. Everyone should exercise and wear seatbelts, nobody should smoke or drink excessively, and everyone should receive childhood vaccines. Not only are these types of recommendations limited in number, they are also neither terribly interesting nor surprising. They would certainly not support a daily, or even weekly, television show. Once we get beyond basic recommendations it becomes difficult to give health advice to large populations.[24]

By this account, the pressures of producing a daily TV show interesting enough to get good ratings just overwhelmed Mehmet Oz's professional scruples. Soon, he was trucking in the same kind of manipulative "here's what your doctor *doesn't* want you to know" framing that quacks throughout the ages have latched onto. With weight-loss and cancer-care content the two surest ways to juke his ratings numbers, Dr. Oz increasingly foregrounded doubtful weight-loss schemes pushed by figures in America's huge, ever-evolving, and ever-so-scammy nutritional supplements industry.

Take raspberry ketone—just one of many iffy diet supplements Dr. Oz took to hyping on his show. Ketones are chemicals that naturally occur in small quantities in raspberries and a number of other fruits that biochemical researchers in Japan suspected might be useful in managing people's weight. So, starting in 2005 they did what researchers do in cases like this: they launched a series of experiments on mice and rats to test the substance's safety and efficacy.[25]

Of course, small-scale tests on mice are the first of *many* steps in the process of developing a new treatment. If the substance shows promise, these exploratory tests are followed up by larger tests involving more lab mice. If they hold up, a long, complex series of progressively larger human trials follow, concluding in a double-blind randomized study, where subjects are given the treatment, a control group is given a placebo, and neither the subjects nor the people administering the drug know who is in which group. *Only* if results hold up after rigorous analysis of a clinical trial like that can the treatment be considered proven.

It may sound unwieldy—it *is* unwieldy—but there are good reasons to go through this entire process rigorously. When you're putting a new substance into people's bodies, it is not a good idea to be cavalier about risks.

All of which explains why the process of testing and approving a new medical treatment takes years. Dr. Oz couldn't afford to wait years, though: he had a full hour of TV to fill every single day of the week. He needed content compelling enough to keep his viewers coming back. And so *The Dr. Oz Show* happily skipped over the entire process, touting a tiny study on a handful of mice as slam-dunk evidence that raspberry ketones were *the hot new weight-loss pill your doctor doesn't want you to know about!!*

How could he get away with it? Aren't new drugs meant to be rigorously tested before they can be sold? Aren't there penalties for doctors who sling pills with no science to back them?

There are, yes. But there are also loopholes. Technically, Dr. Oz wasn't recommending a new drug but a new *supplement.* In the United States, the rules to regulate nutritional supplements are as lax as the rules around new drugs are stringent. Supplement hawkers are not required to show that their pills do what they say they do. They're not required to certify that their pills contain the ingredients the label says they contain. As long as they don't make specific claims of medical efficacy, they can get away with a lot. An awful lot.

Take those raspberry ketones. The word "raspberry" may make it sound like this is a natural product, a kind of fruit extract. In reality, ketones are a trace chemical in raspberries—you would need almost ninety pounds of raspberries to have enough ketones for a single dose.[26] In reality, the product being sold is being synthesized in a lab, much like a new medicine would be, and stuffed into capsules at dosages nobody checks, in manufacturing facilities nobody certifies. What exactly these ketones will do to a human body taken in high doses nobody can really tell you, because nobody has studied it.

Not that any of this was about to stop Dr. Oz.

"I've got the number-one miracle in a bottle to burn your fat," he said, in one later infamous segment. "It's raspberry ketone." The usual scientific word salad followed. "Raspberry ketones," he said, "contain adiponectin; it sounds like a big word, but this is a hormone that naturally tricks your body into acting like it's thin."[27]

Being featured on the Dr. Oz show led to a massive spike in sales, with any number of fly-by-night supplement hawkers piling in on the action in the days after the segment aired.

The effect was so marked that, in the days following the show's airing in April 2012, it became "nearly impossible to find in stores," according to news reports from that time.[28]

This phenomenon, where interest in (and sales of!) a product skyrockets after it's featured on *The Dr. Oz Show*, is so common that for a while it had its own name: the Oz Effect.[29] And it's big. Being featured on *The Dr. Oz Show* can take a product from invisibility to stardom instantly.

Take neti pots, the little ceramic or plastic contraptions people sometimes use to rinse their sinuses with saline water. After Dr. Oz praised the gadget on *The Oprah Winfrey Show* in 2006, a producer boasted that neti pot sales increased by 12,000 percent, with internet searches on the topic increasing 42,000 percent.[30]

By the mid-2010s, a whole ecosystem of sketchy supplement hawkers had grown up around *The Dr. Oz Show*. Its participants would monitor the show every day and race with each other to buy search terms on online advertising platforms related to the products. Within minutes of appearing on *The Dr. Oz Show*, a bidding war would break out for the top search result on Google and Facebook for whatever product he was selling that day.

Needless to say, the people playing this game had no more capacity to produce these supplements than your next-door neighbor—they'd hear about a supplement one minute, start selling it the next, and only *then* figure out how they could source it, package it, and ship it. With no one checking up on the purity or integrity of the products, it's a fair bet that they rarely contained much of the active ingredient listed on the label. Then again, as that active ingredient was untested, that may count as a feature more than a bug: taking a placebo definitely won't hurt you; taking high concentrations of an untested new chemical compound very well could.

Mehmet Oz has always protested that he himself neither sells supplements nor endorses individual supplement products on his show. He hardly needed to: as the host of a wildly popular network TV show, the guy is not exactly short on cash. In testimony to the US Senate, he played the victim, describing himself as powerless against the army of grifter supplement peddlers hanging on his every word; he even urged Congress to pass new laws to ban supplement sellers from misleadingly claiming he had endorsed their product.[31]

Yet the kerfuffle over raspberry ketones and other once-hot diet supplements (açai berries! resveratrol!) pales in comparison to that over the product that, more than any other, cemented Mehmet Oz's status as a medical pariah: the great green coffee bean extract scandal of 2012.

In April of that year, a study appeared in the journal *Diabetes, Metabolic Syndrome and Obesity: Targets and Therapy*. The study claimed green coffee bean extract had caused substantial weight loss for people—not mice!—even when given in isolation: no diet, no exercise, nothing.[32]

In fact, the study cited was tiny, involving just sixteen subjects. Worse, it was financed by a manufacturer of . . . you guessed it, green coffee bean extract. No reputable scientist would jump to conclusions about a compound's effectiveness based on evidence this spotty.

And yet in May 2012 Mehmet Oz took to the airwaves with a bean in his hand. "This little bean," he said, "has scientists saying they've found the magic weight-loss cure for *every* body type. It's green coffee beans, and when turned into a supplement, this miracle pill can burn fat fast for *anyone* who wants to lose weight."

He then welcomed naturopathic doctor and certified nutritionist Lindsey Duncan to the stage to talk more about his, um, magic miracle pill. Duncan began on a cautious note, saying, "You know, I usually don't recommend weight-loss supplements, but this one has got me really excited." After breathlessly hyping up the study for a few minutes, Dr. Oz got down to brass tacks. "What do folks have to do to get the benefits?"

"Eight hundred milligrams, twice a day," Duncan answered, without hesitating.

"And the capsules you can buy where?" Oz prodded.

"You buy them online," he said, going on to stress that consumers should look for *pure* green coffee bean extract, without any additives or fillers. Audiences ate it up, and sales of pure green coffee bean extract pills went through the roof in the weeks that followed.

Years later, when the Federal Trade Commission pursued Duncan as part of a crackdown on manipulative weight-loss products, it would reveal that Duncan was not speaking off the cuff. The specific dosage he recommended happened to match the dosage in the pills his company was selling. And the emphasis on "*pure* green coffee bean extract"? Well, that just happened to be the search term he had recently bought on Google and Facebook for his product.

In effect, Lindsey Duncan had hacked the Oz Effect from the inside. Having gotten invited onto the show, he was then able to squat on what would become a hot new search term before the program even aired. Duncan, who did not admit wrongdoing, agreed to settle with the FTC by paying $9 million in consumer redress and is barred from making deceptive health claims in the future.

But what about the study, the promising nub of human research that got the ball rolling? You know, the one scientists would probably need to replicate and expand on in years to come?

Well, it turned out the study couldn't have been replicated, because it was fake. A later review found that the data in the study had apparently been tampered with so it would show the amazing results the people paying for the research wanted it to show. By 2014 the editors of the professional journal that had initially published it, *Diabetes, Metabolic Syndrome and Obesity: Targets and Therapy*, retracted the study once the authors admitted they could not verify the data.[33]

To be clear, Dr. Mehmet Oz never descended to the fever swamps of conspiratorial thinking that drove charlatans like his one-time guest Joseph Mercola. He never denounced vaccines, for instance, and he consistently urged his viewers to get themselves inoculated for COVID-19 and to give their children the recommended suite of childhood immunizations as well. And, as Dr. Oz never tires of reminding us, he never sold specific products himself, never endorsed a given product, didn't directly profit from the supplement industry he was nonetheless so instrumental in driving.

Yet the charlatan label is richly deserved: Dr. Oz used sophisticated audience research to zero in on his audience's dreams of health and fitness, and he championed the products in ways that served him to his audience's detriment. He hacked into HumanOS with breathless promises he surely knew they were primed to believe and must have known were nonsense, betraying his audience's trust in him with impressive regularity.

And yet the reason to call Dr. Oz a charlatan is not just the obvious hoaxes, the raspberry ketones, and the green coffee bean extracts that a leading scientist like himself must have been able to see through. It's not just the surgical Reiki or the segments he hosted on how astrology can inform your health decisions (spoiler: it can't).[34] It's not even outlandish episodes like the time he had a self-described spiritual medium on air describing how talking to the dead can improve your health.[35] No, the reason we can be sure Dr. Mehmet Oz is a big-time charlatan is something else altogether: science!

In 2014 a team of 14 British doctors, pharmacists, and researchers published a study in the prestigious *British Medical Journal* that systematically scrutinized every health recommendation offered in 40 randomly selected episodes of the Dr. Oz show. They examined 80 separate recommendations and found some evidence to support 46 percent of them.

For 39 percent of the recommendations, they could find no scientific evidence to support the recommendation. And the other 15 percent? That's the interesting bit. For 1 out of every 7 claims on the Dr. Oz show, researchers found scientific evidence *against* Oz's recommendation.[36]

It is perhaps inevitable that a charlatan this prolific and this famous would catch the eye of Donald Trump. Oz is a big supporter, and so he was all ears when in 2022 Trump urged him to run for a powerful seat in the US Senate. Winning the Republican nomination on the strength of Trump's endorsement, he went on to run one of the most inept campaigns in recent political memory, losing a winnable seat to a visibly ailing opponent. Politics, it turns out, is the one thing Mehmet Oz hasn't been successful at.

Of all the charlatans we've written about in this book, none saddens us more than Mehmet Oz. A genuinely gifted surgeon and medical innovator, he did not *need* to go to the dark side to find success. Instead, he turned his back on science purely to gratify his ego, transforming the practice of pretending to know that which he does not know into a ratings bonanza and a money spigot.

At its height, 3.4 million people watched his show on any given day.[37] He became, arguably, the most trusted doctor in the richest, most powerful country in the world, and he used that exalted perch to shower his audience with nonsense day in and day out for years on end. It's just sad.

And yet Dr. Oz's quackery did not go unrewarded. In November 2024, then president-elect Trump appointed him to administer America's public health insurance programs—Medicare for the elderly, and Medicaid for lower-income people. In this new position, Dr. Oz will be one of the most powerful health-care administrators in the world, directly responsible for managing programs that insure the health of 145 million Americans.

But for all of Dr. Mehmet Oz's wealth, for all his reach, for all his power, he's small potatoes compared to the age's standout health-and-wellness quack. To meet the most successful charlatan in the wellness sphere, we'll take you to India.

Baba Ramdev

Think of yoga, and the image that comes to mind first is probably of a well-heeled Western woman in a skin-tight Lycra suit contorted into an impossible position. She is breathing carefully, but her focus is on physical fitness—a sort of sport.

The success of yoga in this westernized form has been so total, people sometimes forget about its roots. In India, where yoga is from, it is a religious practice first, though one that involves the body. In the 2,300 or so years since Patanjali—a quasi-legendary Hindu sage—first set down its principles, yoga has always been first and foremost a devotional Hindu practice—not a way to get a killer bod, but a way to reach nirvana.

Indeed, the convoluted body positions that westerners associate with yoga are relatively new—people had been doing yoga for thousands of years before "downward dog" was invented in the 1930s. For most of its history, yoga was a form of religious observance centered on controlling your breath while sitting in the lotus position: the accuracy with which you recited your sacred *mantras*—or incantations—mattered much more than the position your body was in.

One implication of this is easy to miss: because yoga is a religious discipline, its practice was confined to a pretty small part of India's rigidly caste-based society. The priests and religious scholars known as Brahmans dominated the practice of yoga. That means that even as yoga exploded in popularity around the world, the vast majority of Hindus in India—95 percent of whom are not Brahmans—didn't practice it.

Yoga went mainstream in the West before it broke out of the Brahman pigeonhole in its homeland. Conquering the West brought with it a whole host of glamorous associations. The practice took a multidecade round trip from India to Hollywood, with a stopover in Silicon Valley. Now reintroduced to its home market, its massive potential for profit was just about to be tested.

And who would exploit this gap in a very big market?

Meet Baba Ramdev.

Born Ram Kisan Yadav to a farming family in the central state of Haryana, some one hundred miles from New Delhi, he grew up poor in a typical, deeply religious North Indian village. His schooling proceeded mostly within the Arya Samaj tradition: a nineteenth-century Hindu revival movement that took the ancient Vedas—Hindu scriptures—to be literally true and infallible. Arya Samaj was intent on taking Hinduism's message beyond the elite and spreading the faith to non-Brahman families, which is why its schools could reach even the children of illiterate farmers in the villages of Haryana.[38]

For Arya Samaj, spreading awareness of Vedic spiritual teachings was the central goal, and the yoga Vedas are an integral part of that tradition. As a student in the 1980s and '90s, Ramdev volunteered to teach yoga for free to villagers around him. His piety is not to be doubted.

From early on he hewed closely to the figure of the "god-man," a form of religious asceticism that's always been recognized as a revered component of Hindu practice. Clad in simple hand-spun robes, letting their hair grow unchecked, god-men devote their lives to religious practice and instruction.

In his twenties, Baba Ramdev took a vow of poverty: a solemn oath that he would own no property and have no debt, cementing his god-man bona fides. For devout Hindus, it is customary to treat god-men with the utmost reverence.[39] He set up an ashram, a type of religious school, and built within it a little pharmacy that sold homemade traditional Hindu remedies.[40]

But this particular religious ascetic had a mind for business as well as one for yoga. Baba Ramdev realized early on that Indian society was changing rapidly, and with it, attitudes toward yoga. With India's economy growing fast, hundreds of millions of middle-class Hindus who had always seen yoga as an upper-caste thing began to practice it for the first time.

As the country's cities expanded, these newly urbanized people were looking for ways to reconnect with Hindu orthodoxy outside the traditional village setting where the faith had always lived. And, in 2003, just as India was urbanizing fast, Baba Ramdev persuaded a fledgling religious broadcaster to feature his yoga lessons on the air for the first time.[41]

Ramdev was among the first to realize there was latent demand for yoga instruction from non-Brahmans. The dream he speaks to has some things in common with Mehmet Aydın's weaponization of Turkish people's nostalgia for rural life. Newly urbanized Indians were nostalgic for the countryside—not the real countryside, of course, with its backbreaking toil and hardship, but a better, holier, idealized memory of a godly rural life. And Ramdev knew instinctively how to turn that longing to his advantage.

Charisma drips from Baba Ramdev, and his commitment to his cause has never really been in doubt. It is also true that most Hindu ascetics do not employ a marketing department.

Fully inhabiting his god-man image—orange robes, long beard, a *lot* of yoga—Ramdev came of age technologically at just the right time for a message like this to reach a mass urban audience. Yoga had gone global first; now he was bringing it back, turning it viral and digital in its homeland.

None of this happened in a political vacuum. At the same time yoga was conquering the suburban fitness classes of North America, the Hindu nationalist Bharatiya Janata Party (BJP) was conquering power in India.

A whole ascendent Hindu middle class came of age with Baba Ramdev talking about yoga on the TV screen in the background. He became to India's precarious new middle class what Walter Mercado had become to the same kind of people—mostly women—in Latin America: a flamboyant, near-magical individual they instinctively felt they could trust, who came into their lives with a message of hope and empowerment. Like Kenneth Copeland, Edir Macedo, and Jerry Falwell Jr., he associated the attributes of godliness with his products and in fact put that association at the center of his marketing vision.

If, like millions of devout Hindus do every day, you watch one of Baba Ramdev's classes on TV, what you will see is very different from what happens in a suburban yoga class in the West. You'll see a yogi carefully decked out in the garb of a Hindu saint, all flowing orange robes. But you will rarely see him contorted into spectacular positions.

The form of yoga that became popular in the West stresses asana—the practice of stretching into a variety of body postures. But asana is just one of the elements of the yogic tradition, and by no means the most important.

Baba Ramdev's practice focuses on pranayama—a different aspect of the yogic tradition concerned chiefly with the control of the breath. And within pranayama, he zeroes in on a technique he calls *kapālabhāti*—Sanskrit for "shining skull," which is what the perfect clarity this type of breathwork brings is meant to turn your mind into.

Tune in to one of his classes, and you'll mostly see him sitting in a lotus position breathing *in a very strange way.*

The key to the technique is to use your stomach muscles to produce a short, sharp exhalation. Imagine you're trying to expel something caught in your sinuses using your breath alone, and you have the main idea. That explosive exhalation is followed by a slower, passive inhalation.

This is kapālabhāti.

You can try it right now if you'd like. Sit upright and exhale, hard, from the stomach. Then breathe in normally. Now try doing that thirty times in a row, followed by some slow, mindful breathing. Then do it thirty times again. Then breathe slowly.

Now organize your life around breathing that way for at least half an hour at the crack of dawn every morning.

Congratulations, you are now a Baba Ramdev follower!

To hear him tell it, the benefits you can expect from kapālabhāti breathing are essentially limitless. Some are immediate and impossible to argue with. Kapālabhāti certainly will warm up your body on a cold winter morning: but then, any vigorous exercise will do that. It's claimed that it will clear your sinuses, and that's hard to argue with as well, for purely mechanical reasons.

But we're just getting warmed up. Have you suffered from intestinal gas recently, or digestive problems? Kapālabhāti will clear them right up.

Trouble with your uterus? Kapālabhāti will take care of it. Hepatitis B? Kapālabhāti is the best thing for it. AIDS? Cancer? Kapālabhāti will cure them too.[42] Homosexuality? You know the answer already.[43]

The claims are preposterous on their face. But within Hinduism, where the underlying unity of spiritual and physical health is a matter of dogma, they're not especially controversial. For figures like Baba Ramdev, steeped since childhood in a culture of devout Hinduism, it would be heresy to posit any gap between them.

Physical and spiritual health are one and the same thing.

Now, had Baba Ramdev been satisfied to teach people how to exhale energetically and then inhale calmly, there would be little reason for us to worry about him.

But Ramdev was never content to be just a plain old TV yogi.

Behind the scenes, he leveraged his TV celebrity into one of the most successful consumer brands in India: Patanjali Ayurved, which has grown into a sprawling household-goods conglomerate that will sell you everything from cleaning products and nutritional supplements to cosmetics and soap.

The name of the company is at the core of its pitch. Patanjali, you'll recall, is the name of the ancient Hindu sage who first wrote the yoga sutras. Ayurveda, for its part, is the name given to the traditional Hindu system of medical practice. To call a company Patanjali Ayurved is to inject both Hinduism and yoga deep into its identity.

In India, this sells.

To get a sense of the scale at which Patanjali Ayurved pitches its aspirations, consider its main competitors: Colgate-Palmolive, Unilever, Procter & Gamble. All huge transnationals owned by non-Hindus. For pious believers, it's a no-brainer: one package has a god-man on it; the other one doesn't.

Plus the one from the god-man is less expensive. So: easy choice.

Patanjali Ayurved pitches its products through their association with the god-man. They are holy and therefore a cleaner, healthier, and safer option than those Western brands.

Baba Ramdev's face on the label is crucial here: customers strongly, religiously identify with the brand. By putting products deliberately built around traditional Hindu beliefs into the mass market, the company can penetrate almost any consumer segment. With such hit offerings as an all-purpose cleaning fluid featuring real cow-urine extracts, Patanjali is able to enmesh religious loyalty with its marketing spiel from the word go.

For Hindus, the cow is holy, and its products are holy. No pious Hindu home can be without ghee, a clarified butter that is believed to be blessed through its association with the cow. Not surprisingly, ghee is by far Patanjali Ayurved's strongest seller. But Patanjali's website looks something like a Hindu self-care Amazon, selling anything from sunflower oil to herbal sexual-potency pills for men, recommended for strength and energy.

One herbal pill, we're told, "eradicates sexual weakness, Gout (joint pains or Rheumatoid), diseases related to kapha (Asthma and allergy), semen deficiency, urine and bone-weakness, diabetes etc. problems both in men and women and beneficial for providing vigorous energy. Increases body immunity and overall body strength. Have anti-ageing properties. Shilajit should be taken in a small quantity or take as per the suggestion of the physician."[44]

At just 90 rupees ($1.07 at the time of writing), it's a steal.

The pills, the website says, contain a mix of *shilajit*, described as "a sticky substance found primarily in the rocks of the Himalayas [that] develops over centuries from the slow decomposition of plants," and *amala rasayana*, which has actually been shown to have medicinal effects in scientific medical trials.[45] Of course, since these are technically considered medical supplements rather than medicines, they can be sold even if no one checks to certify the stuff that is in the pill is what it says on the label. This is not a problem limited to India—as we will soon see, the United States suffers from very much the same licensing gap. But in India, where the public profile of god-men is so visible, a recommendation to buy a product like amala rasayana without further medical work is weak.

Other products on offer stress other aspects of traditional Hindu medicine (or "ayurvedics," from which the other half of the company name is derived), including traditional roots, herbs, and extracts. These are liberally spread around in anything from skin creams to deodorants.

The company's communications always stress the scriptural roots of the recipes, trying to draw a direct line between the product in the bottle and the message in the Veda. In 2017 its line of Vedic toothpaste held almost 14 percent of India's huge consumer market.[46] Who is to guarantee that this delicate process of industrializing millennial wisdom is carried out correctly? Ramdev's image beams from the packaging: to his followers, there is no question whom they are buying from.

Running a large commercial empire when you are a religious ascetic who can neither own nor borrow has its complications. To make it all work, Ramdev has had to lean strongly on his (very) nonascetic business partner, Acharya Balkrishna, who legally owns the empire that Ramdev in effect controls. According to *Forbes*, on paper Balkrishna is now the sixty-third-richest person in India, with a net worth north of $3.3 billion.[47] A fellow religious student, Balkrishna appears to operate as the chief operations officer and the chief financial officer of an empire undoubtedly led by a man who owns literally nothing.

Insiders note that Baba Ramdev himself is always involved in top corporate decision-making. "He is involved in all the most important decisions—what to make, how much to make, when to make, how much to sell for. He personally tries out every single product and approves it," one former executive told the *New Indian Express* in 2017.

Those are the strategic decisions: at the operational level, it's all Balkrishna. But Balkrishna is not only a businessman. Like Baba Ramdev, Balkrishna is a dyed-in-the-wool Hindu nationalist with a strong ideological commitment to a politicized take on ayurvedics. Both partners have become major backers of the BJP and close allies of Prime Minister Narendra Modi, who by now has accumulated almost complete political power while bullying India's hundred million Muslims.

In his book *The Science of Ayurveda*, Balkrishna puts out a compelling vision for modernizing and industrializing Hindu traditional knowledge. Promotional videos show traditional Hindu scholars in robes poring over Sanskrit texts to find the original recipes for the products that Patanjali Ayurved scientists go on to standardize and produce in modern factory settings. Balkrishna's goal is to marry millennial Vedic scriptures with modern business practices.[48]

Rumors of financial ties between Balkrishna's empire and BJP party coffers are often reported in Indian media, but the nation's official investigators have mostly steered clear of asking too many difficult questions. One especially consistent set of rumors involves the sensitive issue of land ownership in India's massively overpopulated northern plains. Again and again, BJP-led state governments appear to have made grants of substantial parcels of land to Patanjali Ayurved at substantially below-market rates.

To Ramdev and Balkrishna, the way to parry charges like these is obvious: the success of Patanjali Ayurved is a direct threat to the Western interests that dominate India's consumer-product landscape. Those interests naturally want to trash the reputation of a formidable competitor. And so foreigners do what foreigners do: they conspire, because they fear the power of Hinduism to remake India and the world.

Rather than engaging with details about land valuation around the city of Nagpur, they throw back charges of foreign conspiracy a little bit the way Donald Trump uses the formula "witch hunt": not so much as a defense, but more as a thought-terminating cliché, a way of sidestepping the entire conversation. Similarly, when independent lab tests of products sold under the Patanjali Ayurved label came back showing signs of adulteration—including the explosive result that not all the *ghee* sold comes from *cow*'s milk—Ramdev instantly turned it into an accusation against his competitors, alleging the foreigners had tampered with the product samples sent to labs to tarnish his company's name.[49] As reported by the *Economic Times*, Ramdev said, "Multinational firms like

Hindustan Unilever, Colgate, and Nestle are bribing people to get fake and adulterated Patanjali products tested in labs. Sometimes they even produce reports from fake laboratories to malign us."[50] To be clear, Nestle and Unilever deny the accusation.

Ramdev's defense is undoubtedly Trumpesque, but it also mirrors the communications of Prime Minister Modi, who also imagines himself a champion for the spread of Hindutva (Hindu-ness) in a world hostile to Hinduism. In Modi's political imagination, every criticism can be dismissed as prima facie evidence of a foreign conspiracy against ascendent Hindu power. Ramdev has found that this approach works and uses it liberally.

But in fact, sweetheart land deals, even if true, seem to account for only a small proportion of Patanjali Ayurved's spectacular profits. The company has been hovering around $1 billion in sales in the Indian market since 2019, 30 percent more than Colgate-Palmolive's turnover in the same market.[51]

What really sets Patanjali's profitability on a different plane is its labor relations. The company allegedly monetizes Hindu piety by pressuring employees to accept substantially lower salaries than they could get working for the competition. How does it get them to agree to this? By telling them they should consider their work as *seva*, a form of devotional sacrifice that often takes the form of volunteer labor. A 2017 investigation by the *Economic Times* of India alleged that Patanjali employees work up to six twelve-hour shifts per week for wages well below what competitors offer.[52] This one weird management trick means Patanjali can price its products well below those of many competitors across a variety of markets. By the company's estimate, some two hundred thousand Indians now work for Patanjali Ayurved.

A Bloomberg report found that at the outset of the pandemic in 2016, you could find a Baba Ramdev yoga lesson on free-to-air television in India "for 19 and a half hours every day."[53] His strategy seemed to be to flood the zone with cow urine. His face became omnipresent, his rhythmic-breathing routine a sign of belonging to a wider community of mobilized, politicized Hinduists confidently asserting themselves at the head of a nuclear power.

In fact, perhaps the only time Ramdev has been questioned in ways that might have threatened his empire came amid India's horrendous COVID-19 pandemic. He went on air to question the efficacy of scientific COVID vaccines and urged his millions of followers to take ayurvedic herbal pills instead. Pills that, more than obviously, they should buy from Patanjali Ayurved.

In fact, Baba Ramdev seems to have treated the pandemic as a once-in-a-lifetime opportunity to grow sales. He courted the rage of India's influential medical community saying kapālabhāti—his hokey take on breathing meditation—can cure COVID. Why shouldn't it, when it cures everything else? Of course, Patanjali Ayurved's sales don't rise when you do a funny breathing exercise in the privacy of your own home, so the "cure" would have to be supplemented with a number of . . . well . . . supplements. Which, of course, Patanjali Ayurved sells.

In an explosive May 2021 video, Ramdev called Western medicine "stupid and bankrupt," alleging hundreds of thousands of people have died from taking Western medicines. Soon, the Indian Medical Association, representing 350,000 doctors, served a legal notice to Ramdev demanding a retraction and an apology for the "baseless and unscrupulous claims made for cheap publicity."[54] The doctors' organizations demanded a crackdown on Ramdev from the government, asking the prime minister to "take appropriate action against individuals viciously propagating the message of fear on vaccination and challenging the government of India protocols for treatment for their vested interest in their company products."[55]

India's doctors saw Baba Ramdev's COVID outrage as intolerable, even though it wasn't any worse than the other nonsense claims he'd been making for years. The reason comes down to the scale of devastation COVID-19 left in its wake in India. The official death toll, at 530,000, is almost certainly an undercount of COVID's impact on the country.

At the height of the plague in 2020, a health-care system that is close to collapse at the best of times simply seized up altogether, with patients unable to get treatment, not only for COVID but also for anything else. India was gripped by panic, and the last thing the country needed was a charlatan trying to make a quick buck out of the tragedy. "This in our opinion," said the Indian Medical Association, "is a clear-cut case of a sedition case and such persons should be booked immediately without any delay."[56]

In February 2024 the Supreme Court of India temporarily banned Patanjali from advertising certain products, citing misleading claims about curing COVID-19. The court also issued a contempt notice to the company's founders for violating previous orders. In August 2024 the Supreme Court closed the contempt proceedings after accepting their apology but warned against future violations.[57] In January 2025 a court in the Indian state of Kerala issued arrest warrants against both Ramdev and Balkrishna, over allegations of misleading advertisement of its medicines.[58] Baba Ramdev and Balkrishna have denied any wrongdoing.

So far, there have been no arrests. It helps that Prime Minister Modi's BJP is close to Baba Ramdev and to Balkrishna. Rumors have circulated about financial links between the governing party and Baba Ramdev's company, and though evidence is scarce, one intriguing clue as to how it all works came from a hot-mic moment, or rather a hot-mic near miss. It happened when a BJP politician pressed Baba Ramdev for campaign donations only for the swami to remind him not to ask about such things in front of an open microphone.[59]

Joseph Mercola, Mehmet Oz, Baba Ramdev . . . very different men, but alike in the ways that matter most. They used digital technologies, whether it is TV or the internet, to put a promise of perfect health in front of millions of vulnerable people. They knew those digital promises were scalable, giving rise to businesses that target a mass audience.

Mostly, though, what makes them similar is that they target the same dream. They know we worry about our health—and we do!—and they know how to manipulate us by championing our dreams of optimal health. They know how to mobilize social proof to their advantage: the testimonials on Mercola's website, the swarms of buyers for the products Oz praised, the hundreds of people lined up to breathe oddly behind Baba Ramdev all serve, in their way, to convince their marks that people *like them* believe, so they should believe. Leveraging their audience's credulity into million-dollar paydays for themselves, all three have brought the age-old snake oil grift well and truly into the twenty-first century.

7

Digital Alchemy

The Crypto Grift

For hundreds of years, charlatans in Europe flocked to the practice of alchemy. Before the development of modern chemistry, sages took it for granted that some method must exist for transforming base metals like iron or copper into pure gold. The quest became an obsession, with tinkerers and serious thinkers alike devoting years to the practice. Sir Isaac Newton himself spent two decades trying his hand at it—longer than he spent developing calculus or working out the universal laws of motion that formed the backbone of modern physics.[1] Kings and princes kept court alchemists at hand, none willing to be left behind lest some rival discover the secret first.

Naturally, any number of grifters joined the space: even if gold couldn't be conjured out of iron, it *could* be swindled out of the pockets of unsuspecting dupes. Mamugnà, whom we met at the beginning of this book, bilked huge sums out of the declining Venetian republic's coffers in the sixteenth century—but by then the scam of pretending to create money out of nothing was already well over a thousand years old. The pope tried to ban it in 1317, describing it as an exploitative "crime of falsification."[2] By the eighteenth century, the figure of the alchemist-swindler was fully established in the European imagination.

Reading such tales from the perspective of the twenty-first century, we're liable to shake our heads and tsk-tsk at all this. "Money out of nothing?" we scoff. "How could anyone be so dumb?"

And then, we put all our money in crypto.

The similarities between the alchemists of history and the crypto bros of our day are too many to ignore.

It's a world that draws a volatile mix of financial visionaries and seductive charlatans.

While a handful of hardcore cryptographers and idealistic financial visionaries try to work out a revolution in our conception of money for the twenty-first century, a horde of grifters leeches off their efforts in search of a fast buck. Telling the two apart is often impossible.

The exotic math that underlies cryptography seems custom-made for claims to secret knowledge. Like their alchemic forebears, today's crypto bros talk feverishly about a cutting-edge new way of creating wealth that relies on sophisticated methods many are dazzled by but can't really understand.

Crypto charlatans pander to their marks' prior beliefs by telling them they're far ahead of a curve normal people are too dim to grasp. Time and again, they persuade their marks to exchange actual, usable, real money for a fantastic, chimerical crypto version of money whose value fluctuates wildly and simply implodes with startling regularity.

The criticisms of crypto as a concept are well known. Rather than seeking wealth by producing a useful good or a service others are willing to pay for, crypto is accused of seeking to produce wealth divorced from any purpose that is either legal or useful. Some enthusiasts pitched crypto as a godsend to people in countries facing hyperinflation, but not many countries do face hyperinflation, and crypto has never caught on in those places.

The one case where crypto's usefulness is undoubted is money laundering: if you're trying to hide the provenance of a large sum you've amassed illegally, then a fully unregulated and anonymized currency fits your purposes beautifully. Child pornographers, drug barons, cyber racketeers, and human traffickers love crypto for precisely this reason, though obviously this fact doesn't make for exactly glowing PR from the point of view of enthusiasts.[3]

We don't mean to suggest all of crypto is a scam—it isn't. Many perfectly reputable financial institutions and some very serious investors are betting on cryptocurrencies. Global titans such as Fidelity Investments, one of the world's largest asset managers, have launched cryptocurrency services to allow private and institutional clients to trade crypto.[4] Payments giants such as PayPal and Visa have integrated crypto in different ways into their payment platforms.[5] Professionally managed firms such as MicroStrategy and Tesla have added Bitcoin to their balance sheets, framing the move as a hedge against inflation and currency debasement, particularly in the context of massive monetary stimulus in response to the COVID-19 pandemic.

Even JPMorgan Chase—whose CEO, Jamie Dimon, is among the world's most outspoken skeptics of crypto—has created its own blockchain-based coin to allow cross-border transactions to settle instantly.[6] Plenty of financial professionals are excited by crypto's promise to streamline global payments by reducing costs and cutting settlement times from days to milliseconds.

And crypto may well make it big in the developing world, once it's past its growing pains. Visionary fintech startups such as Stellar are working on blockchain solutions to facilitate low-cost remittances for migrant workers, who often face exorbitant fees when transferring money across borders using traditional services.[7] For millions without access to reliable banking systems, crypto-based services offer a decentralized, low-barrier financial system, which, if scaled, could bring banking closer to billions across the globe.

Major market players are not sitting this one out. The Chicago Mercantile Exchange and the Intercontinental Exchange, which owns the New York Stock Exchange, now offer regulated Bitcoin futures and other crypto derivatives, giving institutional investors the ability to hedge and speculate on digital currencies in a tightly controlled environment.[8] As the regulatory landscape improves, crypto may yet play a growing role in diversified investment portfolios, providing a counterbalance to traditional financial assets and offering resilience against systemic risks in traditional banking, much in the way gold did over the last century.

So, we don't mean to imply that all crypto is a scam. What we do mean to say is that in its earliest incarnation it proved to be an irresistible lure to a wide range of charlatans who pulled some of the most spectacular grifts in recent memory.

But then, this is how it usually goes with innovative financial products. People forget that the early history of Wall Street is full of stories of shoddy exchanges fleecing customers who trusted those exchanges with their savings. The US Securities and Exchange Commission (SEC) was launched precisely to bring some order to markets that had proven serially unable to police themselves.[9]

When new types of markets arise outside the jurisdiction of any regulator, the same old scams seem to get reinvented, leaving a trail of hopeful investors out of pocket. And so it was in the benighted year of 2022, when crypto exchanges began failing one after another.

Many of the crypto implosions of our age are throwbacks to earlier types of financial frauds. Unlike traditional investments like stocks and bonds, crypto assets don't generate any kind of income stream. For now, the only way they make money is if more and more people pile into them. When you are bold enough to buy a crypto asset, your only exit scenario is to sell it to an even more vulnerable mark than you were somewhere down the road. This "greater fool" dynamic is a defining characteristic of Ponzi schemes: they can be profitable, but only so long as they keep growing, and, of course, they can't keep growing forever. Eventually the bubble bursts, and when it does, it's the people who got in late who end up losing out.

Sam Bankman-Fried

Of all the crypto charlatans who have disgraced our newspapers these last few years, none rose to the dizzying heights of one Samuel Benjamin Bankman-Fried. Barely twenty-six when his meteoric rise began, he shared with Elizabeth Holmes (of Theranos fame) an uncanny knack for gaining the confidence of well-established senior figures who would then vouch for his success. And like Bernie Madoff and Arif Naqvi, he knew how to make outlandish promises about the future with the kind of cool, brainy demeanor that made the ideas sound plausible to sophisticated investors who ought to have known better.

Charlatans, we have seen, can rise from all sorts of circumstances, from the very humble to the very much not, yet few grow up as privileged as Sam Bankman-Fried (commonly known by his initials, SBF). Born literally on the campus of Stanford University to parents who were both highly esteemed professors at the university's hyperelite law school, Bankman-Fried had every advantage a young person could hope for, and plenty of talent as well. His father, Joseph Bankman, was an authority on US corporate tax law, while his mother, Barbara Fried (pronounced "freed"), taught both law and philosophy and became known for arguing that many crimes were so fully determined by the perpetrator's background that no moral blame could be assigned to them for committing it.[10] The mind reels at trying to imagine what the typical conversation was like around the Bankman-Fried dinner table.

Showing a talent for math from an early age, Sam spent summers as a teenager at the Canada/USA Mathcamp, an elite academic summer camp where about 120 of North America's brightest young mathematical talents could hang out together. It was at Mathcamp that he met Gary Wang, who would end up owning a 10 percent share of his company.

Bankman-Fried ran into Wang again a few years later at the Massachusetts Institute of Technology (MIT), where the two would deepen their friendship as roommates. Bankman-Fried graduated MIT in 2014 with a degree in physics and immediately went to work in the financial industry, taking a job as a trader for Jane Street Capital, a Wall Street trading firm and market maker for exchange-traded funds (ETFs).[11]

He gained valuable experience in his five years at Jane Street, but Bankman-Fried had bigger dreams than trading ETFs. Soon, he'd left Wall Street to work at the celebrated Centre for Effective Altruism (CEA), a brainy new charity think tank founded by Oxford University professors that was encouraging bright young people to focus on earning as much money as they could so they could donate as much money as possible to good causes.

CEA was, in some ways, the perfect space for Bankman-Fried: filled with arcane theorizing few could fully understand, buzzy, and hugely attractive to more and more of the best and the brightest the Anglo-American elite had to offer, it held out the prospect of a deeply meaningful life to young people who craved meaning more than money.

Bankman-Fried would wave the banner of effective altruism for the rest of his dazzling but short career in finance. But CEA couldn't hold him for long: Sam would leave his mark elsewhere. Like any good finance whiz kid of his time, Bankman-Fried was drawn to the glitzy new world of crypto finance, an exotic, trendy emerging corner of the finance industry where computer code was turned—somehow, no one seemed entirely sure exactly—into money.

Cryptocurrency was launched onto an unsuspecting world by the quasi-mythical collective of anonymous, anarchist math nerds who invented Bitcoin, calling itself Satoshi Nakamoto, in 2008. They (observers tend to believe Satoshi is the pseudonym for a small collective of programmers, though there's always a chance it was a single individual) said they wanted to challenge government's monopoly on the creation of money through new cryptographic algorithms that would allow finance to be radically decentralized, with money created without a central authority and backed from a complex system of cryptographic puzzles captured in a public ledger, or blockchain. The specific technical details have always eluded all but a minuscule mathematical elite, but the upshot was that the blockchain could create a financial asset that was secure even though no central authority had minted it.

Bitcoin's popularity very soon burst the banks of the small number of people who understood its operation. Over the following two decades, crypto grew and grew in popularity, progressively roping in more and more regular people interested not so much in the techno-utopian promise of radically decentralized finance as in the good old-fashioned get-rich-quick dream.

And a number of people did get rich, very rich, and very quickly, as Bitcoin valuations soared from just $13,200 in September 2020 to $76,400 in March 2021 before losing almost half its value in July, then shooting back to a high of almost $81,000 in November 2021.

As the Bitcoin roller-coaster ride continued, a veritable boom in new digital assets (or "crypto coins") began hitting the market, each with a more outlandish set of design principles than the one before. With each new coin vowing to have "cracked the code" on what it would take to make crypto revolutionize the world of finance for hundreds of years to come and stories of newly minted crypto fortunes circulating widely, the atmosphere was ripe for a series of speculative bubbles to develop.

Assets based on increasingly exotic algorithms each claimed to have found the crypto philosopher's stone. In late 2021 a crypto firm called Titan misleadingly promised annualized returns of up to 2,700 percent—the SEC would later fine it for the breach.[12] At a time of near-zero interest rates, when traditional investments had lost much of their lure, capital around the world was on the prowl for returns. Huge sums of capital were itching for growth, and crypto sure did promise growth.

From 2015 new tokens, new public ledgers, whole new crypto ecosystems seemed to be coming onto the market each week along with a dizzying mass of new exchanges, services, and apps all promising to allow regular people to join the now roaring crypto craze.

As more and more "normies"—regular folks—joined the wave, the proportion with the cryptographic chops to fully grasp what exactly they were putting their money into dwindled from small, to tiny, to indistinguishable, to zero.

Social proof was strong: everyone seemed to know someone who had made a killing in crypto. Those looking for confirmation that joining the craze was a good idea were not short on evidence. Every day seemed to bring new stories of people making incredible fortunes with modest bets on crypto. The FOMO—fear of missing out—was rampant. Crypto ticked pretty much all the boxes for attracting all the era's aspiring grifters, fraudsters, and charlatans. What happened next seemed foretold.

In 2020, as the COVID-19 pandemic left more and more people stranded at home, many with money to spend from successive rounds of government financial stimulus, a golden era of crypto fraud dawned. It didn't help that the sector had always touted itself as a refuge from the oppressive thumb of government regulation, which somehow turned the absence of rules and openness to abuse into a feature rather than a bug.

As new tokens were launched, it became increasingly hard for ordinary people to tell apart the legitimate ones from "rug-pulls"—fraudulent schemes in which developers would promote a new token, hype its features, attract a pool of investor money, and suddenly disappear, leaving investors in the lurch. For a time, every old-time scam received a crypto makeover, chief among them the trusty old Ponzi scheme, now in digital guise.

Among the early runners was OneCoin, an online crypto-glossed pyramid scheme developed by the Bulgarian brother-sister act of Konstantin Ignatov and Ruja Ignatova. OneCoin paid early buyers a fee for each new buyer they brought in, and for each new buyer *those* new buyers brought in: a classic Ponzi-style pyramid. The scheme collapsed, as all pyramids are prone to do, in 2017, but not before dupes were separated from $4 billion of their hard-earned dollars. The brother and sister went on the lam. Eventually, Konstantin was arrested and pleaded guilty to fraud and money-laundering charges in 2019.[13] Ruja remains a fugitive. The FBI has offered a $5 million reward for information leading to her arrest.[14]

There were dozens of stories like Ignatov and Ignatova's: half-baked (or hardly-baked-at-all) coins popped up all around the world with names like Thodex, AnubisDAO, StableMagnet, and Luna Yield.[15]

Some were promoted by celebrities or online influencers. Swipathefox was launched by basketball star De'Aaron Fox.[16] CryptoZoo, an NFT-based game, was promoted by Logan Paul, a hugely popular heavyweight boxer and influencer.[17]

Some of the coins appear to have been projects originally launched with honorable intentions that went wrong for reasons ranging from infighting between members of the launch team to just plain mismanagement. Others were more brazen, like the notorious DeFi100 project, which sucked in $32 million before the coin's website suddenly went offline and displayed a message reading simply, "We scammed you guys, and you can't do shit about it."[18] Its promotors deny wrongdoing and insist their site was hacked.[19]

The outright fraudsters went to great lengths to simulate the look and feel of the more reputable crypto exchanges to dupe people into sending money directly to them before misappropriating it. Others simply put a crypto cherry on top of a well-established criminal cake.

One especially damaging scam originating in Asia got dubbed "pig butchering"—a combined romance-crypto scam that would see fraudsters slowly and methodically entrap people into what they thought were long-distance romantic relationships with beautiful but far-off women. Scammers would scan dating sites for potential marks, strike up a conversation, and then begin to "fatten the pig"; that is, they would get the men—the victims were all men—to fall in love with fictional single women.

The long-distance "relationships" that resulted could get spun out over a period of weeks or even months before crypto was first mentioned. Then, just casually, the "girlfriend" would start dropping hints about friends of hers who'd gotten very rich off crypto investments, and she'd subtly goad the mark into following suit. She would then persuade punters to put increasing sums of their own savings into fictional crypto accounts, showing larger and larger gains each time. Eventually, with the promise of a sweet life together in the offing, the fictional woman would persuade the mark to take out large loans in the mark's name to double down on the "investment." If he did, she would disappear altogether, pocketing the money. Devastated marks would find themselves humiliated, heartbroken, and swimming in debts incurred to fund this dream.

In 2021 alone, the American Federal Trade Commission received a staggering 46,000 reports of this kind of abuse.[20] But most fraud victims are too embarrassed to report the crimes perpetrated against them, meaning the real sums involved are certainly much larger—as much as $14 billion in 2021 alone, according to an estimate by crypto data analytics firm Chainalysis.[21] By another estimate, the total had risen to $75 billion by 2024.[22]

Pig butchering is not charlatanry—it's just fraud. Other crypto scams operated more in the gray area, at times by hiding truly scandalous conditions of service in the dense, interminable terms-of-use documents that exchange users had to "agree" to before they could sign up.

Presuming (in the vast majority of cases, correctly) that few users would actually take the trouble to read the agreement in detail, or to submit it to a lawyer for review, shady exchanges sneaked all kinds of unconscionable conditions into such agreements.

This created some very strange situations.

When the Celsius Network crypto exchange collapsed on June 12, 2022, thousands of depositors lost millions in value. The bewildered US bankruptcy judge who oversaw the bankruptcy case found that the Celsius Network had not broken its contract when it simply stole its customers' assets, because the agreement customers had clicked "agree" on when they opened their accounts, explicitly allowed Celsius to do exactly that.

As *Gizmodo*'s Lauren Leffer put it, "Celsius' incredibly shady terms of service also explicitly warned signatories that if Celsius chose to steal all your assets, 'you may not have any legal remedies or rights,' to get your money back."[23]

It will surprise no one who has ever clicked "agree" to terms and conditions that virtually no Celsius customer had taken the trouble to carefully study the terms-of-service document involved. If they had, they would have found that buried in Section 13 was a clause making the crypto assets they deposited in Celsius accounts legally little more than a gift to Celsius. When Celsius did collapse in June 2022, those same users suffered paper losses of almost $5 billion worth of crypto assets that—if it's any consolation to them—hadn't actually belonged to them in the first place.[24] Judge Martin Glenn, the chief US bankruptcy judge in the Southern District of New York, had little choice but to rule that "based on Celsius's unambiguous Terms of Use . . . when the cryptocurrency assets (including stablecoins . . .) were deposited in Earn Accounts, the cryptocurrency assets became Celsius's property."[25]

Crypto's White Knight: SBF

The stories were appalling, and idealists were duly appalled. True believers thirsted for a leader who could help the ecosystem graduate out of its Wild West days and complete its transition from anarcho-utopian dream to real financial alternative for everyday people. Meanwhile, figures in the traditional financial system, stunned at the fortunes being made (and lost) in the crypto space, were themselves trying to figure out ways into the space but were hampered by the absence of figures trustworthy enough to do business with.

Sam Bankman-Fried seemed to fit the bill. Stuffed with elite credentials and reputed to be something of a genius, he stunned the sector by calling for *more* government regulation, not less. Rejecting crypto's founding anarchic core premises, he positively called on financial-market regulators to adopt new rules to ensure customers couldn't be cheated. Better yet, SBF claimed he knew how to develop algorithmic solutions to the underlying problems, solutions that could be used as the template for regulating the system as a whole.

To the grown-up US financial and political elites, he was a godsend: precisely what an older generation of investment professionals had been hoping for as a bridge into the bright, new crypto future.

By doing away with the antisystem ethos, SBF's calls for increased regulation of crypto painted him as a different kind of crypto founder. For the head of a buzzy new crypto firm to actively encourage regulating the industry made for a man-bites-dog story, instantly casting him as a more thoughtful, more serious sort of player.

Positioning himself brilliantly as the *antidote* to all the crypto scamming, SBF sold a vision of a different kind of crypto company, one experienced investors could take seriously. Developing cozy ties to politicians and philanthropies too, Sam Bankman-Fried seemed to feel instinctively at ease in the haunts of traditional power.

That someone in his position would need to donate handsomely to America's political establishment almost goes without saying. SBF contributed handsomely to the election campaigns of dozens of American power brokers. Most of his spending went to help Democrats; it was not surprising when we learned his mother—Stanford Law professor Barbara Fried—ran Mind the Gap, a fundraising network of more than eight hundred donors that was channeling tens of millions of dollars to congressional candidates in contested US House races.[26] The average crypto-exchange founder spent his days trading, coding, and gaming—not sending fat checks to Washington.

But Sam Bankman-Fried was different.

In December 2021 he turned up to testify in front of Congress, holding forth on the need for regulation to protect consumers from the kinds of frauds that were increasingly making their way to the front pages and touting his exchange's 24/7 risk-monitoring practice as more sophisticated and safer than those in use in traditional financial markets. Throughout his testimony, Bankman-Fried hinted heavily that the practices he was pioneering would make an excellent blueprint for new regulatory rules that would need to be applied to the entire industry.[27]

He spoke movingly about the exorbitant costs poor people without traditional bank accounts face in trying to send money to their relatives in other countries. In public comments at the time, he claimed he had made it his life's mission to make as much money as possible purely so he could donate as much as possible over the course of his lifetime to the world's neediest people.

All the while, he was perpetrating perhaps the biggest crypto scam of all time: FTX.

Founded in Hong Kong in 2019 by SBF alongside his old Mathcamp buddy Gary Wang, FTX was short for Future Exchange. The firm was often shorthanded as a crypto-trading platform, but that wasn't exactly right. It was a crypto-*futures* trading platform, one devoted largely to letting people buy and sell contracts whose value would fluctuate *alongside* those of crypto assets.

The terminology can be confusing, but the key is in the word *futures*—nobody has to actually buy or sell any crypto to bet on what would happen to the price of Bitcoin in the future. As analyst Stephen Diehl put it, perhaps the easiest way to think of it is to think of FTX as a casino where you put in dollars, are given chips, and are then invited to gamble on the price of crypto.[28]

FTX's value proposition was entirely straightforward: they were selling confidence. While Wild West exchanges like Celsius might collapse and run off with all your money, FTX was different. Idealistic. Politically engaged. Smart. Responsible. Run by math geniuses who'd created a unique risk engine that never stops and cannot be gamed, it was a risk engine so foolproof that US regulators and politicians would do well to deploy them throughout the industry. That's how good it was.

Futures markets of this type aren't at all new. Their forerunners date back to the nineteenth century, when traders in Chicago realized that they could secure contracts for wheat, cattle, and other agricultural commodities that had not yet been produced: in essence paying farmers now for delivery of their goods in six months' time. Those contracts could then be bought and sold in an open market, creating a price today for goods to be delivered at some point in the future. Refined, extended, financialized, and reinvented any number of times in the 170 years since, futures contracts today take a bewildering variety of forms, and futures exchanges allow you to bet on everything from the price of copper to the price of semiconductors.

FTX proposed a platform for extending this idea to the sphere of crypto.

That FTX was first set up in Hong Kong was no coincidence. US securities laws take a dim view of unregulated securities trading. Many exchanges went venue shopping, their leaders racking up hundreds of thousands of miles on their frequent-flier accounts looking for the jurisdiction where the regulators would be least likely to come pester them. For a while in the late 2010s, Hong Kong—with its deep pool of financial talent, any number of software developers, and regulators signaling they wouldn't ask many questions—looked like the ideal place.

SBF soon realized any exchange with a reputation for fairness and honesty stood to make big money. And so it did. As brave prodemocracy protesters faced down the authorities on the streets in 2019, Bankman-Fried was in his office high above, making his first billions.

The financial press couldn't get enough of the spunky kid with the messed-up hair in shorts and tube socks, who was then leading one of the world's fastest-growing firms. "The World's Richest 29-Year-Old," blared one *Forbes* headline, touting Bankman-Fried's goal "to position his risk-taking two-year-old financial firm as something safe and mature," after luxuriating at length on his radical philanthropic views.[29]

Describing Bankman-Fried as "perhaps the most interesting new billionaire in the world," the magazine noted that no one, not even Mark Zuckerberg, had earned as much money before the age of thirty as he had.[30] In 2021 *Cointelegraph*, an influential industry publication, had him as the third most powerful player in crypto worldwide.[31]

The stories about him fall over themselves in praise, such as one by *Nikkei Asia* in June 2021:

> Sam Bankman-Fried is worth $8.7 billion, according to Forbes. But that number could get "a lot bigger" depending on the outcome of a fundraising round that he says will sharply increase the valuation of FTX, the Hong-Kong based crypto derivative exchange he founded in 2019. Despite his wealth and the lavish lifestyle the financial hub has to offer, the former Wall Street trader

> lives like many millennials—he swears by his vegan diet, shares an apartment with roommates, wears T-shirts and shorts to work, and makes sure every room in his office in Hong Kong's central business district has beanbag chairs to sleep on.[32]

And how was he making those billions? By charging customers small fees for the privilege of using the exchange he had conjured out of pure code. In just three years, FTX rose to be the second-largest crypto exchange on earth, attracting hundreds of millions of dollars' worth of investment with elaborate promises of cutting-edge risk-management practices that would ensure your money was safe with them.

If you believed, say, that the price of Bitcoin would rise in the future, the FTX platform would match you up with someone else who believed the price would fall. You both placed your bets by funding your accounts with actual money—good old greenbacks—and FTX would issue futures contracts that would rise or fall in value alongside the price of Bitcoin. If you bought a "long" contract—one betting the price of Bitcoin would rise—and the price actually did rise, the exchange would show the value of your position increasing. At the same time, of course, the value of the "short" contracts bought by those who had gambled on Bitcoin going down lost value.

Because futures exchanges have been around for more than a century, the basic principles of how to run them soundly are well understood. Key among them is the idea that no trader's balance on the exchange can be allowed to dip below zero. If a trader makes a bad bet, and the value of their position reaches zero, the exchange needs to move quickly to either demand the trader put in more capital or close out the account.

Outside the Wild West world of crypto, those principles are professionally enforced by regulators. In a normal exchange, government watchdogs would be formally charged with ensuring the total amount of actual money the winners are winning wasn't more than the total amount the losers are losing.

In a properly regulated market, whenever winners decided to cash out their earnings, the exchange would be sure to have enough money on hand to pay out. This makes sense, because it's from the funds put in by "losing" traders that the exchange can afford to pay out earnings to the winners. If losing accounts are allowed to go below zero, the exchange will be left without enough money to pay the winners. Much computing talent and much regulatory zeal go into ensuring this situation can never arise, because if it does, the exchange itself will ultimately collapse, facing demand for withdrawals it just doesn't have the money to pay out.

Just like a casino can't risk issuing more chips to its customers than it has dollars on hand to pay them out, FTX promised its customers there would always be enough money for them to cash out. But even as Bankman-Fried talked up the need for regulation, FTX was operating with no effective oversight, and Bankman-Fried was determined to keep it that way.

That seems to have been the key reason persuading SBF to move his entire operation out of the sleek downtown office towers of Hong Kong and into a palm tree–shaded suburb in the Bahamas in late 2021. Lax though the regulatory regime had been in Hong Kong, in the Bahamas it would be laxer still: the small island nation's government was working hard to position Nassau as a crypto-innovation hub, and when a big fish like FTX expressed interest, the government was determined to get them to come. Once FTX was ensconced in the Bahamas, it was expected that no regulator would dare come close to Bankman-Fried's books . . . or his secrets.

When it all came crumbling down, exposés would luxuriate over Bankman-Fried's lifestyle at Nassau's hyperexclusive Albany community. Described as a gated community for the yachting class, it pitched itself shamelessly to the global elite, attracting the likes of Tiger Woods and Justin Timberlake with such amenities as a seventy-one-slip marina dedicated exclusively to megayachts, an eighteen-hole golf course designed by Ernie Els, and eleven closed-to-the-public restaurants.[33]

Even by the over-the-top standards of Albany, the FTX crowd lived it up there. SBF bunked down in the compound's $30 million penthouse with a shifting cast of around ten employees, partners, sex buddies, and collaborators in a setup that seemed like the world's most expensive college dorm. At Albany, FTX executives coded late into the night and took naps in the beanbag chairs strewn about the place as needed. Getting peckish, they'd order thousands of dollars' worth of vegan high cuisine delivered to their desks every single day from one of the development's restaurants. They'd knock back amphetamines as needed to stave off sleep (though always using them "on label," Bankman-Fried was careful to note, lest we think him a libertine), play video games to blow off steam, and, many sources allege, jump in and out of one another's beds with startling regularity as part of a freewheeling culture of polyamory that pervaded the firm.[34]

It wasn't exactly the lifestyle he had claimed to want in interviews in which he'd told reporters he was "not that much of a consumer, exactly" or that he planned to keep no more than 1 percent of his earnings.[35]

For more than a year, the getting was good. Bankman-Fried's paper fortune swelled from $8.7 billion during his stint in Hong Kong to some $26 billion at its peak in the Bahamas. With money coming in at an unprecedented pace, no spending seemed too extravagant to a company determined to become a household name throughout the world. Bankman-Fried paid $7 million for an ad in 2022's Super Bowl LVI, featuring comedian Larry David dismissing the great ideas of history from the wheel to the light bulb, to suggest those who doubted FTX's claim to be "a safe and easy way to get into crypto" would look just as silly in retrospect.[36] But that was chump change for FTX: the company offered $135 million for a nineteen-year deal to rename the home of the NBA's Miami Heat as the FTX Arena until 2040.[37]

FTX's very wealth became the core of its social-proof strategy—proof enough that crypto was here to stay. The very messaging in the Larry David ad was a brilliant twist on social-proof marketing—one turned on its head. The ad inverted the usual formula; instead of showing you that people like you believed in things like this, it showed you that fools did not believe in the idea. "Don't be like Larry," the ad counseled. "Don't miss out."

Thanks to stunts like these and SBF's image as a boy savant, FTX soon had the kind of grown-up credibility other crypto projects could only dream of. NFL legend Tom Brady and his wife, supermodel Gisele Bündchen, took an equity share and soon found themselves doing FTX commercials, and New England Patriots owner Robert Kraft and billionaire hedge fund manager Paul Tudor Jones were soon along for the ride as well.[38] Brady and Bündchen were on hand, of course, for an FTX-sponsored Web3 conference in the Bahamas in May 2022 that also included the likes of Bill Clinton, former British Prime Minister Tony Blair, pop superstar Katy Perry, and hundreds of other luminaries.[39]

By this point, FTX's claim to be the "safe, easy way to get into crypto" was winning over not just Super Bowl fans but the kinds of staid, conservative financial institutions that are meant to have elaborate safeguards against being conned.

The Ontario Teachers' Pension Plan—which, behind its modest-sounding name, hides a $250 billion global investment behemoth—took equity stakes in several FTX-linked companies and ended up having to write off every penny of the $95 million it had put in.[40]

Kevin O'Leary, the tech entrepreneur and celebrity investor known to millions from the TV series *Shark Tank*, lost almost $10 million on his equity stake in FTX—a loss made perhaps less bitter by the $15 million fee he received from the company to act as its spokesman. And those were just FTX's famous backers; the company also raised money from institutions whose names you may not know, but which investment professionals recognize and revere—names like Temasek Holdings, Sequoia Capital, Sea Capital, Tiger Global, and Lightspeed Venture Partners—huge, fully professionalized investment-and-research powerhouses tasked with husbanding the resources of the world's richest people.[41]

Maybe they were all in the grip of FOMO. So scared were they to be left out of the FTX gold rush, they never stopped to really scrutinize the company's accounts. Nor did anyone take a close look at FTX's sister firm, the firm that, in time, would bring the entire house of cards down: Alameda Research.

This was the name of the crypto hedge fund Bankman-Fried and Wang had set up in 2017—two years before FTX came onto the scene—to buy and sell crypto futures for profit.

To hear the 2021-era puff pieces tell it, FTX was born specifically out of SBF's disappointment with the services offered by the pre-FTX exchanges. Remember, SBF had been a professional trader for Jane Street—he was used to the full-service trading platforms of Wall Street—sophisticated platforms allowing him to make all kinds of complicated bets across a range of securities. Before FTX, there was nothing like that for the crypto market.

As *Forbes* put it, SBF "soon grew frustrated with the quality of the major crypto exchanges. They were geared toward making it easy for individuals to buy and sell a few bitcoins, but they were in no way equipped to handle professional traders moving large sums at rapid speeds. Sensing his moment, he decided to start his own exchange."[42]

Once FTX was established, Alameda began doing much of its trading *on* the FTX platform. The overlapping ownership of FTX and Alameda was . . . not ideal. It was a little like having one of the casino's croupiers also playing at the blackjack table. Well aware of this, Bankman-Fried publicly distanced himself from the leadership of Alameda Research, appointing a young math-wizard friend of his, Caroline Ellison, who—later reports would suggest—was also Bankman-Fried's sometime girlfriend.[43]

Both of Ellison's parents were professors at MIT's world-famous economics department. A math prodigy from a young age, she spent her days listening to her parents talk about economics, just as Bankman-Fried had spent his childhood overhearing his parents discussing corporate law. There was a neat mirror-image parallelism to their academic careers: Bankman-Fried, the son of Stanford academics, graduated from MIT, while Ellison, the daughter of MIT academics, earned her degree from

Stanford. In time, Ellison, Bankman-Fried, and Wang seem to have become the central nub of a leadership cadre that grew to oversee dozens of subsidiaries and hundreds of employees around the world. Old friends, they were roommates as well as business partners and had been for years. To people in their social circle, the pretense of a corporate separation wall between a company headed by Bankman-Fried and one headed by his sometime girlfriend Ellison was, at best, difficult to believe.

In public, FTX was adamant that it did not "commingle" customer funds, meaning it didn't take risks with them. It wouldn't invest them, it wouldn't lend them out, it wouldn't do anything that risked them becoming unavailable when customers wanted to withdraw them.

It couldn't, it said, due to the crown jewel of the FTX empire: its aggressive, proprietary risk engine, which would automatically close out positions when an account threatened to come near a value of zero.

FTX was at pains to emphasize that it was, after all, an exchange, not a bank: its terms of service were clear in saying each customer's funds belonged *to* that customer. FTX did not offer to extend credit; that was not its role.

US federal prosecutors would eventually come to believe that was strictly true for all FTX customers but one: Alameda Research. In early 2023 a federal indictment would charge FTX-directed software developers with coding a series of special rules that exempted Alameda from key protections baked into the normal FTX risk engine.[44]

If you made a wrong bet on the future of, say, Ethereum, and the value of your account dropped to or near to zero, FTX would automatically close out your position, but not if you were Alameda. If you were Alameda, your account could go negative. Deeply negative. And the software wouldn't do a damn thing about it. Nobody would.

In effect, this meant Alameda could illegally "borrow" FTX's customers' funds essentially without limit, directly in contravention of FTX's terms of service.

By allowing Alameda to hold negative balances, FTX created a heads-I-win, tails-you-lose dynamic on its platform. When Alameda made a trade and it went well, it could withdraw its earnings in real, noncrypto cash and sprinkle it around its shareowners. When it made a bad trade and lost, its position could go negative—*deeply* negative, billions-of-dollars negative, and it wouldn't matter: Alameda would always get another chance to make the money back, in effect by gambling with other FTX customers' money.

If, like Celsius, FTX had had the foresight to tell its customers in its terms of service that their money was already no longer theirs, it might not be so bad. But as it was, FTX's entire marketing strategy was based on a promise to shield customers from risk through sophisticated safeguards that applied to everyone. The reality was it did apply to everyone . . . except the CEO's girlfriend.

The risk engine SBF had wanted to make a model for crypto regulation turned out to have one rather big asterisk appended to its end. It was as though FTX were enticing people to come swim at a totally safe, guaranteed 100 percent shark-free beach . . . but refused to disclose to them that a single very big, very hungry great white shark would be allowed special permission to swim among them, simply because the people who owned the beach happened to also own the shark.

As so often happens, the scheme might have worked like a charm if asset prices hadn't moved decisively against Alameda . . . and against SBF. In May 2022 a wide and deep crypto slump hit, knocking back prices for all sorts of crypto assets of the type Alameda was invested in. In May 2022 one of the year's hottest crypto projects—TerraLuna token—collapsed in a scandal of its own: the first domino in a chain that would eventually bring FTX tumbling down.

Hilariously misdescribed as an "algorithmic stable coin," it was composed of two related tokens: Luna and Terra, which were described as helping to stabilize each other the way the moon stabilizes the wobbles in the earth's orbit. Luna's value would fluctuate, but it would always be exchangeable for Terra, which, in turn, was supposed to always trade one-to-one with the US dollar, with investors continually reassured that thanks to the supersophisticated algorithm behind the whole thing, the whole package was algorithmically stable. It was bunk: as any monetary economist could have told them, such pegs are inherently open to speculative attack. Terra was indeed attacked at the start of May 2022 and, within a few weeks, it was worth effectively zero.

According to crypto analysis firm Nansen, the TerraLuna collapse was bad news for Alameda, sending its negative position at FTX soaring.[45] If it had been anyone else, FTX would've closed the account and wiped out the investors. But that's not how FTX would treat Alameda: instead of closing out its position, FTX called in Alameda's collateral. On paper, the collateral Alameda had offered should be good enough to back Alameda's negative balance as it grew first to the hundreds of millions and then into the billions of dollars.

Everything would now turn on the value of Alameda's collateral, and it would very soon become obvious that was not enough. On paper, those assets were very substantial indeed—billions of dollars' worth. Asked, in the weeks that followed, how he could have allowed Alameda to get so far in over its head, Bankman-Fried circled back to Alameda's collateral time and again, saying he hadn't worried because he had believed Alameda's collateral was good and capable of making right much of the mess Alameda had created.

Collateral Damage

It's here, when you actually scrutinize the collateral backing FTX's loans to Alameda, that the real cherry on top of SBF's grift comes into focus: the collateral Alameda was holding consisted largely of FTT. And what was FTT? It was an in-house crypto token FTX had created as a sweetener for its customers. The asset backing FTX's billion-dollar loans to Alameda amounted to a bunch of computer code FTX itself had written and that had barely traded in the market.

FTT amounted to an FTX customer-loyalty program: FTX customers earned FTT, and those FTT allowed them to pay lower trading fees on FTX. Beyond that, it was also just a speculative crypto asset, subject to all the same greater-fool dynamics as every other crypto asset. Worse, FTT was in no way liquid. It traded little. As collateral goes, it was fishy at best.

Why? The answer lies in the fact that FTT could be expected to fluctuate alongside FTX's popularity: a crypto asset whose main wow factor was that it entitled customers to lower fees on FTX wouldn't be very attractive in a world without FTX, would it? This feature made investing in FTT tokens a rough parallel to investing in FTX stock—although, to be clear, FTT was not literally stock and didn't entitle customers to share in FTX profits.

FTT was more like a betting slip on the future of the exchange itself. The basic point was that if FTX became worthless, FTT would be worthless too.

Finance professionals know what to call this: wrong-way risk. Insuring an Alameda loan with FTT tokens is a little like taking out a fire insurance policy that says that, in the event your house catches fire, you will be compensated with $10,000 in cash, which is to be stored inside that same house. Obviously, if the house burns, the $10,000 in it burns too: an insurance policy built on wrong-way risk is no insurance policy at all.

In any case, the mountains of FTT that Alameda had turned over to FTX couldn't be liquidated to pay out FTX customers' withdrawals. Few actual FTT trades were ever made, in fact leading to a widespread suspicion that the per-unit price had been manipulated precisely so the holdings of FTT in Alameda's books could support huge loans from FTX. This kind of market manipulation would've been illegal in any properly regulated futures exchange, but let's not forget, FTX had gone far out of its way—halfway around the world, indeed, from Hong Kong to the Bahamas—to ensure it wouldn't be properly regulated.

It was more than obvious that any attempt to liquidate the FTT would deeply depress the price of the FTT token, leaving a huge hole in the balance sheet. In balance sheets SBF would frantically circulate in the days before FTX's collapse, those liabilities turn up to be worth negative $8 billion in a line infamously labeled "hidden, poorly internally labeled 'fiat@' account." If ever a criminal defendant has managed to include a complete confession in a single cell of an Excel spreadsheet, this was it.[46]

It would take several months for the $8 billion hole Alameda Research blew in the FTX balance sheet to lead to its collapse, much in the way the *Titanic* stayed afloat for a few hours after it hit that iceberg. But from that moment on, FTX's fate was sealed. Eventually, customers would demand their money back, and if FTX didn't have it, if it had siphoned it off to its sister trading firm and then lost it, well, FTX wasn't going to be able to pay them. And indeed, it wasn't able to pay them.

The collapse of FTX, when it did come at the end of 2022, was swift and brutal. It dominated financial headlines around the world, making Sam Bankman-Fried the villain of the piece for weeks on end. His personal net worth collapsed from $26 billion to, in effect, $0 in just a few hours, as word got around that FTX was seeking a bailout after finding an $8 billion hole in its finances. Rather than offering to bail it out, savvy exchange participants rushed to withdraw their funds from the exchange before it collapsed. That rush created a run-on-the-bank effect, with all depositors suddenly clamoring to withdraw their funds at once. The detail is that FTX was not supposed to be a bank: had it been run the way its terms of use said it would be run, everyone would've been paid just fine. As it was, the exchange couldn't afford to meet all the requests for withdrawal. Alameda's collateral was largely made up of FTT and other illiquid assets: try to sell them all at once, and their value would plummet to zero . . . which is what it would do in any case, given that without FTX around, the token would be worthless.

Faced with close to a million angry customers who'd lost, in some cases, their entire life savings in FTX, Bankman-Fried again went counter to stereotype. Corporate leaders on the hook for billion-dollar frauds are supposed to shut up. Tightly. Any good lawyer—hell, any *bad* lawyer—will instruct clients that anything they say in public could be brought up against them in court. Bankman-Fried, who grew up under two parents who were both among the most accomplished attorneys in American academia, can hardly have failed to know what *everybody* knows: talking while under federal investigation is a losing game.

And yet he talked. Boy, did he talk! He talked and tweeted and gave interviews, as usual in his tube socks and from his lavish Bahamian penthouse. Frank, open interviews in which he seemed at pains to look humble, to admit he'd gotten in way over his head, but then also to characterize the entire affair not as a crime, not as a swindle, but as a mistake: the outcome of good intentions, bad recordkeeping, and his own lack of adequate experience.

At times, Bankman-Fried's postbankruptcy candor seemed almost suicidal: a determined campaign to destroy the reputation he'd spent years trying to foster.

In a remarkable text message–based interview with *Vox*, Bankman-Fried more or less explicitly admitted that his claimed interest in effective altruism was a ruse, a public relations pose designed to bolster his credibility and ease his campaign to open investors' pocketbooks.

Asked about his knack for talking about ethics, he expressed some contrition, saying, "It's what reputations are made of, to some extent," and adding, "I feel bad for those who get fucked by it," describing all his ethical posturing and Effective Altruist proselytizing before the FTX collapse as part of "this dumb game we woke westerners play where we say all the right shiboleths [*sic*] and so everyone likes us."[47]

The bankruptcy administrators soon hired to manage FTX after its collapse would agree that SBF's recordkeeping was bad. Very bad. John Ray III, brought on as CEO to replace Bankman-Fried after the collapse, came in with four decades of experience in trying to sort out the messed-up accounts of failed companies, including ENRON. He was unsparing: "Never in my career have I seen such a complete failure of corporate controls and such a complete absence of trustworthy financial information as occurred here," Ray would say in the days after taking over as boss. "From compromised systems integrity and faulty regulatory oversight abroad," he went on, "to the concentration of control in the hands of a very small group of inexperienced, unsophisticated and potentially compromised individuals, this situation is unprecedented."[48]

FTX, Ray would soon make clear, had only the vaguest notion of what it owned and what it owed, to whom, when, or why. Million-dollar expenditures at the company were approved not through a rigorous documented decision-making protocol, as would happen at a regulated Wall Street bank, but through a system of "personalized emojis" shared on an in-office messaging app.[49]

And why didn't FTX's board of directors stand up and put an end to the nonsense? Oh, did we forget to mention? FTX had no board of directors. SBF sidestepped the whole thorny issue of dealing with board members' uncomfortable questions through the inspired choice of simply not having a board. Hundreds of millions of investment dollars, many from sophisticated institutional investors, ended up sloshing around a company that didn't have a formal human resources department or even a proper accounting department.[50]

If you would expect FTX to run the way a bunch of glib, hyper-privileged finance-bro roommates would run a major crypto-futures exchange, that's because that's precisely how it did run. Or, at least, that's how Bankman-Fried sought to portray things. They weren't criminals, he pleaded to anyone who would listen; they were just disorganized.

For a few days after FTX's collapse, this defense seemed like it might possibly fly. Certainly, the recordkeeping chaos John Ray III said he found in FTX's books was dire enough to account for much mischief. But, of course, disorganization could also be used tactically, as an excuse. So, which one was it?

On December 21, 2022, prosecutors at the Southern District of New York—the fabled American prosecutorial authority with jurisdiction over Wall Street—announced that Bankman-Fried's two closest collaborators, Caroline Ellison and Gary Wang, had agreed to plead guilty to a whole string of conspiracy and fraud charges and to collaborate with prosecutors in return for a reduced sentence. The story broke the same day Bankman-Fried, arrested days earlier in the Bahamas, was flown to New York after declining to fight extradition.

With Ellison declaring in court that she of course knew the special exceptions for Alameda "were wrong," and with Wang pleading guilty to charges that could theoretically land him a fifty-year sentence, prosecuting Bankman-Fried was relatively straightforward.[51] He was found guilty on seven counts of fraud and conspiracy.[52] Before handing down his sentence on March 28, 2024, the court heard dozens of victim impact statements, with one investor after another describing the financial chaos and emotional anguish the saga had put them through. "Beyond the monetary loss," one wrote, "this crime has shattered our sense of security and trust in the systems meant to protect us."[53] Bankman-Fried was sentenced to twenty-five years in federal prison.[54] Ellison was sentenced to two years in prison.[55]

During his trial, Bankman-Fried wore an ankle bracelet while he remained on house arrest at his parents' Palo Alto home, whose value was pledged as collateral for the $500 million bond he was released from jail on.

He shared, for those few weeks, a roof with a legal-scholar mother who famously didn't believe on a philosophical level in the concept of blame. In a remarkable 2013 essay titled "Beyond Blame" for the *Boston Review*, Barbara Fried argued that because criminals' behavior is fully determined by their environment and circumstances, it makes little sense to punish them for their crimes. She illustrated this view with a striking example, meant to show the senselessness of punishing an underprivileged everyman—Smith, she calls him—for his crimes:

> Suppose that Smith grew up in a neighborhood where drug dealing was the most common form of gainful employment. He was raised by a single mother who was a cocaine addict, and by the time he was twelve was supporting his family by selling drugs. When he was seventeen, he got caught up in a drug deal gone bad, and in the altercation that ensued, he shot and killed the buyer. How should we think about Smith's level of moral responsibility? Is there some magical moment at which Smith was transformed from the victim of his circumstances to the author of his own story? If so, when was it?[56]

Interesting. A paraphrase, with a bit of rearranging, might give you this: Suppose that Bankman-Fried grew up in a neighborhood where teaching law and philosophy were the most common forms of gainful employment. He was raised by law school–professor parents who were also major authorities on tax law, and by the time he was twenty-four he was supporting his family by selling derivatives contracts. When he was twenty-nine, he got caught up in a crypto-derivatives exchange deal gone bad, and in the altercation that ensued, he destroyed $1 billion worth of people's savings. Is there some magical moment at which Bankman-Fried was transformed from the victim of his circumstances to the author of his own story? If so, when was it?

When, indeed?

Out of all the charlatans discussed in this book, Sam Bankman-Fried was probably the smartest and certainly, at his peak, the wealthiest. His ascent had all the hallmarks of a charlatan's arch—he played ruthlessly to people's dreams of wealth, engineered social proof of his company's success in the form of expensive endorsement deals, laid claim to special knowledge and privilege, and made his customers feel like they were the elect even as he ruthlessly stole from them.

But he seems unlike many charlatans too, in his almost obsessive need to continue talking in public about his grift even after it had begun to unravel. Unlike so many other charlatans, he doesn't seem to have grasped how manipulative and criminal his approach was until the very last minute. Like Dr. Mercola, to some extent, the accusation of grifting is complicated by his apparent belief in his own grift.

When it's all said and done, Joseph Mercola at least gives his customers the supplement pill they asked for. Sam Bankman-Fried, for his part, promised security and provided nothing. Those who trusted him are $1 billion poorer for his efforts. He'll have two and a half decades in prison to think about what he got wrong.

8

Charlatans in High Places

A SPECTER IS HAUNTING THE PAGES OF THIS BOOK: THE SPECTER OF Donald J. Trump.

The American leader poses an impossible conundrum to an observer of charlatanry.

On the one hand, everything that could be usefully written about him has already been written, many times over. On the other hand, that an out-and-out charlatan rose to become the most powerful man in the world remains so startling, so strange, so epoch-making that our hand is forced.

We could not pass him by even if we wanted to.

This is not a manifestation of political animosity. The prepolitical, pre-2015 Trump would have comfortably earned a spot in these pages even if his presidential campaign had flamed out in a few weeks. And Trump is not the only one to have risen to high office in recent years only to use his power to derail investigations against him and to line his pockets. In this chapter, we'll read about those who blazed the path Trump would follow.

In reality, Donald Trump is not so unique. All around the world, but with special virulence in the United States, power-hungry charlatans are finding their way into the political sphere. Employing the same tactics we have chronicled here, they're finding ways to raise huge sums of money and mobilize a sizable segment of public opinion behind them. They corner sections of the political sphere and embed themselves in them, exploiting their followers to further their purposes.

The guardrails that used to keep the most shameless charlatans out of political influence have shown they can fail—and the results could be dire for all of us. Political science has its own rich vocabulary to describe charlatans who manage to gain control of the state, subtly graduated by the level of danger they pose to democracy: populists, demagogues, despots, tyrants. Often they'll begin by, in Alexander Hamilton's phrase, "paying an obsequious court to the people" and then climb that ladder as though it were a career path, "commencing demagogues, and ending tyrants."[1]

The first step, though, is that "obsequious court to the people." The process of winning over "the people"—or at least *enough* people—has plenty of common ground with the tactics normal charlatans use. Motivated reasoning is rampant in the political sphere, and pandering to people's political dreams has always been the quickest way to earn their votes. Once they have their hooks in, well, they can get their followers to follow them far. Very far indeed.

The same vulnerabilities that leave people open to charlatans in their business and spiritual lives leave them just as vulnerable as political beings. As Italy's Silvio Berlusconi famously discovered, the same techniques you can use to sell dish soap you can use to attach people to a candidate for office.

Motivated reasoning is a central concept in research on voting behavior.[2] And it figures: our dreams guide our actions in the voting booth as much as or more than in any other sphere of life. Giving voice to people's political dreams is as much a way to earn their confidence as it is for any other dream a charlatan might want to exploit. The real wonder isn't that there are so many charlatans in office, but that there are so few.

Yet the few there are can do lasting damage. To see how, we need to begin with a detour through a very peculiar, very revealing university.

Trump U

Consider a university that was not, in fact, a university. Although it offered "graduate programs, post graduate programs, and doctorate programs," it was chartered nowhere and accredited nowhere. Legally, it was a for-profit company. Its correspondence came out of a glamorous address: 40 Wall Street, in the heart of Manhattan's financial district.

Its pitch was simple: to teach students the hugely profitable money-making secrets of its world-famous founder.

The venture ran into trouble from the very beginning.

In New York, as in every American state, use of the term "university" is closely regulated. An institution without a proper charter and without accreditation cannot legally use the term to describe itself. It can legally use plenty of close synonyms—institute, school, academy—but not the *U*-word.

Which is why beginning in 2005, the New York State Education Department sent the first of a series of official letters demanding the organization cease using the term in its communications within New York. The university that was not a university, however, never replied, instead continuing to develop its curriculum and launching a hugely ambitious marketing campaign to advertise its offerings.

Management for the nonuniversity initially developed a "Real Estate Investor Training Program," described in a later affidavit by one person involved in its design as "an online program with some interactive aspects (conference calls and video conferences.)"[3] Management, however, soon realized that producing and imparting online education is expensive. Teachers are expensive, monitoring student performance is expensive. Why bother?

So, beginning in February 2007, then, the university pivoted away from distance education and toward an in-person model that, nonetheless, looked nothing at all like a traditional in-person education.[4]

The "university" offered a series of in-person live seminars and events around the country that promised big profits to anyone ready to put into use the secrets of its founder. It wasn't exactly subtle. "Unheard-of Real Estate Market Factors Have Created A PERFECT STORM of Profit Opportunity!" read one newspaper ad, followed by "FREE INTRODUCTORY CLASS!"[5]

What followed is a pattern familiar to anyone who's been persuaded to sit through an hour-long pitch for a time share: hard-sell tactics that are as old as time itself.

Prospects attracted by this marketing campaign would call a phone number, where a sales representative would guide them to sign up for the university's free introductory one-day course. Once there, they would be welcomed by a motivational speaker who would vaguely describe the way the "university" could help them to become successful real estate magnates.

The first activity asked students to begin planning their real estate investments by carefully laying down the basics of their financial situation on paper—including all their assets and all their liabilities. Staffers for the university that was not a university would collect these, and while the motivational speaker continued to talk, carefully separate them into high- and low-priority piles. Knowing precisely how much money each mark had to devote to his real estate "education" allowed them to be strategic on whom to prioritize for the hard sell.

After lunch, the speakers would explain that the most valuable secrets of the real estate game couldn't, of course, be explained in a day. Then, staffers would move into the hard sell: now that they knew exactly which of their marks could be exploited, they would focus narrowly on the most promising leads, applying hard-pressure tactics to get them to sign up for the next course offered: a three-day intensive seminar retailing for a mere

$1,495—peanuts compared to the huge windfalls they promised their marks they could expect.[6]

Surely you can guess what that three-day seminar was actually for.

Amid more vague talk of real estate strategies and a double helping of motivational pap, speakers would dangle just enough information to keep attendees wanting more. Naturally, toward the end of day two, the staff had had plenty of time to size up the marks; they had plenty of information to work with and knew exactly whom to squeeze to sign up for the elite-level courses where the *real* secrets of real estate fortune hunting would be revealed. Elite-level courses came in three tiers, bronze, silver, and gold, ranging from a downright modest $9,995 for the lowest tier to an astonishing $34,995 for the gold tier, including a three-day in-field mentorship and retreats on everything from wealth preservation and creative financing to commercial and multiuse real estate.[7]

The commitment ladder was fine-tuned. Once you'd spent $1,495 for a three-day course, those more expensive offerings didn't look so outrageous. At the final day hard-sell session, staff members were trained to talk marks through the process of calling their banks to request a credit limit increase right then and there so they could pay for these more expensive courses.[8]

Plenty bought the pitch, handing over tens of thousands of dollars for courses that offered nothing that couldn't be found for free in a focused afternoon on Google. Students took on thousands of dollars in loans to attend these courses, sometimes tens of thousands, and sometimes through home equity lines of credit backed by the homes they lived in.

According to sworn testimony by Ronald Schnackenberg, a former salesman for the not-a-university, its seminars were "a scheme involving a constant upsell." He testified that "the whole goal of the free seminar was to persuade consumers to sign up for the $1,500 seminar . . . the whole purpose of the $1,500 seminar was to get people to sign up for the $35,000 Elite seminars. And the whole purpose of the $35,000 Elite seminars was to get people to buy additional books, seminars and products."

Schnackenberg added that he had received many calls from students after they had taken the seminars, and "virtually all students were dissatisfied with the program they purchased." To his knowledge, none of the customers who paid for the university's programs "went on to successfully invest in real estate" based upon the techniques that were taught. He called the university "a fraudulent scheme" and said that it "preyed on the elderly and uneducated to separate them from their money."[9]

By now, you've realized we're talking about Trump University and the thick tangle of lawsuits for fraud and deceptive advertising that would follow it for years.

But just imagine for a second that the name in front of it had been anything other than Trump—that the name in front of the university that was not a university had been Gates or Musk or Jobs or Buffett. Imagine, if you can, a case like this one apart from the extreme polarization and partisan rancor that attaches to Donald Trump's name. Would we have any trouble seeing the scheme as standard-issue charlatanry? We wouldn't . . . and courts, before 2015, didn't either.

To be clear, Trump U was not, like so many other Trump-linked ventures, a franchising operation involving him renting his name to a separately controlled company. Trump University was directly owned and operated by the Trump Organization.[10]

Between 2010 and 2013 three separate state investigations into the organization's deceptive practices were launched on behalf of some six thousand students who alleged they had been defrauded. The investigations were eventually settled out of court, in the heat of the 2016 campaign season, for $25 million.[11] As part of the settlement, Trump admitted to no wrongdoing.

The sordid story of Trump University is well known. It was fully established by 2014. We find it interesting not only because it took place before the strange politics of the Trump era compromised everyone's ability to talk about him measuredly but also because the tactics used feel so familiar after researching charlatans for the better part of four years.

The same tactics—the big, attention-getting promises with scant follow-up, the serial deception, and the obsession with money—would become the hallmarks of a new way of doing politics in America, with consequences that continue to spiral to this day.

These tactics have been most obvious on the American right, precisely because Trump's enduring popularity normalized them, made them seem almost patriotic. But they are visible on the left too. As we'll see in the next chapter, new left orthodoxies are just as open to abuse by talented charlatans as are any of the ideas on the contemporary right.

In its two and a half centuries the United States has seen plenty of bad presidents, but never before has executive power been handed to a straight-down-the-line charlatan, in the sense we've explored in this book.

Of course, all politicians seek to connect with voters' dreams; that is the core of their job description. What marks Trump out as different is not his knack for saying out loud the things his listeners privately think. That's a talent every politician aspires to. What marks Trump out as unique is the aggressive way he uses that identification to seek political power to further his personal interest—including his interests in making money, in expanding his power, and, above all, his interest in not going to jail.

That the man behind a scam such as Trump University would end up fighting multiple prosecutions can hardly be called a surprise. If there's one subject in which Trump University really did provide an education, it was in understanding Trump's behavior toward those who look up to him.

His university had latched on to people's dreams of wealth to rob them of millions, providing nothing of substance in return. His presidency latched on to a different, more widespread dream but did the same thing with the identification: using it as a means of separating his marks from their money—now labeled "campaign contributions"—while also attaining power for himself, and no ordinary sort of power: executive power over the government of the United States of America, arguably the single most powerful entity the planet has ever known.

The mark-to-charlatan wealth transfer involved is direct. In March 2024 a *New York Times* investigation reported that the work of defending Donald Trump was generating some $90,000 per day in legal fees for the army of lawyers defending him in three separate criminal prosecutions, plus other fees relating to civil suits that had found him liable for sexual assault.[12] The investigation shows that in 2023 Trump had paid a shocking $60 million for legal services, and $48 million of that sum had been paid not by him but by rank-and-file donors to his political campaign, as well as donors to his political action committee. These donors are limited to $5,000 per year, so it is not a small number of rich individuals contributing this money, but rather an army of small donors across America, each making an average donation of $71.[13] Trump's donors, the same analysis shows, are much more likely to be concentrated in less affluent counties than his opponents'.

For all of Donald Trump's undisputed charlatanry before the famous escalator ride that brought him into the political limelight, his first term was relatively restrained. Trump certainly parlayed his political office into profit, but often in indirect and plausibly legal ways. For instance, Democrats in the US House of Representatives disclosed an investigation showing officials from thirty-three countries had stayed at Trump's upscale Washington, DC, hotel, with foreign governments spending a total of $3.75 million for the privilege of staying there.[14] High rollers from Saudi Arabia, the UAE, Qatar, Turkey, China, and Malaysia paid as much as $10,000 per night for luxury suites at the hotel. The Malaysian prime minister topped up his bill with an additional $1,500 nightly fee for a "personal trainer."[15] Almost by definition, a foreign dignitary on official business in Washington is trying to influence the decisions of the executive branch, giving the transactions the look and feel of corruption. But then, it's not as though traveling Saudi princes would've stayed at the airport Motel 6 if Trump had not been in power. Such behavior may have stayed within the limits of the strictly legal, but that is more a function of the laxity of American anticorruption law than of his probity.

Indeed, there's an argument to be made that the strength of American institutions did much to prevent Trump's abuse of power from his inauguration in 2017 to January 5, 2021. When the president tried to unduly influence his attorney general and his FBI directors into stopping investigations against figures in his favor, it didn't work. The former recused himself from the investigation, and the latter wrote a memo to document the abuse and was eventually fired in apparent retaliation.[16]

Trump's contempt for the rules—written and unwritten—for how a president of the United States is meant to behave have been discussed at great and almost tedious length for a decade now. Everybody already knows everything about Donald Trump, and none of it prevented 77,302,580 Americans from casting their ballots to reelect him to the White House in 2024. What he will do with the power they have entrusted him with we cannot yet say.

Berlusconi

There are examples around the world. But patient zero in our times is Italy under Silvio Berlusconi—a Mediterranean Trump from the 1990s. If, as Marx wrote, "history repeats itself first as tragedy and then as farce," then Berlusconi is the tragedy, Trump the farce.

Unlike Trump, Berlusconi genuinely was a self-made man, having built a property, media, and insurance empire in the 1980s that had made him a billionaire and Italy's richest man, before he descended into the field of politics.

He created a political party, Forza Italia, and staffed it with his companies' middle managers.[17] He told Italians that he alone could fix Italy, that he was on their side against the loafers and communists that littered Italy's bloated state bureaucracy and led its left-wing parties.

Championing the dreams of Italians left behind by the elite in Rome, he won his first election in 1994. Berlusconi controlled much of the best real estate in Milan, Italy's economic capital, as well as the bulk of the country's private TV and a good chunk of its financial services. Nor was he a stranger to political power: he had been the best man at the prime minister's son's wedding, that "socialist" PM who controlled the state-owned banks that financed his breakneck expansion.[18] Already, then, Berlusconi was suspected of a whole array of illegalities, but his wealth afforded him an army of elite lawyers who knew how to beat a rap in Italy's sclerotic court system.

It was easy for Berlusconi, a media baron with his finger on the pulse of what everyday Italians really wanted, to connect with voters' dreams. The same marketing know-how his TV empire, Mediaset, had used for years to understand what Italians wanted so they could sell ads was put to the task of convincing them candidate Berlusconi stood for them. To conservative Italians disgusted with the values of the postcommunist Left, Berlusconi became an object of adulation. And Berlusconi knew exactly how to turn that adulation into power, and that power into cold, hard cash.

He was the head of a government determined to overhaul the nation's outdated broadcasting laws and, at the same time, was the owner of the country's dominant private media company. Throughout the 1980s he had skirted Italy's strict laws against media concentration with a series of quasi-legal maneuvers, like having different stations he owned start broadcasting the same cheesy American dramas and game shows at slightly different times so he could claim they were not operating as a network.[19] *Baywatch*, dubbed, might start at 7:28 in Turin, 7:30 in Rome, and 7:31 in Palermo—see? It's not a network!

But all that skirting of the rules was so troublesome. If only, Berlusconi seems to have reasoned, he could secure the office of prime minister, he could get down to the business of rewriting inconvenient laws rather than having to tiptoe around them.

In 2004 he named a new communications minister: Maurizio Gasparri, whose acquaintance with the world of media came from his time as editor in chief of the daily newspaper for the Movimento Sociale Italiano, the successor organization to the Fascist Party of Italy.

That same year, Minister Gasparri put forward in parliament the law that would bear his name. The Gasparri Law created lucrative new opportunities for Mediaset. It raised the ceiling on how much of a country's TV market could be concentrated in a single company from 30 to 45 percent, a change that could *only* benefit the nation's biggest media owner, a.k.a. his boss, the prime minister.

Although Maurizio Gasparri was not accused of any wrongdoing in connection with the controversy, the law that bears his name caused an uproar in Italy for what seemed to be its brazen abuse of public authority to line the prime minister's pocket. The Italian president—normally an entirely ceremonial figure—took the highly unusual measure of refusing to sign the law as approved by both chambers of parliament, demanding amendments. He did not get amendments, and under Italian law he had little choice but to sign. By 2006 the European Union (EU) was notifying Rome that the Gasparri Law infringed on European legal principles because its provisions blatantly favored existing media owners, or "incumbent operators."[20]

Of course, in this context, incumbent operators could mean none other than Silvio Berlusconi: the law unshackled Mediaset, allowing it to use its monopoly power in ways that would have been illegal before and solidifying the prime minister's stranglehold over media in the country. New rules to divide up the digital broadcasting rights when Italy switched to digital television seemed written specifically to allow Mediaset to hog more and more of the spectrum, entrenching its dominant position. Surely, it was not in regular Italians' interest to live in a media monoculture—but Berlusconi bamboozled them into giving him the power to promote his interests over theirs.

At one point, Berlusconi attempted a radical new law that would have required Italians to obtain a license before uploading videos to YouTube—an attempt to protect Mediaset's monopoly so brazen it led to protests in the streets.[21]

And this wasn't only in media. Berlusconi also owned an important bank, Mediolanum, that was interested in branching out into insurance but couldn't due to financial-sector regulations. No problem—the Berlusconi government would champion financial deregulation, passing a law that allowed Mediolanum to offer products it would've been barred from offering otherwise. Under the guise of "structural reform" and "market liberalization," the Italian government kept promoting policies that, coincidentally, benefited the head of that government.

Of course, when the prime minister is also the country's main industrialist, conflicts of interest start to arise in all sorts of places. Berlusconi pushed labor-market liberalization schemes that made it easier and cheaper for his companies to hire and fire regular Italians. The Berlusconi government responded to the 2008 financial crisis with an industrial policy that favored large firms (like his) over small- and medium-size firms.[22] Even when they weren't narrowly tailored to benefit Mediaset or Mediolanum, these decisions continually placed Silvio Berlusconi's business interests in opposition to those of his voters. He kept making decisions in ways that benefited his interests over theirs . . . and they kept voting for him.

It's impossible to put a precise figure on the impact that Berlusconi's legal and regulatory reforms had for the bottom line of Berlusconi-owned companies. Yet time and again, Italian governments led by Prime Minister Berlusconi made regulatory and policy decisions narrowly tailored to the interests of citizen Silvio Berlusconi. Worse, despite facing charges on dozens of irregularities over a long career, and even being convicted on some of those charges, Berlusconi was able to spin out Italy's appeals process long enough never to have to spend a night of his life in jail.

Throughout, Berlusconi's media empire portrayed him as a champion of the little guy, sticking it to the left-wing elites in Rome and championing individual liberty and the values of hard work. Berlusconi never lost sight of that Italian dream and was careful to always portray himself as the champion of those who held fast to it.

To Berlusconi, money and power were not everything. Berlusconi was a man in full, reaching for the trifecta. His pharaonic sexual appetite became mixed up with all the other allegations against him. Witness his infamous "bunga bunga" parties. These soirées took place at the private residence of a Group of Seven leader, but they would not have been out of place in a Roman emperor's court.

The scene was Mr. Berlusconi's sumptuous eighteenth-century Villa San Martino near Milan, a setting straight out of a Fellini film. Italian prosecutors spent years assembling evidence of a sprawling pimp ring operating out of the prime minister's house for his benefit. The parties would start with a lavish meal—this is Italy, after all—with the menu sometimes color coordinated with the red, white, and green of the Italian flag. The meal would be followed by a floor show featuring stripteases by women dressed as nuns, nurses, and even public figures. After this the prime minister would reportedly choose a young woman to spend the night with, then shower her with gifts of cash, jewelry, or a luxurious apartment to live in rent-free.[23]

At the heart of the investigation was a list of thirty-three young women, primarily aspiring starlets aiming for gigs on Berlusconi's TV empire, who told prosecutors they had attended these soirées. Italian law protects many of their names. Their testimonies painted a picture of modern-day bacchanalia that was over the top even by Berlusconi's standards. At their peak, these parties took place three times a week at Villa San Martino.

The star witness at the first of the many trials the parties gave rise to was one Karima El Mahroug, known professionally (that is, in her stripping role) as "Ruby the Heart Stealer." Ruby, it later transpired, had been underage at the time of her first liaisons with the prime minister. Her account to prosecutors included the rather startling claim that Mr. Berlusconi had explained the "bunga bunga" as his personal harem, inspired by his friend Muammar Gaddhafi.

It sounds like lurid tabloid nonsense, but the stories were meticulously substantiated by Italy's magistrates. Over a ten-year period, they deployed wiretaps with an enthusiasm usually reserved for mafia investigations. Bank records were scrutinized, revealing curious patterns of generosity toward young women. Computers were seized, leaving no hard drive unprobed. Prosecutors came to understand that Berlusconi wasn't just paying dozens of women for sex; he was then paying them again to lie about his having paid them for sex. The prosecutors charged Berlusconi with bribery and witness tampering. They put him on trial. He beat the rap.[24]

As this was all going on, Berlusconi was at the same time the richest man in Italy and its prime minister. It's perhaps not surprising that his large and extravagantly resourced legal team managed to secure his acquittal on the most serious charges stemming from the parties. The statutory rape charge didn't hold after courts ruled that there was insufficient proof he knew that Ms. El Mahroug—Ruby—was underage at the time of their encounters. In the fog of "bunga bunga," details such as birth dates may well have been overlooked.

Italy's political scene was consumed with debate about this debauchery for years. Berlusconi never exactly denied the parties had taken place—he just preferred to describe them as "elegant dinners" at his ornate palazzo. There was a nod-and-a-wink quality to his denials, a sense that Berlusconi *loved it* that everyone knew his bed was a parade ground for Italy's most beautiful women. Italian men loved him not despite of it but because of it: he was living their dream, incarnating a vision of perfect success that they admired.

When it came to hacking HumanOS, Berlusconi was a master. He turned his life into a bright, garish display of the unlimited money, sex, and power his followers dreamed of. He turned their enduring fascination into votes, and then turned their votes into more money, more sex, and more power: a conjuring act he kept up for the better part of three decades.

In June 2023, at the age of eighty-six, Silvio Berlusconi died in bed, his party still part of Italy's government, having never spent a day in prison for any of it. He received a state funeral, with the archbishop of Milan giving the eulogy and Italy's president on hand to lead the mourning, along with Italy's prime minister and nearly the whole cabinet; two former prime ministers; the leaders of five foreign nations; and a long list of Italian soccer stars, entertainers, and business barons. A day of national mourning was declared in his honor.[25]

Few charlatans in history have ever gotten away with it as comprehensively as Silvio Berlusconi did.

Brexit

If Italy saw a charlatan turn the state to his benefit, our next story is darker. In the United Kingdom, an outbreak of coordinated charlatanism forced one of the most calamitous decisions any developed democracy has made in years, taking Britain out of the European Union, cutting it off from its most important market, and leaving it much poorer and much more dissatisfied, with large majorities regretting the blunder.[26]

The story of the populist movement that propelled anti-EU sentiment ahead of the 2016 Brexit referendum is telling. British isolationism and Euroskepticism are not new. For Britain, which had for centuries been a world-leading great power, the idea of being dictated to by "Brussels bureaucrats"—as it was inevitably framed—had long rankled. Yet the movement that took that diffuse sentiment and galvanized it into an unstoppable political force was not some spontaneous outbreak of Little Britain nationalism: it was a movement led and organized by a constellation of outright charlatans aiming to manipulate public opinion for their own gain.[27]

The first was the then conservative foreign minister, Boris Johnson, who had launched his career on a series of articles about the European Union that seemed to stretch journalistic ethics beyond their breaking point. As Brussels bureau chief for conservative daily the *Telegraph* in the 1990s, Johnson had been among the earliest exponents of a type of journalism that sold tons of newspapers but had only the most tenuous connection with the truth. In story after story, Johnson roasted Brussels bureaucrats for crazy decisions they hadn't actually made. In one story, he claimed the EU wanted to impose a single standardized condom size. Later, he said it would ban recycling tea bags and forbid the sale of prawn-cocktail-flavored snacks. One particularly fanciful tale had the EU forbidding children from blowing up rubber balloons.[28] It was all nonsense, of course, but it didn't matter: Johnson wanted to make the EU ridiculous in readers' eyes. And he succeeded.

The image of the EU as a mindless rulemaking machine thoroughly devoid of common sense became mainstream in Britain. So much so that when Nigel Farage, a hard-edged right-wing Euroskeptic, began to campaign for a referendum to separate Britain from the European Union, he couldn't be contained. Claiming—absurdly—that Brussels was seeking to snuff out British independence, he began drawing conservative votes away from Britain's generally moderate Conservative Party.

Farage's style was full of bombast and overstatement, and British voters ate it up. Farage embodied a certain image of British nationhood—a dream that quickly showed itself politically potent. He would campaign wearing "a tweed jacket, tan corduroy trousers, check shirt, knitted red tie, every garment a cultural signal," as the BBC once put it.[29] Looking every bit the British everyman and downing one pint of warm beer after another, he sold a powerful vision of Britain regaining its vital strength once it was freed from the weight of what were always described as "barmy Brussels bureaucrats."

His campaign took years to develop, and it grew along the way. To try to meet this challenge from the Right, Britain's moderate prime minister, David Cameron, was cornered into agreeing to hold a referendum on the matter. Cameron did not favor Brexit, but the groundswell of opposition to the EU could not be contained. It was a bad miscalculation. The referendum campaign that followed was a festival of charlatanry, with one Vote Leave spokesperson after another making claims about the future that just didn't have any grounding in truth.

Experts, of course, cried foul, seeking to communicate with voters the costs to Britain of erecting trade barriers with its predominant economic partner. In a rebuke that turned into an emblematic moment in the referendum, when asked to name any economic expert who supported Leave, the then Justice Secretary Michael Gove told a TV interviewer simply that "the British people have had enough of experts."[30]

A Leave campaign bus toured Britain with a slogan emblazoned in huge letters on its side: "We send the EU £350 million a week. Let's fund our National Health Service instead. Vote leave. Let's take back control."[31] It wasn't true. One pro-Brexit politician claimed a post-Brexit free trade deal with the EU would be "the easiest in human history."[32] It wasn't. It took eight years after the vote for the sides to manage a cumbersome trade and cooperation agreement that 77 percent of British exporting firms say is not helping their ability to do business with the continent.[33] Overall, the Leave campaign had promised prosperity, but since 2019 Britain had been the worst-performing of the world's advanced industrial economies, shrinking an average of 0.4 percent per year between 2019 and 2024.[34]

It is true that Britain had been in secular decline as a world power at least since the 1956 Suez Crisis. But Brexit accelerated that decline, turning what was until recently one of Europe's major economies into a contracting basket case, increasingly irrelevant not just economically but militarily and diplomatically as well.

The charlatans who perpetrated the campaign that pushed Britain off this cliff, for their part, did very well indeed. Farage enormously enjoyed his moment in the limelight, turning the course of history (for the worse). Michael Gove held a succession of senior cabinet posts, from lord chancellor to cabinet office minister, while Johnson rode the popularity his hard-Brexiteer stance brought him all the way to 10 Downing Street, where he spent a scandal-plagued handful of years.

Anyone who doubts whether runaway charlatanism can really change the world should take a closer look at the scandalous history of Brexit. Again and again, senior British political figures manipulated regular people's dreams of a return to British greatness to further their careers, leaving millions of livelihoods blighted in the process.

Today, in polls, Britons regret their choice in that 2016 referendum, with twice as many saying the decision to leave the EU was bad for Britain as said it was good.[35] The damage is done. And there's no going back:

even if British governments had the stomach to try to return to the EU fold, the existing members wouldn't have them.

In the United States, Donald Trump's opponents sometimes imagine they are dealing with a uniquely corrosive figure. And it's true that, given America's huge geopolitical weight and massive military power, the stakes involved in Washington far exceed those anywhere else on the planet. But if the stories of Silvio Berlusconi and Brexit teach us anything, it is that, in his first term, President Trump was comparatively restrained in his abuse of state power for his own benefit. Had he the razor-sharp mind for profit of a Silvio Berlusconi or the sheer recklessness of the Brexiteers, he might have done far more damage.

9

QAnonsense

Where We Go One, We Go Nuts

#FiveJobsIveHad was one of those fun, screwball trends that started making the rounds on social media. It spread like wildfire in April 2019: one of those instantly sharable viral crazes that arise every few weeks and is forgotten almost before it's quite finished. Lots of people—from everyday folks to celebrities—took part in it for some harmless fun. Among them was James Comey, the former FBI director.[1]

> Mulling on what looks to have been a colorful past, Comey tweeted, #FiveJobsIveHad.
>
> 1. Grocery store clerk
> 2. Vocal soloist for church weddings
> 3. Chemist
> 4. Strike-replacement high school teacher
> 5. FBI Director, interrupted

Unbeknownst to Comey—unbeknownst to anyone—this harmless tweet was about to make life very weird for the people of Grass Valley, California. News crews soon began to arrive in the pretty little town, located about sixty miles east of Sacramento in the Sierra Nevada foothills. And it wasn't just news crews: armed activists began to converge on Grass Valley, and not just on Grass Valley generally, but on the Grass Valley Charter School Foundation, which was planning a fundraiser for May 10.

To the townspeople, the whole thing was baffling. Grass Valley is the kind of place where nothing much ever happens. The town's charter school fundraiser, for its part, seemed as uncontroversial as an event can be: a yearly small-town ritual bringing neighbors together for a nice meal to raise some money for improvements to a local school. The foundation had been doing these fundraisers for years, never calling any particular attention to itself.

The volunteers who ran the Grass Valley Charter School Foundation were just regular folks as well.

Yet one day, out of the blue, emails, phone calls, and texts started pouring in. Many of the communications were concerned and offered support in protecting the fundraiser from violence. Others were simply baffling, coded as they were in complex terminology that made little sense to the foundation's staff.

It must have been an entirely bewildering few days, as the folks who run this tiny charitable foundation pieced together what had happened: some lunatic had read James Comey's #FiveJobsIveHad tweet and decided it contained a hidden clue to a heinous, soon-to-be-perpetrated monstrosity.

Grocery store clerk, **V**ocal soloist, **C**hemist, **S**trike-replacement high school teacher, **F**BI Director: GVCSF. It's a relatively obscure acronym. So much so that if you punch that into a search engine the top result tends to be **G**rass **V**alley **C**harter **S**chool **F**oundation.

Not convinced yet? The hashtag itself has the word *jihad* in it.

Really!

Look again: #Five**J**obs**I**ve**Had.**

It's *right there*, staring at you.

It was on the basis of this "research" that hundreds of internet sleuths had concluded that the former FBI director was tipping his hand about an upcoming gun massacre, staged by the deep state to provide a rationale to disarm the region's lawfully armed citizens. The threat was pure fabrication, but the fundraiser had to be canceled. The parents of 700 children at the school, perhaps 95 percent of whom had never heard of QAnon, saw the buzz of reports about possible violence and freaked out.[2]

Let's begin with the obvious: this conspiracy really makes no sense even on its own, deranged terms.

Why on earth would James Comey want to not only attack a small-town school fundraiser but also *cryptically brag about it beforehand?!* Since when are acrostics a recognized means of intra-elite communications? What kind of deranged state of mind makes a human being fall for blatant nonsense like this? What makes it appear even plausible, let alone so compelling you would take a multihour road trip, bringing your guns along, to go check it out?

This last question, at least, we can answer.

People took this shard of internet detritus as gospel truth for one reason, and one reason only: they'd read about it on the QAnon social media accounts they followed.

Now, if you've been fortunate enough to have made your way on this planet this long without knowing what or who QAnon is, then congratulations to you: you've lived a blessed life. We are about to make it a little bit worse.

The QAnon phenomenon has always been difficult to summarize. One influential author, Mike Rothschild, in his thoroughly researched book *The Storm Is Upon Us*, summarizes it as "a conspiracy theory of everything."[3]

The core idea is that a shady cabal of enormously powerful Democrats and Jews run a sprawling secret organization that kidnaps and tortures children to harvest a secret drug called "adrenochrome" from them. The fact that there isn't even a shred of a hint of evidence to back up any of what it suggests means, to Q aficionados, not that the theory is untrue but that the cabal's stranglehold on media and law enforcement organizations is so total that they will not look into it.[4]

Thankfully, a resistance movement has come together under the leadership of Donald J. Trump and is secretly plotting to overthrow this shadow government and imprison or execute its leaders, beginning, obviously, with Hillary Clinton. This, in Q lore, would be "the storm"—a final apocalyptic showdown between the forces of good and the forces of evil that would end with thousands of arrests and executions, the collapse of the Democratic Party and the deep state, and the restoration of America to its rightful owners: Q believers.

That, insofar as it's possible to summarize briefly, is the core of the QAnon conspiracy theory. Yet that description barely scratches the surface. Speaking to *The Washington Post*, Kevin Grisham, the associate director of the Center for the Study of Hate and Extremism at California State University, San Bernardino, described it as "just this amorphous blob of conspiracy theory that can adapt to any situation."[5]

The Q blob has absorbed conspiracy theories ranging from the belief that John F. Kennedy Jr. is secretly alive and plotting to overthrow the deep state to devotion to NESARA, a mythical set of radical economic reforms secretly already adopted into law that will soon be instituted and make everyone rich instantly.[6]

It's just one layer of nonsense on top of another, forever.

That properly grown-up human beings can believe this stuff has always been unsettling, and the movement that those people eventually converged around has always been hard to categorize. QAnon is not precisely a cult, though it has many cultlike elements. It is not exactly a new religion, though it has obvious religious overtones. It is not exclusively a political movement, though its adherents are ardently political. It is far more than just an internet-based live-action role-playing (LARP) game, though most of what its adherents seem to spend their time doing is playing roles online.

Most intriguing, for our purposes, is that QAnon is *not* the work of a single charlatan going by the name Q. Instead, it is the product of a radically decentralized community of charlatans, all manipulating one another and cheering.

There is one possible world where QAnon is the future of charlatanry—the way charlatanry could metastasize, unless appropriate guardrails are put into place. That is why it's important to come to grips with the phenomenon: if we don't, the next iteration, amplified by artificial intelligence—will be worse.

A Man Called Q

At the center of this cesspool is a man called Q, short for "Q-Clearance Patriot"—a self-described military intelligence insider purporting to be embedded at the highest level of the US government right alongside President Trump.

The term *Q-clearance* relates to the highest level of intelligence access within the US Department of Energy, responsible for safeguarding America's nuclear arsenal. Eagle-eyed readers will already have spotted the first of dozens of inconsistencies about this story: Why would a *military* intelligence officer have a *civilian* top security clearance? It is but one of the many, many obvious questions you'll just have to agree not to ask if you decide to get into the world of Q.

Q began posting cryptic messages on the anonymous message board 4chan on October 28, 2017, and that right there gives you a second big hint as to how this whole thing got started. What precisely is 4chan? Think of it as the bathroom stall door of the internet: a message board designed from the ground up to preserve anonymity and render censorship impossible.

There are no login screens on 4chan, no profile pictures, and there's certainly no content moderation. As a result, the boards are awash with some of the most horrifying material on the internet: virulent misogyny and racism, gore, extreme pornography, and rampant antisemitism and thousands upon thousands of swastikas: so many that when people first see the site their initial impression is usually that they've stumbled onto a neo-Nazi hangout.

Again, this poses another of those very obvious questions Q believers seem never to stop and wonder about: If some high-up national security professional with direct access to the president needed to get information out to the public anonymously, could he really do no better than to use a Nazi meme site?

For QAnon, making exactly no sense at all, even on its own terms, seems to be not so much a weakness as a recruitment strategy. The story being peddled is so outlandish, it could only be seriously entertained by the most credulous people. Its tenets are so silly that anyone with a minimum of common sense will dismiss it right away.

But then, that's precisely the point. QAnon is a kind of echo chamber for unchecked confirmation bias: a place for people eager to one-up one another in the arts of aggressively seeking confirmatory evidence and resolutely shutting out any consideration of alternatives. Don't believe us? Ask the members of the Grass Valley Charter School Foundation.

But why put QAnon in a book about charlatans? Is it because Q himself is a charlatan, or because the grifters who made a quick buck selling merchandise to Q's legions of followers are charlatans? Both those things may well be true, but they're not the reason we wrote this. Our conclusion is much darker than that: Q represents the future of charlatanry, a dark future where regular people aren't just passive victims of a charlatan but are algorithmically empowered to become charlatans to one another in a swarm.

The LARP That Went Nuclear

QAnon almost certainly got its start as a LARP—basically an internet lark where people have fun pretending to be who they are not.

In this sense, Q's origins are not at all remarkable or even particularly unusual. Anonymous message boards like 4chan are awash with people goofing off and LARPing. With no way to connect given posts to individual people, the boards are a natural magnet for people who enjoy making wild, unverifiable claims about who they are and why they are there.[7]

The original Q-Clearance Patriot who posted content was one of many. Every day, across anonymous boards that attract tens of millions of users from all around the world, some bored teenager is posting on one of these boards pretending to be anything from an out-of-work arms dealer to the grand wizard of a secretive offshoot of the Ku Klux Klan. A whole culture of LARPing and trolling thrives on these sites, with posters trying to one-up one another with more and more outlandish stories and earning clout for getting people outside the site to believe them.

As Nicky Woolf, the QAnon researcher behind the investigative podcast series *Finding Q: My Journey into QAnon*, is keen to underline, the prime directive for LARP culture is *thou shalt not take thyself too seriously*.[8] Marked by an ethos of relentless cynicism, LARPers take it for granted that nothing written there is true. That's part of the fun of the hobby: the message boards are a safe place to create fictions as outlandish as you want to make them, in the sure knowledge that nobody would possibly believe them.

The original batch of Q posts, then, were the opposite of original. They were also comprehensively wrong, right from the very first line: "HRC extradition already in motion effective yesterday . . ." Hillary Clinton was not, in fact, arrested, or extradited, or anything of the sort. Obviously.[9]

It was an unpromising start, to be sure, and yet being continually wrong about everything never seemed to hurt the budding movement. Exercising their confirmation-bias muscles to hypertrophy, QAnon followers always found a way to argue that each thing Q got wrong was only *apparently* wrong but was pointing at a deeper, more meaningful rightness.

Perhaps the biggest mystery is why this particular LARP should have gone on to become the cornerstone of a massive, world-spanning conspiracy theory movement while thousands of other LARPers see their posts get zero response.

With Q-Clearance Patriot, though, things quickly took a turn. Much of the fun of LARPing, for 4chan devotees, consisted in exporting their practical jokes outside the anonymous-board fever swamps and onto mainstream sites like Reddit and Twitter (now X) where "normies"—that is, regular folks not steeped in the lore and culture of the anonymous boards—might actually believe them. A small core of 4chan trolls soon began proselytizing for Q, posting about his "drops" on normie sites. They succeeded beyond their wildest dreams.

Throughout the second half of 2017, hundreds of thousands of normies—people who wouldn't know how to get onto 4chan and would bolt for the exits after five swastika-saturated minutes there—came across Q-related content on mainstream social media. They came to the conspiracy theory without any kind of understanding of LARP culture, about the context where Q first arose. And a shocking number of them believed it, falling down an all-encompassing internet rabbit hole where up is down, black is white, and where, as in George Orwell's *Nineteen Eighty-Four*, we have always been at war with Eurasia.

Q continued to post through the winter of 2017–2018, then suddenly moved from 4chan to a competitor site, 8chan, which somehow has even fewer moderation rules. Q watchers agree that at this point the original Q poster appears to have been replaced by a new Q: the writing style in the new posts was different, the predictions less specific (though just as wrong).

It was this second Q, starting in early 2018, who really took the LARP to the next level. Under his guidance, the movement took off, penetrating deeply into mainstream US political culture and running away with the minds of untold numbers of supporters.

Who exactly was this new Q? We can't say for sure. Anonymous message boards are, well, anonymous. A cryptographic system allows a poster to prove that he is the same person who posted a given previous message, but not to link that stable identity to anyone's real-world identity.

But that prompts the question: Who can guarantee that the cryptography is sound and that the person posting as Q today is the same person who was posting as Q yesterday? Only the board owner can do that.

And who owns 8chan?

Funny you should ask.

To go by his résumé, Jim Watkins was just a humble pig farmer, albeit one who had made the somewhat eccentric choice to move to the Philippines to run a hog farm there. This he did soon after wrapping up a decade-and-a-half-long stint as a helicopter mechanic for the US Army, and after he'd made some money with the first of many forays into the internet economy.[10]

Back in 1998, during the Wild West days of Web 1.0, Watkins spotted a gap in the online pornography market. Japanese censorship laws made pornography there, let's say, less than satisfying to customers. Watkins realized that if he ran a Japanese porn site from servers hosted in the United States, he could skirt the rules and make a quick buck.[11]

That's when he set up the now-defunct Asian Bikini Bar: a porn site aimed at the Japanese market, hosted in the Philippines but—this is the key—hosted on servers located in the United States.[12] It seems to have been a hit, the first of many business ventures, and enough to allow him to buy that dream hog farm in the outskirts of Manila.

So, a pig-farming pornographer is the only person able to vouch for the integrity of the cryptography behind Q's posts, adding yet another layer of insanity to the official Q story.

Why a high-level intelligence official in the White House would choose to communicate with the world through such a website is one of those questions that answers itself. He wouldn't. Obviously. Naturally enough, then, early speculation about Q's identity pegged Jim Watkins as the most obvious candidate.

As journalists dug into the Q story, however, doubts soon arose about this theory. Jim Watkins wrote prolifically under his own name, including in the far-right political opinion website he founded, The Goldwater, named after conservative politician and 1964 presidential candidate Barry Goldwater. His posts there seemed entirely different in style from Q's clipped and cryptic utterances. Where Q communicated in short, vague sentence fragments, Jim Watkins's writing meandered. Most Q watchers concluded that while Jim Watkins would certainly know who Q was, he was likely not Q himself.

But Jim wasn't the only Watkins in the picture. His son, Ron, was listed as the system administrator for 8chan, meaning he was, if anything, even more directly involved in the site's operation than his father. Very little was known publicly about Ron's life. After an uneventful youth in a small town in Washington State where he sang in the high school choir and barbershop quartet, he moved to Sapporo, Japan, and then the trail runs cold.

It was only years later, after Donald Trump lost his bid for reelection and Q stopped posting, that it became clear that it had been Ron Watkins who had been posting as Q all along. In the mad months separating Joe Biden's election as president and the January 6, 2021, Capitol insurrection, Ron stepped out of the shadows, becoming one of the key public voices pushing an absurd conspiracy theory accusing Dominion Voting Systems Corporation of perpetrating a complex electronic election fraud. Unlike his father, the younger Watkins's writing sounds *just* like Q—the cryptic clues, the clipped syntax, the oddball use of brackets around the letter *s* to suggest possible plurals, it was all there. Ron even took to describing his upcoming posts as "drops"—just like Q used to.

To be clear, both Jim and Ron Watkins strenuously deny being Q or even knowing who Q may be. In one interview with British podcast series *Finding Q*, Jim Watkins claimed the only thing he knew about Q was the fact that he was a user of one of his boards.[13] And Ron has denied being Q so many times now that doing so has become part of his internet persona.

Yet for all their denials, the case that Ron Watkins was Q appears quite solid . . . not least because Ron is not a very disciplined figure and has at times slipped up during interviews, referring to Q in the first person. Most (in)famously, during an interview with documentary makers from HBO, Ron at one point said, "It was basically three years of intelligence training, teaching normies how to do intelligence work. It was basically what I was doing anonymously before—"[14]

Then he realized he'd screwed up and sought to backtrack, awkwardly saying, "But never as Q . . . I am not Q."[15]

The tacked-on denial, pasted over a terrified smile, seems to give it away. If this interpretation is correct—and we believe it is—a former high school barbershop quartet singer in his early thirties played the pivotal role in launching a worldwide movement from his apartment in the northern Japanese island of Hokkaido.[16]

Essentially nothing is known about Ron's life in Japan or about his reasons for choosing that locale, though we know of course his father had, um, long-standing business interests there. Yet to give all the credit for running the world's biggest, craziest LARP to Ron Watkins would be to miss the point.

QAnon was never really under Ron Watkins's control.

QAnon belonged to every person who believed in QAnon.

Ron Watkins is, in many ways, the *least* interesting aspect of Q. A charlatan he may well be: with his emphasis on "knowing things he did not in fact know," Ron fits the classic definition. Yet out of all the charlatans that the Q universe has generated, Ron is far from the most successful, or the most interesting.

Q's success seems to have been a function mostly of his author's style, with its propensity for asking heavily laden questions that invite his followers to take part. QAnon wasn't so much a conspiracy theory as *an invitation* to believers to create their own conspiracy theories—as one observer put it, it's a "choose your own adventure" conspiracy theory.[17]

Q's corpus of work, the so-called Q drops, consisted of broad hints, purported codes, and then gibberish: it was an open invitation to decode. As a result, much of the Q content that reached the masses wasn't actually Q's writing itself. Instead, it arose from esoteric "research" performed collaboratively by members of the community: just regular folks reading Twitter and spinning theories about the codes elites use there.

In a world where paeans to citizen participation are so common, the Q community became all about participating in this collective endeavor of "decoding Q" and understanding deep truths about the world they would have been blind to in isolation.

The ubiquitous metaphor used in this regard is the "red pill"—a reference to the iconic scene in the 1999 sci-fi classic *The Matrix*, in which the protagonist, Neo (played by Keanu Reeves), is presented with two pills—one red, one blue—and invited to make a transcendent choice: "You take the blue pill, the story ends, you wake up in your bed and believe whatever you want to believe. You take the red pill, you stay in Wonderland, and I show you how deep the rabbit hole goes."[18]

Those who joined the Q community believed themselves, like Neo, to be courageous fighters for the truth, willing to look in places and make connections that the loathed mainstream media would not.

There's a bitter irony here for those who urge educating young people in the art of critical thinking to overcome such outbreaks of mass credulity. Two decades of wholly well-intentioned critical thinking curricula urging folks to evaluate the evidence and think for themselves led up to this: a mass movement of people all convinced they were practicing critical inquiry, all latching on to a series of absurd beliefs, clutching desperately to anything that looked like confirmation, and seeking to proselytize on behalf of their faith.

It all amounted to a kind of mass spasm of motivated reasoning: thousands upon thousands of people convincing one another of things they were already convinced of on day one.

For Q community members, participating in this community made good on the promises that normal politicians never made good on: it allowed anyone to participate and add their grain of knowledge "that *they* don't want you to know."

It was open to anyone, and the good ideas were chosen by the algorithm.

At QAnon's peak in 2020, hundreds of Q acolytes were posting "possible decodes" on Twitter on any given day, proposing avenues of "research," validating one another's claims, drawing attention to ever more outrageous conjectures. Because there were so many, it was impossible for the vast majority to gain a hearing outside a Q researcher's immediate circle. But if there's one thing that social media algorithms are extremely proficient at, it is identifying the kinds of content users mostly interact with. So, the algorithms themselves—particularly Twitter's—became *the* place where the visibility of a given idea would be decided.

The result, in the Q sphere, was a kind of evolutionary process in reverse: starting from a pool of conspiracy theory ideas, the algorithm would identify those ideas users would engage with the most. As a mechanism for identifying truly *terrible* ideas and persuading hundreds of thousands of others to believe them alongside you, you could hardly do better.

The problem, of course, is that more extreme content drives stronger engagement than duller fare. (Of course!) Load a social media site with thousands of Q decodes, and the algorithm will identify the 1 percent that will drive the most engagement with exquisite precision. Deploy them to 10 million users, and you'll very quickly notice which 1 percent of them are most likely to be watched all the way through. The only problem is that those outliers, those most engaging of decodes turned out to be reliably the craziest of the crazy.

Why? Because craziness drives engagement.

Let's go back to the example with which we started: the ill-fated collision, in time, of James Comey's #FiveJobsIveHad tweet and the wholly innocent residents of Grass Valley, California, and its charter school's fundraising group. It's worth noting that while Q had written often about James Comey, he had never written anything about #FiveJobsIveHad and certainly not about the Grass Valley fundraiser.

That entire seam of ridiculous conjecture—what Q followers call "research"—had been fished out of the fever swamps of the internet by Twitter's algorithm, which, noticing the engagement it drove, served it to more people, helping the idea spread. Back in Sapporo, Ron Watkins could not have guessed that half a world away somebody would make an acrostic out of James Comey's tweet and link it to some school fundraiser in a town in California. That was not his doing. The decode was one patriot's contribution to the cause, nothing more.

To really see how corrosive algorithmic amplification can be in a situation like this one, consider the story about adrenochrome. In Q lore, adrenochrome is a hyperpowerful drug favored by the superpowerful deep state cabal: the chemical key to sustaining their unnatural vitality, a sort of fountain of youth for the global elite. Crucially, in their telling, the drug must be harvested from living children under torture.

Did Q simply make up this tale? He did not. The whole story is lifted more or less straight from Hunter S. Thompson's classic 1971 novel about the joys and terrors of drug abuse, *Fear and Loathing in Las Vegas*.[19] There, adrenochrome is described as a hallucinogen so intense that "it makes pure mescaline seem like ginger beer." As the drug-addled character Dr. Gonzo says in the book, "There's only one source for this stuff . . . the adrenaline glands from a living human body. It's no good if you get it out of a corpse."

Thompson made it amply clear that this was all fiction. Adrenochrome is indeed a substance produced by the human body—a by-product of the breakdown of adrenaline—but it's not a hallucinogen at all: as the few (idiot) souls who have tried it can attest, all it tends to do is bring on a massive headache.

The part about how it can be gotten only from a living body is purely made up as well: adrenochrome can be readily synthesized in a lab, and there's no chemical difference between the stuff your body makes and the man-made type. None of this, again, should come as any kind of surprise given that the adrenochrome story comes out of a novel written by America's most famously drug-loving fantasist. It is and always has been fiction.

Yet for all this, and despite the absolute absence of evidence to support the madcap notion that senior Democratic politicians literally feast on the bodies of children, the story that deep state elites torture children to "steal their youth" through adrenochrome took hold. An actual researcher looking to verify the claim would discard it in a matter of minutes. And yet millions of people devoted to the importance of critical thinking and "doing your own research" came to believe that this obvious falsehood is true.

The overlap between the adrenochrome story and the oldest of antisemitic tropes is impossible to place in history. Starting in twelfth-century

England, the belief took hold in Europe that Jews performed a secret ritual that involved putting the blood of Christian children into matzo balls. The blood libel, as it came to be known, never had any basis in fact but nonetheless spread throughout Europe and remained dominant as a belief in the minds of Christians for a millennium, driving pogroms and systematic violence and discrimination against Jews. Then again, it's perhaps not so surprising that a LARP spun on 8chan, a message board suffused with Nazi imagery and rampant antisemitism, should be the one to reinvent the blood libel for the social media age.

For years, the front QAnon had presented to the world was that of a movement against pedophile abuse. Who could possibly be against a movement against child abuse? When questioned about their commitment, Q devotees constantly circle back to their concern for the children they imagine themselves to be saving. This framing helped bring in new converts, the first step on a ladder of radicalization.

But, in time, the story about a massive secret child sex trafficking ring turned out not to be sensational enough to drive engagement. Algorithmic amplification rewarded with clicks stories of ever more sordid and absurd abuses. And so, a rebooted blood libel narrative based on a twisted version of a Hunter S. Thompson novel ended up gathering a mass following among patriotic Americans committed to doing their own research.

The key algorithms involved here—Facebook's, YouTube's, and what was then Twitter's—were optimized for audience engagement throughout the period, since audience engagement is the product these firms sold to advertisers. Anything that will keep a viewer watching or reading longer will drive profits in this business, and social media firms have strong incentives to optimize for it.

It's just that, in doing so, they end up promoting a twenty-first-century blood libel.

It is no surprise that the adrenochrome story drives clicks: it ticks off all the emotional drivers for online engagement. The emotions that most drive user engagement have been exhaustively studied, and the results of that research do not make for happy reading. Content that plays to our anger always outperforms, as does content that demonizes the opposing side. In Q world, the more extreme the crimes ascribed to liberal elites are, the more engagement they drive. Stories like adrenochrome perform well not *despite* being insane but *because* they are.

With stories as sordid as these, algorithmic amplification can take hold rapidly. Begin watching a Q-related video in 2018, and you would soon find yourself watching another, and another, each more extreme than the one before. What began as a LARP spiraled entirely out of control, coming to be believed by millions.

How Many Millions?

According to the Public Religion Research Institute (PRRI), a nonprofit, nonpartisan organization dedicated to conducting independent research, belief in QAnon held steady throughout 2021, even as President Trump receded from power and the Biden administration took control of the government.[20] Belief remained despite Q disappearing from view, and despite the very obvious fact that no storm came, Hillary Clinton was not tried and executed, thousands of liberals were not put in jail, and the constitutional government of the United States continued more or less unencumbered. At the end of 2021, as at the beginning, 16 percent of survey respondents strongly or mostly agreed that "the government, media, and financial world in the United States are controlled by a group of Satan-worshiping pedophiles who run a global child sex-trafficking operation." A disquieting 22 percent of respondents—corresponding, if the survey is accurate, to the views of 37 million Americans—completely or mostly agree that "there is a storm coming soon that will sweep away the elites in power and restore the rightful leaders." That's more people than live in any one American state, representing something close to the population of Poland. Perhaps some 8 million Americans—the population of the state of Virginia—completely agree that satanist child traffickers secretly run the United States government.

Who are these Q believers, anyway? Popular narratives tend to paint them as solidly Republican—natural, given the movement's devotion to

Donald Trump—but according to PRRI's research, educational factors seem to explain more of the disparity than purely political ones. Yes, 43 percent of QAnon believers are Republicans, but a substantial 20 percent is made up of Democrats, along with 27 percent political independents. In terms of educational attainment, 57 percent had a high school degree or less, while 29 percent had attended a university but had not obtained a bachelor's degree. Nine percent did graduate from university, and a further 5 percent, intriguingly, had postgraduate degrees.[21]

It's impossible not to think of Grete De Francesco's old insight about the choicest audience for charlatans being "composed of the semiliterate, those who had exchanged their common sense for a little distorted information and had encountered science and education at some time, though briefly and unsuccessful."[22]

When these followers had asked the mainstream institutions of society—the media, the universities, the schools—how the world worked, they "had not received satisfying answers and had come away full of resentment yet hankering for more knowledge." It is this particular mix of curiosity and resentment, together with a deep thirst for meaning, that turns certain people into easy prey for charlatans.

Radically Decentralized Charlatanry

QAnon represents a real sea change in the world of charlatanry, and for reasons that have nothing to do with Ron Watkins's overactive imagination. What the Q community achieved has little precedent that we can find: a framework for radically decentralized charlatanry. Q followers are not passive victims of a charlatan; they have democratized charlatanry and made it available to everyone . . . with a little help from the algorithm.

On social media, on Reddit, and in lightly regulated Facebook groups, Q enthusiasts formed virtual communities where everyone was invited to take part in creating a collective fiction that would be fervently believed in. QAnon's structure, its emphasis on "asking questions," and its followers' militant commitment to treating wild conjecture as plausible one minute and then, very soon afterward, as the acknowledged truth is a strange twist on an old phenomenon. Q followers created a community of charlatans, with each "pretending to know that which he does not know" in front of an audience committed to the shared world.

It's as though, to paraphrase Andy Warhol, in the future, everyone will be a charlatan for fifteen minutes.

In Q world, exegesis was what mattered most. Q drops themselves weren't much fun, often amounting to little more than gibberish or "codes" created by randomly hitting keys on a keyboard alternately with the left and right hand. The whole fun of the LARP came down to the task of interpretation, to the decodes. These could come from anyone, anywhere and were often worked collaboratively by teams of "researchers."

The most successful Q decoders soon amassed audiences in the hundreds of thousands or millions of users. They launched people like Dave Hayes—an earnest, serious Christian paramedic in Arizona whose YouTube channel grew to a following of 750,000 under the title "the Praying Medic"—to the status of minor celebrity.[23]

Q influencers like Hayes were instrumental in aligning the world of Q with America's huge evangelical Christian community. Hayes, who believes God speaks to him nightly through prophetic dreams, leaned heavily into those private nighttime chats with the divine to guide his Q decodes.

This approach turned parts of QAnon into an offshoot of America's fundamentalist evangelical movement, with Q conferences adopting much of the look and feel of an evangelical church; Q converts even took to citing Q drops by their sequential number, as though they were Bible verses. Remember Q 48:71?

"NAT SEC concerns re: blackmail **[gain control]** of J. Biden by Russia, China and/or other foreign **[or domestic]** entities? US Intel apparatus **[reports?]**? Clear and Present Danger?"[24]

But Q's appeal was not limited to the evangelical hard right. As with the original big-tent conspiracy theory, the Q sphere was only too happy to absorb other beliefs and roll them into the Q canon.

The apogee followed the onset of the COVID-19 pandemic, which brought an entirely new demographic into the fold. Long-standing skepticism about the safety and efficacy of vaccines in progressive circles soon congealed into vaccine conspiracy theories, and where there is a conspiracy theory, there will be Q.

Anti-vax sentiment had been bubbling away in progressive Democratic circles in the United States for many years when COVID-19 hit. Stuck at home during long lockdowns, whole new demographics soon found an on-ramp to the Q community. Natural-health enthusiasts looking for alternative views on the pandemic found a supportive, like-minded community in the QAnon universe. Soon, vaccine-hesitant moms who had once voted for a candidate of the Left like Bernie Sanders found themselves getting red pilled, falling down the QAnon rabbit hole and devoting themselves to this strange online world. A good number of them, it must be said, seem to have found their way into the Q sphere through the influence of our good friend Joseph Mercola, whose own anti-vax sentiment deposited him in a mind space virtually indistinguishable from QAnon's.

The cost of all this in the lives of Q believers is hard to overstate. On the same platforms that had once supported the rise of QAnon—Facebook, Twitter, and Reddit—family members of converts congregated to support one another as they shared tales of heartbreak about the loved ones they'd "lost" to QAnon. The testimonies on these Q-casualties boards are devastating, and they come in the tens of thousands. Here's just one:

> After these past two years, I feel like my parents are strangers. [. . .] I told my mom that her QAnon obsession was breaking us apart, and her response was "There is so much you don't know out there, and one day you will learn the truth". That was the day I realized that my mom was more concerned with the 2020 election than the mental health of her daughter. I don't dare confront them, because that has blown up in my face plenty of times. I just don't know how to move on in my own life.[25]

Another, married to a Q believer, writes,

> My Q is consuming QAnon and tons of other conspiracy theories online every day. He's got headphones on watching videos for hours every day. And he believes whatever he hears on a video with zero proof. I tried to tell him that *anyone* can stand in front of a camera and say something. That doesn't make it true. He hates me—well, it seems like he does sometimes—because I refuse to believe all this nonsense. [. . .] I've spent 15 years with him. 14 years married. The last several dealing with his blind devotion to Trump and then the insane devotion to Q. I've waited for him to figure out for himself that these are all lies. But he just goes further down the rabbit hole.[26]

Testimonies like these are devastatingly common. Q has destroyed thousands of lives, tearing families apart as devotees soon find it impossible to tolerate those outside the cult. Massively democratizing the practice of charlatanry, Q became a huge experiment in the destructive potential of runaway confirmation bias. It became a space full of lies trumpeted as truth, where earnest people could fool and be fooled, by turns, in the context of a supportive community. For many socially isolated people, Q became not just an interest but an obsession, an online community that could inject meaning into their lives. And in its last act, QAnon took a real stab at destroying American democracy as well.

By the first few days of January 2021, QAnon had already amassed a long and inglorious track record of failed prophecies. The Democratic Party had not replaced an ailing Joe Biden at the top of the party's presidential ticket, as Q had predicted they would. Donald Trump had not crushed Biden in an Election Day landslide, obviously. Trump-appointed judges had found no evidence of fraud. And more than obviously, the "storm" had not come: no Democratic child trafficker had been tried or executed, no rooms full of trafficked children had been unearthed—basically nothing that Q had prophesized had come to pass. It was almost enough to make you conclude Q wasn't a White House insider at all. Come to think of it, he sounded much more like a shut-in fantasist in Japan.

Unwilling to accept this obvious conclusion, a good number of Q believers decided that if Q wasn't going to unleash the storm for them, they'd have to do it themselves. On January 6, as Congress met to certify the results of the previous November's election, a large contingent of Q believers congregated on the ellipse just south of the White House before setting off to storm the Capitol. As people waving Q banners or wearing Q T-shirts breached Capitol police lines and roamed free inside the Capitol, terrified lawmakers scurried for safe rooms. This homemade storm, rigged up out of the fevered dreams of a Q-addled rump, obviously failed to overthrow the American republic . . . but not for lack of trying.

Q stopped posting in 2021, as his followers struck out in different new conspiratorial directions. What began as a LARP, a role-playing game, metastasized into an all-consuming passion for thousands. Algorithmic amplification ensured that the nastiest, most destructive, most extreme conspiracy beliefs would receive the widest possible distribution. The toll has been staggering.

And yet Q seems likely to be remembered less as the culmination of something than as proof of concept. Now the world knows how charlatanry can be decentralized, democratized, and viral, put within the reach of the masses and unleashed to do staggering harm. In its structure and its methods, QAnon is an unprecedented phenomenon. We have been warned. What comes next could be worse.

10

How Charlatans Took Over the Culture Wars

DONALD TRUMP'S ENTRY INTO AMERICA'S POLITICAL SCENE HAS HAD some strange effects on the nation's political culture. America's polarized politics is built around two contrasting images of what the country could be and what it should be. Partisans on both sides build identities around these contrasting ideals, and a sizable minority of the population is passionately committed to those creeds. These idealized visions of what America can and should be are rocket fuel to a large coterie of culture-war charlatans. Ruthless people find it easy to manipulate partisan dreams for profit or power. Which is why America's culture war is such a rich seam of charlatans.

In planning whom to cover in this chapter we faced an embarrassment of riches, on both the right and the left. For our American readers this chapter could be especially instructive: whichever side of the culture wars they are on, the obvious signs of charlatanry that spring up in the loudest corners of the public sphere are impossible to miss.

This is not likely to stay an exclusively American problem for long. More often than not, America ends up exporting its political dysfunctions to the rest of the world. In Brazil and Chile, politicians discuss gun rights as though the Second Amendment were part of *their* constitutions. American-style controversies over gay and trans rights take center stage in the politics of Uganda, Russia, Hungary, and many other places. The dark side of America's still formidable soft power is that it exports its political anxieties just as effectively as its technology, music, or films. The trends that infect the US public sphere don't often remain confined to it.

Brian Kolfage

Brian Kolfage loves America and has the wounds to prove it. An Air Force veteran, Kolfage earned his Purple Heart on his second tour of duty in Iraq, when an insurgent rocket landed about a meter from where he was standing in Baghdad on September 11, 2004. That he survived at all was a miracle: doctors had to amputate both his legs and his right arm to secure his life, making his body a kind of testament to the sacrifices he was willing to make for the country he loved.

After a long recovery at Walter Reed Army Medical Center in Washington, DC, Kolfage rebuilt his life as a public speaker and philanthropist, telling audiences about his experiences of war and the vision of the country for which he'd been fighting. He launched a coffee company and vowed to donate 10 percent of sales to veterans' charities. Soon, though, he realized he could spread that vision much more effectively online than in the real world.[1]

Over the following years, Brian Kolfage would launch a whole slew of hard-right websites and Facebook pages, joining the sprawling web of conservative online players already out trying to turn conservative outrage into clicks—and dollars.

During the Obama years, his websites (with names like Freedom Daily and Wounded American Warrior) pushed out a steady stream of shrill headlines and aggressive conservative clickbait. The stories they peddled were always hyped and sometimes plain old fabricated—"Muslim Teen

Refugee Charged with MURDER for Beating 97-Yr-Old WWII Veteran to Death"[2] went one typical offering, or "Bad News for Barack After What Malia's Caught Doing in Chicago—No Hiding Her NASTY Secret Now."[3]

Kolfage had a staff of at least ten people producing fake news before people called it that: the stories were popular and soon the network of sites Kolfage ran were grossing hundreds of thousands of dollars per month. But Brian Kolfage was dreaming bigger, and the increasing polarization and partisan rancor that came with the Trump years created all sorts of new opportunities for him.

It was sometime in 2018 that Kolfage came up with an inspired idea: We Fund the Wall. The GoFundMe pitch was simple: if the liberals in Washington were going to hold up the funding for President Trump's visionary wall on the border with Mexico, Brian Kolfage would get his readers to put up the cash for it.

Kolfage involved big names in the conservative movement behind this quixotic idea, bringing Trump's one-time strategist Steve Bannon on board alongside Erik Prince, head of the private military company Blackwater and brother of Trump's secretary of education. A slick online media operation followed, built around a GoFundMe site seeking to raise *$1 billion* from private donors for the wall.[4]

There was obviously plenty that was fishy about the campaign from the start—for one thing, there didn't appear to be any legal way for a private organization to donate money to the government earmarked specifically for a single purpose, such as building a wall. That's just not the way government finances work. Yet for Trump supporters who fully bought into the dream of keeping America safe from the polluting blood of foreigners, this didn't matter. Kolfage championed their dreams, so they willingly handed him their money.

The bureaucratic hurdles were real, though. Under GoFundMe's rules, if the campaign didn't reach its absurdly ambitious $1 billion goal, all donations would be returned to the donors. As the fundraising pitch started to take off and attract millions in donations, Kolfage pivoted, founding a new nonprofit corporation not only to fund the wall but also to privately *build* the wall using donor cash.

To do this, he had to convince donors to endorse their earlier cash pledges to the new organization. Thousands did.

Brian Kolfage was adamant in his fundraising that all donations would be devoted only to building the wall, but because you know what book you're reading, you can guess what became of *that* promise. Soon his wife, Ashley—herself a model and budding Instagram influencer—was parading around in front of their new $100,000 Range Rover.[5] (Ashley Kolfage has not been accused of any wrongdoing.)

Kolfage insisted that the money was all coming from his coffee business, but with fundraising for We Build the Wall nearing $20 million, federal prosecutors began to have their doubts. As US Department of Justice charging documents would later show, in December 2018, when serious money began to pour into We Build the Wall, bigger fish in Republican politics just about elbowed Kolfage out of control of the organization. Steve Bannon, in particular, seems to have brought in his own people, but not before remunerating Kolfage handsomely, though it was through a circuitous route involving a number of shell companies. Under the secret arrangement, Kolfage would allegedly receive $100,000 up front, and then $20,000 per month.[6]

In April 2023 Kolfage pled guilty to conspiracy charges and agreed to return the $17 million he had raised before being sentenced to 51 months in federal prison for his role in, as the government put it, "carrying out a scheme to defraud hundreds of thousands of donors." His associate Andrew Badolato received a 36-month sentence.[7]

And how about their brand-name coconspirator, the former White House strategist who allegedly got the biggest payout from the deal? Steve Bannon walked away without a scratch, because Donald Trump pardoned him on his last day in office in 2021. New York state prosecutors would later revive the case under state rather than federal jurisdiction. As we write, Bannon, who denies wrongdoing, is awaiting the start of his New York State trial over these charges.[8]

Brazen though Kolfage and Bannon's wall scheme was, a $17 million fraud is small potatoes compared to some of the charlatanry that has blossomed in a universe dominated by post-truth. The worst cases reached genuinely ghoulish extremes at gobsmacking scale. None was more shocking than the empire Alex Jones built.

Alex Jones

To those familiar with Jones's shtick, little introduction is needed. To those not familiar with it, little we can say can illustrate how extreme his rhetoric could get. On a series of linked media properties, including a hugely popular podcast, all under the banner of Infowars, Jones became a force in conservative media by positioning himself at the very furthest extreme of the right-wing fringe: a place where conspiracy theory is the common currency and assertions that would get you laughed out of any other room are seriously debated on a daily basis. That he thought the September 11 attacks were an inside job almost goes without saying. For years, he argued that the government can control the weather, including setting off floods specifically to punish right-leaning areas, explaining that the government can "create and steer groups of tornadoes."[9]

It's a worldview where *everything* is a conspiracy. To Jones, the rising visibility of gay people is the result of a government campaign to manipulate people's sexuality through chemicals in the water. In one notorious rant, he charged that government experiments were turning frogs gay by altering their hormonal balance.

"The government is turning frogs gay" came to be seen as the furthest extreme of Jones's lunacy—though in fact, the claim was notable for an entirely different reason: unlike most of his stranger claims, this one actually did have a (distant) grounding in fact. A small scientific study had shown that runoff from the pesticide atrazine can alter the hormonal balance in male frogs and "feminize" them anatomically, which of course in no way means that "the majority of frogs in the United States are now gay," as Jones claimed in 2017.[10]

Jones would, of course, jump into the same QAnon fever swamp we discussed in the previous chapter, but his charlatanry was on a whole different level from the bit players discussed there: Jones built and monetized a mass audience that made Infowars a kind of money machine.

As you'd expect, Jones's worldview is one where a major civilization-shaking catastrophe is always just around the corner, and as such, well, his fans are primed to start preparing for it. Never fear, the Infowars website sold a complete suite of products to help you survive Armageddon, from emergency-survival food parcels to water- and air-filtration devices.[11] The gig was profitable—insanely profitable—to the tune of $165 million in sales in the three years between 2015 and 2018, as revealed by court filings first accessed by the *Huffington Post*.[12]

And why was Jones in court in the first place?

That . . . is one dark tale.

On December 14, 2012, when twenty first-graders plus six of their teachers were mowed down by a lunatic with two rifles and a handgun at Sandy Hook Elementary School in Newtown, Connecticut, the nation united in grief for the murdered children.

Not Alex Jones.

All that week, Jones took to the airwaves saying that the attack at Sandy Hook Elementary was fake news, a government conspiracy designed to create a pretext to disarm good, God-fearing Americans in contravention to their constitutional rights. Jones's charges weren't just generic—he got personal, attacking, by name, parents who had lost children to the massacre just hours before. He called them crisis actors engaged in an elaborate, government-orchestrated ruse.

The lie wasn't any more outrageous than many others in the Jones arsenal, but this one had real-world consequences in ways the others did not. People intimately connected with victims of the shooting, naturally, spoke to the press. And Jones's legions of fans soon made it a kind of mission to destroy their lives.

One such life belonged to Robbie Parker, whose daughter Emilie had been a happy, healthy six-year-old in kindergarten until cut down by the killer's bullets. Parker gave an emotional statement to the press the day after the tragedy only for Jones to pounce, calling him out by name for being a fraud.

Almost immediately Robbie Parker's world, which had already been turned upside down once that week by his daughter's murder, was turned upside down again, as a deluge of angry abuse from Jones's listeners came pouring into his life. At perhaps the most emotionally vulnerable moment in his life, Parker was besieged with angry messages calling him a fake, a phony, and in many cases *threatening his life* for the fearsome crime of . . . mourning his murdered daughter in public.[13]

Parker and his wife hoped the harassment would die down after a few days. Or weeks. But it didn't. Jones's followers continued to hound them month after month until, two years after the shooting, they decided to move across the country, thousands of miles, to Washington State to try to distance themselves from the abuse. Soon, though, Jones's troll army found records of the sale of their Connecticut home, pieced together where they had moved to, and published their new address as well. And the abuse wasn't just online. Parker described how a Jones follower spotted him on the streets of Seattle one day in 2016, nearly four years after the shooting, and began shouting at him right then and there.[14]

Erica Lafferty, for her part, described getting rape threats from Jones's followers after she spoke to the media about her murdered mother, Dawn Hochsprung, who had been the principal of Sandy Hook Elementary.[15] Jeremy Richman, the father of another murdered six-year-old, was so distraught by the campaign of hate unleashed against him and his family that he would go on to take his own life in 2019.[16]

If we know about the damage Jones's lies about the Sandy Hook massacre caused, it's because the parents eventually banded together and launched an epochal defamation suit against him. After hearing in minute detail about the scale of the havoc he had caused in their lives, a jury found Jones liable for defaming the victims' families and ordered him to pay them $965 million in compensation. Enough to wipe out all the profits he had made over the previous two decades three times over.[17]

Months later, the trial judge found that the evidence clearly supported the plaintiffs' contention that Jones's conduct had been "intentional and malicious," adding a further $473 million in damages to the settlement, bringing the total to $1.44 billion.[18]

When politics gets highly polarized and passions run high, it becomes easier for charlatans to ply their trade. And that's true regardless of ideology; if you think only right-wingers grift in America, well, you have another think coming.

Rebekah Jones

Rebekah Jones knew something was wrong.

The Florida geographer and data scientist had been working on the State Department of Health's COVID-19 dashboard at a time when pandemic policy was profoundly polarized, with conservatives pressing to lift lockdowns as quickly as possible while liberals continued to favor a cautious approach to managing the pandemic. Florida's conservative governor, Ron DeSantis, was pushing to end pandemic restrictions as quickly as possible, and news of an ongoing pandemic could only get in the way of such a policy.

And then, it happened.

As Rebekah Jones put it in an incendiary series of Twitter posts, she was asked to "manually change data to drum up support for the plan to reopen," and Florida's deputy secretary for health told her "to delete cases and deaths."

Soon afterward, in May 2020, Jones was fired. Before long, she had launched her own competing dashboard including what she portrayed as the *real* COVID-19 statistics in Florida: you know the drill, the ones *they* don't want you to know about. Rebekah Jones's allegations had all the makings of a gigantic scandal, full of political interference in public health data in the middle of a pandemic and retribution against employees who refused to play along.[19]

Eight months after she was fired, in January 2021, thousands of Floridians heard their phones sound an emergency alert—the same type of alert the state uses to send out hurricane warnings or to alert about an impending tornado. Reaching for their phones, they saw a message that looked like no emergency message they'd seen before. "It's time to speak up before another 70,000 people are dead," the message read. "You know this is wrong, you don't have to be a part of this. Be a hero. Speak up before it's too late."[20]

Florida State officials traced the message to an Internet Protocol address linked to a computer used by . . . Rebekah Jones. Soon, armed state police raided her house to look for evidence. Jones denied sending the message, and she posted video of the raid on social media and garnered a new outpouring of liberal support. She denied having any involvement with the emergency message.

This is when Rebekah Jones's story became national news. National Public Radio, the august voice of the journalistic mainstream, gave her story extensive and very positive coverage, uncritically accepting Jones's version of the story.[21] *Cosmopolitan* gave her a huge spread.[22] She was named one of *Fortune Magazine*'s 40 Under 40 and *Forbes*'s Technology Person of the Year for 2020, calling her "the latest technologist who stepped up to fill the vacuum left by governments during COVID-19."[23]

The mainstream media was unanimous: Rebekah Jones became a bona fide media darling, constantly portrayed as a daring truth teller staring down a powerful GOP rising star. And boy, did she raise money on the back of that image!

Jones set up a series of legal-defense funds through GoFundMe, the same crowdfunding app Brian Kolfage had relied on. She raised some $325,000 in her first go and a further $23,000 in a second legal fund. Soon, her profile was high enough that she announced plans to run for a seat in the US House of Representatives, the lower chamber of the American Congress. She looked to have a fair shot at being elected, too.

Much of the mainstream media piled onto the Rebekah Jones platform without ever really stopping to scrutinize whom it was they were lionizing, which is a shame. Had they done so, they might have found out about Jones's, shall we say, "colorful" past.

Her escapades included the time when, as a graduate assistant at Florida State University, she had an affair with one of her students. Though she hadn't been convicted, she had been charged with stalking the former student, who was also the father of her child, after posting a sixty-eight-page document online describing the intimate relationship with this former boyfriend, including explicit texts and nude photographs. Jones had been fired from the university after retaliating against her ex by threatening to give his roommate a failing grade. The local newspaper, the *Gainesville Sun*, covered the story and said that, according to police, Jones wrote in emails to the man, "You're going to be famous. We're going to destroy each other. This is never going to end."[24]

All of this was a matter of public record. None of it, oddly enough, found its way into the *Cosmo* spread about her.

So, her character was spotty, but it was worse than that: on closer inspection, her allegations about political manipulation of the Florida State Department of Health's COVID-19 dashboard didn't appear to make much sense. Jones, colleagues said, never had access to the underlying data and could not have altered it even if she had been asked to, which, to be clear, she wasn't.

As reporters looked more closely at her story, much of it fell apart. Remember her tweet claiming Florida's deputy secretary for health told her "to delete cases and deaths"? She deleted it. Then she tweeted that "deleting deaths was never something I was asked to do, I've never claimed that it was." Then she deleted *that* tweet as well.

The more you dug into Rebekah Jones's stories, the more they seemed to come apart. Her own COVID-19 dashboard, which she peddled as a truth-telling competitor to the Florida State Department of Health's dashboard she was fired from, showed sharply higher numbers of infections than the official database.

Why?

She included not only data from positive polymerase chain reaction (PCR) tests to identify COVID but also positive antibody-test numbers, leading to double and triple counting of individual cases, because a person would continue to test positive for COVID antibodies months after recovering from COVID itself. Every public health expert knew this . . . but then, Rebekah Jones had no training in public health.

Nonetheless, Jones parlayed her "whistleblower" bona fides into a large online following full of people of a mind to disregard negative stories about her. And the mainstream media, so diligent about digging into the fibs and crimes of a Brian Kolfage or an Alex Jones, wasn't willing to go deep on a liberal hero in the same way. Even after journalists dug up Jones's shocking record of run-ins with the law, including allegations she'd assaulted a police officer and charges for cyberstalking and criminal mischief, major outlets continued to run credulous stories praising her courage as a resistance hero.[25]

It's easy to see why Jones got so little scrutiny from a journalism profession that leans heavily to the left. Journalists are just as vulnerable to HumanOS hacking via confirmation bias and motivated reasoning as anyone else. Tell a liberal newsroom that some right-wing yahoos are raising private money to build a border wall, and they'll be immediately suspicious. Tell them a brave truth teller is blowing the whistle on a conservative governor, and they'll line up to write glowing profiles.

This is natural, indeed; this is the way all charlatans work. They target people who share their prior beliefs, because people who share their priors will naturally be far less suspicious and far more trusting than those who don't. Any set of prior beliefs can be targeted in this way. Including prior beliefs we hold sacred, like anti-racism.

Regina Jackson and Saira Rao

Meet Regina Jackson and Saira Rao, the crusading anti-racism campaigners behind Race2Dinner. The basic pitch behind their organization is so strange, it must stand out for oddity even among the many oddities in this book. The long and the short of it is this: you pay them $2,500, and they'll come to your house to show you and your white girlfriends exactly how racist you are.

Race2Dinner is an outgrowth of the most militant faction of American anti-racism. If by anti-racism you understand something simple and milquetoast like "treat everyone the same, whatever their race may be," then Jackson and Rao have some disquieting news for you: you're a racist.

Theirs is an ideology that sees all of society as riven, top to bottom, with racial oppression. From their standpoint, even the presumption that you can opt out of racism just by treating people the same regardless of race is a pernicious form of racism. There is no such thing as "regardless of race"—any time you are failing to acknowledge the pervasive reality of racism, you are perpetuating racism. You cannot opt out.

To be sure, no real racist would consider paying Jackson, an African American, and Rao, an Indian American, $2,500 to come to their house and tell them they and their friends are, well, racists. No political moderate would either. In consequence, Jackson and Rao ply their trade exclusively in the homes of wealthy white women already strongly committed to fighting racial bias. That's their market. And, it turns out, it's a surprisingly big market.

At Jackson and Rao's dinners there is an essentially endless list of things you, as a wealthy white woman, can do or say that will be pinned as rooted in white supremacy. Disagreeing with anything Jackson and Rao say is, obviously, white supremacy and strictly verboten. More confusingly, agreeing with them is *also* white supremacy, an expression of patronizing contempt. Talking about your Black friends is more than evidently tokenizing them, which is white supremacy, but also giving money to Black causes and organizations in an attempt to expiate white supremacy will itself be labeled as white supremacy.

Trapped in a maze where you have no good moves, you might be tempted to cry, but beware—white tears, you'll be instructed, are one of the most potent weapons in the arsenal of white supremacy. As you sit there trying desperately to keep things together, you'll be reminded how the tears of white women were often enough to get a young Black man lynched in the South, and you'll be ejected from the room, thrown out of the dinner party *you paid $2,500 for*, and sent to a special designated crying room, where your white tears are apparently cordoned off from doing yet more harm.

Racism, at these dinners, is treated like nothing so much as original sin: a deeply shameful, ingrained guilt white people are born with, live with their entire lives, and can expiate only through a sort of introspective sacrament.

"You've got to acknowledge that you're a problem, that you have all this extremely toxic behavior inside of you, and you need to deconstruct your Whiteness and start being in community with each other around this," says Rao.[26] In Christian theology, the sacrament you undergo to cleanse yourself from original sin is called baptism; in anti-racism, it's called Race2Dinner.

Yet the virulence with which Jackson and Rao confront their customers suggests other analogies as well. If descriptions of Race2Dinner sound suspiciously like Maoist self-criticism rallies from the Chinese Cultural Revolution, well, you would be partially correct. But only partially: Chinese communists never went so far as to charge bourgeois scum money to be told they're bourgeois scum. Then again, fixating on the ludicrous cost of Race2Dinner is—you guessed it!—white supremacy, a sign that you "see this work as charity. You doing us a favor. White supremacy culture has you believing that you are doing us a favor by even caring about racism or antiracism. This results in your incessant demands that we educate you—on your own racism, on a system you created to harm us for your benefit. For free."[27]

The dream that Jackson and Rao target is a powerful one, and a noble one. Race2Dinner promises "a world free of White supremacy, caste, patriarchy, misogyny, all the isms, all the phobias and hate." Once in their charge, their customers are treated to a carnival of motivated reasoning, where essentially any behavior can be interpreted as an expression of the evil they seek to extirpate. Yet such is the guilt that so many white Americans experience over the dark past of racial oppression that the two are flush with customers.

Their website is peppered with the sloganeering and phraseology of nonprofit anti-racist activism. Yet the company that actually pockets the $2,500 is a for-profit limited-liability company, meaning Jackson and Rao get to personally benefit from their anti-racist work.[28]

Ludicrous as Jackson and Rao's take on anti-racism is, the pair benefits from the same kind of liberal media credulity that has shielded Rebekah Jones over her long record of questionable shenanigans. Because anti-racism is a cardinal value for the kinds of elite professionals that staff major media in the United States, Jackson and Rao continue to be valued members in good standing of the liberal elite. A strong halo effect envelops their work, protecting them from the kind of skeptical reporting they could expect if they were engaged in a less socially valued form of charlatanry.

Jackson and Rao can be accused of many things, but deception is not one of them. Like Chani Nicholas, they are quite straightforward about what it is they're selling: they promise one supremely uncomfortable dinner at a given price, and if people pay it, they get exactly what they asked for. In the grand spectrum of charlatanry, we're toward the more benign end: peddling nonsense to willing customers is, after all, not a crime.

Like Rebekah Jones, the sums charlatans like Jackson and Rao charge tend to be in the thousands or tens of thousands of dollars, not in the tens or hundreds of millions of dollars charlatans on the right go after. In the United States, at least, right-wing charlatans play on a much bigger stage, make grabs for vastly larger sums, and face much more stringent media and legal scrutiny. Charlatans on the left may be fewer in number, and they get away with less . . . but they do get away with it.

11

Ten Million Psychopaths

TODAY, CHARLATANS ARE EVERYWHERE. THEIR SCHEMES ARE DIGITAL, viral, and scalable. In this book we have seen them at work in all kinds of circumstances, with all kinds of different aims and goals. Chances are, most of the charlatans here struck you as ludicrous: the kind of obvious huckster only a fool would fall for.

But, if we have done our job right, somewhere along the way, we made you squirm.

At least a little.

One or two of our charlatans spoke to you. Perhaps someone close to you has fallen into their clutches. Maybe you have. And, chances are, those chapters made for some uncomfortable reading for you.

If you're a devout Christian, you probably had no trouble spotting that Baba Ramdev, the yoga teacher, is up to no good. You were outraged at the way he has exploited devout Hindus' beliefs to build a commercial empire. But then you were terribly uncomfortable reading about the evangelical preachers doing much the same in Texas, Lynchburg, or Brazil. Or maybe it's the other way around.

Perhaps you're a spiritual seeker, happy enough to see crypto bros skewered, but you couldn't help but get defensive when you read our accounts of the online spiritual gurus who speak your language, whether it's Holland's Bentinho Massaro's algorithmic cult or Canada's Chani Nicholas's app-based astrology. Or maybe you're a rationalist and you laughed at the dumb kids who follow those woo-woo New Age gurus, but you had to sweat your way through our description of Pakistan's Arif Naqvi bamboozling the great and the good at Davos, or you wept through our telling of the crypto capers, ruing the money you lost to FTX or to TerraLuna.

If, somewhere along the way, you found yourself rebelling against some part of this book, well, then you already know why virtually everyone is vulnerable: the really remarkable thing about charlatans is that we can meet ninety-nine of them and find them laughably obvious scammers . . . and still be in grave danger from the one hundredth, who speaks to our dreams.

We began this book with dark suspicions that there must be something wrong with the victims. By now, we hope we have persuaded you that that's not the case. Instead, something is wrong, *very* wrong, not with the victims but with the perpetrators. The pattern of behavior charlatan after charlatan exhibits is obviously quite abnormal—but abnormal in specific, consistent ways.

We have now looked at a broad cross section of charlatans. What are they like? Most are described as intensely charming, though perhaps glib. Most of them appear to be highly intelligent, have enormous egos, and build their charlatan empires on assertions of special powers or secret knowledge. Some show themselves to be prone to boredom and struggle to tolerate frustration. Essentially all engage in systematic deception, lying to victims with abandon and showing no remorse or guilt about it.

They never show empathy for the people whose lives they wreck; they're often short-tempered and struggle to control their behavior. A good number of them are prone to having sex with a lot of different people. Many are impulsive, often struggling to formulate realistic long-term plans, which is why so many dig themselves deeper and deeper into schemes that have no realistic possibility of long-term success.

Charming, glib, egomaniacal, intolerant of frustration, deceptive, manipulative, remorseless, devoid of empathy, short-tempered, promiscuous, impulsive, short-term oriented—this isn't just a list of insults; it's the diagnostic criteria set out in the Hare Checklist, a long-established psychiatric test for psychopathy.

The latest version of the *Diagnostic and Statistical Manual of Mental Disorders*—the official tool that psychiatrists use to diagnose their patients—has dropped the use of such words as *psychopathy* and *psychopath* out of a perhaps medically justified concern about stigmatization. What amounts to the same condition is referred to now by the coldly bureaucratic label of *antisocial personality disorder*.[1] The disorder is defined as

> a pervasive pattern of disregard for and violation of the rights of others occurring since age 15 years, as indicated by three (or more) of the following:
>
> 1. Failure to conform to social norms with respect to lawful behaviors as indicated by repeatedly performing acts that are grounds for arrest.
> 2. Deceitfulness, as indicated by repeated lying, use of aliases, or conning others for personal profit or pleasure.
> 3. Impulsivity or failure to plan ahead.
> 4. Irritability and aggressiveness, as indicated by repeated physical fights or assaults.
> 5. Reckless disregard for safety of self or others.
> 6. Consistent irresponsibility, as indicated by repeated failure to sustain consistent work behavior or honor financial obligations.
> 7. Lack of remorse, as indicated by being indifferent to or rationalizing having hurt, mistreated, or stolen from another.

We are not psychiatrists. We cannot diagnose the people we have written about in these pages. What we can do is point out what's perfectly obvious: the charlatans we have written about meet many of the classic criteria for antisocial personality disorder. What, colloquially, people still think of as psychopathy.

And not just psychopathy. For some years, researchers have zeroed in on what's been dubbed the "dark triad" traits: a personality structure that combines aspects of antisocial personality disorder with Machiavellianism and narcissism. Machiavellianism—which the American Psychiatric Association defines as "the tendency to view other people as objects to be manipulated in pursuit of your goals, if necessary through deliberate deception"—is a thread that runs through many of the stories we have told, and so is narcissism, meaning excessive self-love or egocentrism.[2]

Think of Edir Macedo at his huge, Old Testament–style temple in São Paulo relentlessly telling the faithful at his Universal Church of the Kingdom of God that God will perform big miracles for them only if they give him big donations, or of Joseph Mercola's mania for putting his name on every product he comes near. Most charlatans are anything but self-effacing. These are people for whom being at the center of attention matters and for whom manipulation is normal.

The bundle of traits that define psychopathy have been recognized by historians going back to antiquity and across a wide variety of cultures. As one study put it, "It occurs and is recognized by every society, no matter what its economic system, and in all eras, showing that it is not purely an indication of a modern 'sick' society."[3]

Many of our charlatans take huge risks, are aggressively promiscuous, and struggle to make realistic long-term plans. Think of Mamugnà, partying with the young daughters of Venice's noblemen, all of whom are desperate to marry said daughters off to the alchemist. Yes, he did end up under the executioner's sword, but how many babies did he father in the process? From an evolutionary point of view, his approach was nothing if not "live fast, die young." Think of Mehmet Aydın cruising around in his

Ferrari in Uruguay—as a farmhand in Turkey, he could never have had the choice of partners he had as a charlatan in these times.

Charlatans rush to accumulate prestige, wealth, and distinction without seeming to care who gets hurt in the process. They live for the now.

Some researchers have suggested that evolution may select for psychopathic traits in a minority of the population, simply because a willingness to take risks may help them ensure their genes get passed on to the next generation.[4] This does not appear to be the majority view among psychologists. We are not qualified to try to arbitrate this dispute. There may be other, better ways to account for the stable recurrence of psychopathic traits generation after generation. But what we do know for sure is that when a smart, ambitious person exhibiting these traits gets connected to the internet, bad things are bound to happen.

The Hyperconnected Psychopath

Deep in the past, having one out of every hundred people display psychopathic traits might not have been so destabilizing. Looking through our long evolutionary history, at those first two hundred thousand years when *Homo sapiens* lived mostly in small, hunter-gatherer groups of maybe fifty or one hundred people, all kin, psychopathy would have been a rare and manageable oddity—throwing up the rare, ruthless, but perhaps very effective leader in its wake.

Many people may have lived their entire lives without ever coming across a psychopath, while others will have been exposed to one or at most two in their lifetimes. Their very callousness and willingness to take risks may have made some of them quite valuable as leaders, charismatic people able to make the tough decisions their more sentimental peers shied away from. Perhaps this too accounts for their persistence in the gene pool: groups that consistently produced one psychopath out of every one hundred children may have seen their survival rates improve as a result.

Fast-forward two hundred thousand years, and we find ourselves in a completely transformed social universe. We interact with many, many more people. Coming across one psychopath in a lifetime might be unpleasant, but it would normally be manageable. But what happens when we create a society where regular people can expect to run into a couple of charlatans before breakfast?

Their strategies haven't fundamentally changed in all these millennia, but their tactics have been completely reinvented, their influence amplified. The communications infrastructure our societies have built makes vast audiences available to anyone at the click of a mouse. Encountering a psychopath is no longer the once-in-a-lifetime event it was for most of our evolutionary history. And encountering that tiny subset of psychopaths who go on to build a successful practice as charlatans is no longer the occasional occurrence it was in sixteenth-century Italy or nineteenth-century America, where snake oil salesmen were still rare enough to be memorable.

Technological advances have made charlatans' access to potential marks explode. Today's charlatans are digital, viral, scalable, and, in some cases, global. They know how to leverage cutting-edge digital-marketing techniques to identify and cultivate marks. In some cases, the recruitment mechanism is carried out entirely online. Just a matter of numbers.

And the math, when you look at it forthrightly, is scary.

According to the consultancy Kepios, as of 2024 there were some 5.22 billion users on social media worldwide, and that number is rising fast.[5]

The American Psychological Association estimates some 0.3–0.7 percent of women exhibit significant psychopathic traits, alongside 1.2 percent of men.[6]

A smaller percentage of the population—perhaps 0.2 percent—exhibit signs of the dark triad.

Assuming psychopaths are as likely to seek internet access as the rest of us, that suggests there are now *forty million psychopaths* on social media, and perhaps something like ten million social media users exhibit all the traits of the dark triad.

Of course, the vast majority of them are not using social media to turn into full-fledged charlatans. Most live relatively normal lives, in which their peculiar psychological makeup will prove an advantage in many ways, though often causing great pain to the handful of people closest to them. But a tiny percentage of them will find, in today's communications cornucopia, a perfect outlet for their psychopathy.

The explosion of charlatans that now crowd our public sphere is one of the most notable features of our times. Affluent modern societies give rise to a startling number of beliefs, hopes, and dreams.

After all, who wants to live life without a dream?

So, day after day, you will encounter any number of charlatans targeting any number of marks with any number of messages tailored to an infinite variety of dreams. Many of the messages will sound outlandish to you.

The problem, of course, won't come when someone approaches you with a bizarre message. The problem will come when you hear a message that really resonates with your dreams, because your dreams are grounded in the kinds of beliefs you just don't doubt. When you hear your dreams reflected back to you, you will react instantaneously, within two hundred milliseconds, at the gut level. It's just the way HumanOS is wired. It's inevitable.

For most people, nothing is more natural than feeling warmth toward those who passionately champion your dream. When you meet a charming, intense person who charismatically speaks up for your dreams, you will find it unnatural to imagine they are purely out to exploit you. Their lure is irresistible.

Normal people really struggle to imagine the way charlatans think and the way they act.

So, when someone vibes with us, we trust them. And once you trust a little, it's always easier to trust a little more than to stop trusting altogether. Before you know it, you are in way over your head.

Worse, today's technologically hyperempowered charlatans learn from each other, picking up cues from those who came before to refine their own pitches. The most dedicated among them stay abreast of the latest marketing techniques, constantly trying new things in their quest to identify marks, target their vulnerabilities, and hijack their dreams.

Right now, today, someone somewhere on Earth is studying the tactics of a charlatan far away to try to adapt them to their here and now. And some of them will succeed, concocting new schemes designed to be digital, viral, scalable from day one and, therefore, able to operate globally.

A practice that used to be marginal to society is moving in toward its center. An experience that used to be rare and memorable has become routine. The days when someone could reasonably expect to live a lifetime without ever meeting a charlatan are long gone. Today, the barrage is relentless, and the discipline and vigilance it takes to shield oneself from all of them are beyond most people's abilities. The golden age of the charlatan is upon us.

With artificial intelligence developing terrifying new capabilities at unprecedented speeds, the toolbox at charlatans' disposal is only growing. The days of the first AI-enabled charlatan are surely not far off. The tools being used to enlist our trust are growing in power and sophistication. Our defenses are not keeping pace.

In some ways, charlatans aren't the puzzle; their victims are. Successful charlatans tend to be highly intelligent and are guided by self-interest. However vicious some of their tactics might be, their motive is no mystery. They are, in a twisted way, rational in their pursuit of money, sex, power, followers, and ego-gratification. As we've seen again and again, the techniques they deploy to get these things *work*. They certainly work in the short run, and sometimes they work for decades on end, even whole lifetimes. Charlatans may be despicable, but their motivations are not mysterious.

The bigger mystery, really, is the marks. Again and again we see them behaving in ways that are plainly against their interests. They give up their votes, their life savings, their bodies, their whole identities to charlatans who everyone around them can see are just out to exploit them. They believe their charlatans will put them on a path to a better life. In doing so, they give their trust to people peddling stories that seem patently absurd to anyone who doesn't share their dream.

Everyone Is at Risk

"They must just not be so smart." This is almost everyone's gut reaction when they hear about the victims of the charlatans in this book. It was our reaction too. It seems automatic, a product of fast thinking that's impossible to suppress when you hear of people falling for stories that seem plainly, obviously far-fetched. And then, quick on its heels, comes its more polite variant: "Maybe they're just ignorant." Could it be that people who didn't benefit from a good education are especially at risk?

We know that can't be it. Among the victims of the charlatans we have learned about are some of the most highly educated and intelligent people in the world today. The investors who ended up in the grips of Sam Bankman-Fried's FTX scheme included dozens of elite-educated investment professionals, among them the managers of some of the world's biggest public investment bodies like the Ontario Teachers' Pension Fund. The same goes for Arif Naqvi's Ponzi scheme.

Wealth managers, activist investors, and institutions fell for Arif Naqvi's "doing well by doing good" scam, pouring billions of dollars into his Growth Markets Health Fund without really checking where the money was going: the Obama White House, the Gates Foundation, the former CEO of Britain's National Health Service. Clearly, a high IQ and an elite education do not inoculate believers against the charlatans and their scams.

Could it be the opposite, then? Could it be that charlatans peddle the kind of story so outlandish only an intellectual could fall for it? No. Many of the charlatans we examined target those who aren't highly educated, from Edir Macedo's Universal Church of the Kingdom of God, which specializes in trawling the shantytowns of the Third World for converts, to Jerry Falwell Jr.'s Liberty University, which promised people precisely the education they wanted.

In this book we have met twenty-four supremely talented contemporary charlatans—and Mamugnà, a long-ago one. It's not a huge number—far from a statistically representative sample—but even with such a small set, it's already clear that victims are incredibly varied. They include the following:

- slum-dwelling Brazilians
- people on the brink of suicide
- patriotic Turkish Facebook gamers
- struggling middle-class suburban American Christians
- poor Italian immigrants in 1920s New York
- fanatical Donald Trump supporters
- vaccine-hesitant moms
- wealthy woke white women in America
- the US, French, and British governments' international development corporations
- seasoned Chicago-area real estate investors
- women seeking the love of their life
- devout yoga-practicing middle-class Hindus
- the Venetian nobility of the late sixteenth century
- the US government's Overseas Private Investment Corporation
- young spiritual seekers in Europe and the United States
- the Ontario Teachers' Pension Fund
- just about everyone's mom in Latin America
- Tom Brady and Gisele Bündchen
- Tony Blair
- Usain Bolt
- Bill Gates

In an age that cherishes diversity, we've seen no list more diverse: socially, geographically, economically, ideologically, demographically, there's all kinds of everything in there. Whatever the commonalities may be between all these different groups of victims, they don't seem to come at the demographic level. They come at a deeper, more intimate level.

They all *had a dream*. They *trusted* someone who affirmed that dream.

And they got taken advantage of because of it.

That's not to say, of course, that you shouldn't believe in anything, or that you should give up on your dreams. That would be absurd: throwing the baby out with the bathwater. Trust is modern society's secret sauce; our dreams are the ultimate source of human progress. In any case, you can't help it: unless you're a psychopath, you have a dream and a propensity to trust the people who share it.

But we must remember that our dreams double as our vulnerabilities. Dreams engender trust in those who reflect them, and trust can be abused. When we fail to scrutinize our own dreams, fail to see the way our dreams leave us open to manipulation, we become vulnerable. And exploiting those vulnerabilities is what charlatans specialize in.

All Conviction, No Persuasion

We began this book wondering how victims could be so gullible. But the more we've learned about charlatans, the less it feels like gullibility is the problem.

To be gullible means to be easily *persuaded* to believe something. Persuasion is baked into the definition of gullibility. Yet what's remarkable about the charlatans we have seen is how little actual persuasion they seem to do. For all the extreme and bizarre beliefs that charlatans' victims come to espouse, what is amazing is how little time charlatans spend getting people to discard one belief and adopt another one. Persuasion is not in their wheelhouse.

None of the charlatans we have looked at wasted time with anything so old-fashioned as persuasion. Walter Mercado, the extravagantly successful Puerto Rican TV astrologer, didn't exhaust himself trying to demonstrate to skeptics that the position of the stars in the heavens really can predict the future of every person on this planet. Joseph Mercola didn't build his $100 million online supplement empire by bogging himself down trying to convert science enthusiasts into anti-vaxxers.

What charlatans do is something different. They embody a dream, knowing that by doing so publicly, they will attract people who are already of a mind to agree with them. They don't have to persuade, because they address themselves exclusively to those who are already persuaded the moment they come through the door.

Baba Ramdev *knows* millions of Hindus are primed to believe yoga is the road to perfect health and happiness. He doesn't need to persuade them of anything to get them to trust him; he just has to reflect their dream back to them.

Joseph Mercola knows that millions of Americans are leery of scientific medicine and primed to believe Big Pharma is part of a vast conspiracy against them. He doesn't need to persuade anyone of this; he just has to broadcast a set of beliefs and let the people who already agree with him come forward, let them select themselves as his victims.

Mehmet Aydın, who allegedly stole millions through his brazen Farm Bank video game cum get-rich-quick scam, knew millions of patriotic Turks were nostalgic for the rural lifestyles their grandparents had lived and eager to support their country's farmers. He didn't have to persuade Turks to share those feelings; he knew those people were out there and that the way to get their trust was to mirror their values back to them.

Once charlatans have connected with their marks' dreams, they earn their trust without having to *persuade* them of anything at all. So, it's not that charlatans' victims are gullible, exactly. It's not that they are easy to persuade. It's that they're easy to identify. And once identified, they're easy to exploit simply by parroting their preexisting beliefs back to them.

Convincing someone to abandon a preexisting belief in favor of a new one is extraordinarily hard and vanishingly rare. But getting people to double down on what they are *already* convinced is true is the easiest thing in the world.

That initial rush of identification you feel when you hear someone champion your dreams is powerful, effortless, automatic. As we saw in the first chapter, it is a result of what Nobel Prize–winning psychologist Daniel Kahneman described as *fast thinking*—an unconscious, automatic reaction, driven by intuition that comes to your mind before you've had the time to formulate a rational thought.[7] To question such a conclusion requires *slow thinking*: the cumbersome, effortful deployment of our critical thinking abilities. Alas, slow thinking is hard work, and thousands of laboratory experiments show conclusively that people avoid it if they can. Except, when you are faced with a charlatan, relying solely on fast thinking can bring disastrous consequences.

Ensnared by the charlatan's charm, followers always seem to find it easier to go just one tiny step farther down the path the charlatan is guiding them on than to turn all the way back to the beginning, questioning the entire path they have followed. With each small step, they're asked to extend what they already believe just that little bit further. Each time, they think fast—going along to get along—rather than face the tremendous effort involved in thinking slowly and the pain of reconsidering a long line of terrible mistakes.

This process of drawing victims deeper into the charlatan's reality is gradual. No single step feels like a big leap. Compounded over time, the results of so many mistakes can be dramatic. This process of slowly reeling in a mark accounts for why perfectly nice, educated, reasonable people come to believe extremely bizarre things.

Nobody, of course, would sign up to take dating advice from some lunatic who claims to be the Messiah from day one. Yet by drawing their followers in little by little, Jeff and Shaleia Ayan managed to convince their marks that Jeff was, quite literally, Jesus Christ. This gradual process explains why otherwise perfectly well-adjusted American conservatives can come to believe Democrats participate in the ritual torture and murder of innocent children to extend their own lives, and why otherwise unexceptionable Hindus can come to expect that expelling air rhythmically from their lungs will cure AIDS.

None of them had to be persuaded that these things were true. They just trusted someone who gave voice to their dreams, and that someone abused that trust.

Conviction without the need for persuasion also explains how charlatans manage to prevent their followers from expressing or acting on any doubts they might have. Nearly all the charlatans in this book took positive steps to stigmatize doubters, to define them as the enemy that good, convinced followers should shun, if not hate. Those who don't share your dreams are the "other"—the bad guys, outsiders, the "they" who don't get it. The enemy.

Naysayers are often attacked with a heavy hand. For evangelical charlatans like Edir Macedo and Kenneth Copeland, those who question them are *literally* Satan, or at least satanically possessed. Ironically, some New Age spiritual leaders, such as Bentinho Massaro, also teach that those who question them must be possessed by demons. In the QAnon world, they're pedophiles and child torturers. To Regina Jackson and Saira Rao, the women behind Race2Dinner, those who would question their approach to radical anti-racism can only be racists and white supremacists. Horrible people; the very worst. To follow these charlatans is to claim your identity as a good person, willing to fight the forces of evil that naysaying represents. In each of these cases, charlatans use victims' fear of being identified with that reviled "they" to keep control over their marks.

In these pages, we have repeatedly seen how closely victims come to identify with the charlatans who exploit them. This identification becomes a powerful new defense mechanism binding victims to them and extending their exploitation. For marks, rethinking their commitment to their charlatans becomes not just a question of rethinking what they've been told, but of shifting their allegiance, coming to trust a group that's been demonized, sometimes literally. That's a tall order. It's always easier to keep believing in a group you've learned to identify with than to shift your allegiance to those you've come to see as the enemy.

We are not, of course, at risk from *every* charlatan. If twenty-three of the twenty-four cases we've looked at struck you as ludicrous, that's normal. Charlatans don't cast a net; they cast a line. They choose a message the way an angler chooses a fly: not to attract any fish, but to attract a specific kind of fish.

Charlatans' indifference to persuasion also explains why their message so often seems absurd to everyone outside their target group. Charlatans can't make you believe what you don't already believe, so they don't try. A message laser focused on potential marks will always sound ludicrous to those who aren't marks.

And so, charlatans who snooker *other* people always strike you as laughable, silly. Their victims strike you as ridiculously gullible and rather pathetic.

Paradoxically, that doesn't in any way make you safe from charlatans yourself. Just the opposite; it lures you into a false sense of security. However good you may be at spotting the mistakes other people make when their dreams are reflected back to them, you have your own dreams. Your fast-thinking circuits are just as ready to jump to conclusions as theirs, and you're just as unwilling to subject your dreams to critical scrutiny as they are. You think you're immune—you've just read a whole book about it! You delude yourself.

You're not immune.

No one is.

What Can Be Done?

What can be done? First, we must treat the subject with a dose of humility. Charlatans have plagued humanity for thousands of years and will probably continue to plague us for a thousand more. This is not a problem that can be fixed. It can, though, be managed such that the damage it inflicts can be contained.

One avenue is legal. Charlatans are not, first and foremost, criminals, and yet they often do break the law. Many of the charlatans in these pages committed fraud of some kind, and in cases where they have been brought to account, it's most often by prosecutors pursuing charges of fraud and conspiracy to defraud.

Ensuring that white-collar crime investigators are properly resourced and incentivized to crack down on charlatans' frauds is, therefore, the first line of defense against them. To the extent that charlatans commit crimes, fighting charlatanism means fighting crime, pure and simple.

This is the beginning of a response, and often a useful one, but it's obviously far from complete. Law enforcement approaches tend to become relevant mostly in cases of obvious, over-the-top financial abuse. Ponzi schemes, in particular, tend to end up in prosecution simply because of the brutal arithmetic of exponential growth: once they run out of new victims to recruit, they tend to collapse, and when they do, it becomes very obvious who's been cheated.

But these Ponzi-style dynamics are not what we see in many of the cases we've dealt with. In many cases, charlatans go to great lengths to enlist their victims' consent—indeed, their enthusiastic collaboration—in their victimization. This can create a difficult conundrum for law enforcement.

The viewers of Dr. Mehmet Oz's blockbuster television show offering medical advice were surely taken for fools many times during the years the show was on the air. Collectively, they will have wasted millions of dollars on worthless cures and gadgets hyped through the show. But few of them seem to be aggrieved, or even to realize that they were taken for a ride. His over-the-top claims generated huge audiences that brought in massive advertising revenues. It's clear there was something manipulative about and just plain wrong with his show, but whatever that wrong thing was, it probably didn't meet the legal definitions of fraud or conspiracy.

If the law is only a very partial answer to the question of how to defend victims, what other avenues are open?

One obvious pressure point is the tech giants: Google, Facebook, TikTok, and X are some of the most important players in modern charlatans' recruitment strategies, and their parent companies must be pressured to introduce friction into those recruitment strategies. This, again, is complex: to these companies, charlatans aren't enemies; they are lucrative customers. Yet because these platforms are so central to the process of signing up new marks, they can no longer shirk their responsibilities in this regard.

The "how" is tricky.

Deception is at the heart of the charlatan's business model, and those deceptions take considerable resources to unearth. Tech giants will always resist devoting resources to discrediting the claims of their clients: that is natural. It is tempting to want to hold tech companies liable for the harm done to their users by the charlatans their algorithms serve up to them, but this is difficult to do well in practice. Tech giants will face difficult problems both with false positives (wrongly labeling legitimate groups as possible charlatans and limiting the spread of their content) and false negatives (wrongly failing to label charlatans' content as dangerous).

A lot of attention recently has been devoted to "prebunking"—trying to warn victims that they're about to be exposed to a manipulative message before they're exposed to it. Google, for instance, has experimented with including prebunking messages in its results for especially fraught searches.[8]

The exact mechanics of this are complex. For instance, attempts to prebunk anti-vaccine messages often feature doctors and scientists reassuring audiences about the safety and efficacy of vaccines. As we have seen, though, this can backfire, as vaccine-hesitant audiences are often primed to believe the worst about doctors and scientists. Indeed, almost all anti-vax messaging is designed specifically to win over those who, for whatever reason, don't trust the mainstream medical profession. To be effective, prebunking needs to be just as tuned in to the cultural cues of the at-risk audience as charlatans themselves are. Too often, we fear, this will not be the case.

Governments and tech giants both have a role to play in introducing friction into charlatans' schemes, but they're limited roles. The more important lines of defense come closer to the individual.

In many of the cases we've looked at, what the victims really could have used is a second opinion: a reality check from a reliable outsider able to warn them they were at risk of being scammed. Social isolation, lack of access to those reliable reality checks, looks very much like a hidden risk factor for victimization. No one is better positioned to warn potential victims away from dangerous charlatans than those nearest and dearest to them. Friends, colleagues, coworkers, classmates, and family members may be the people best positioned to protect those close to them from victimization.

People need to look out for one another and learn to intervene, tactfully, at the earliest sign that someone is coming under the sway of a charlatan. Training people to spot the signs of victimization and intervene with their loved ones to interrupt the process may be one of the most promising avenues for preventing victimization by charlatans.

But these answers are partial. In the end, the only one who can really protect you from a charlatan is you.

It's natural to assume it is governments' job to protect us from charlatans. Or maybe it's the courts, or Google and Facebook, or even our friends and family. We are skeptical.

The ultimate line of defense, the battleground where it's all to play for, is inside each and every one of us.

That's why the oldest, most stereotypical advice about charlatans is still the best: if it sounds too good to be true, it probably is.

Everyone has heard that old chestnut, and yet people keep falling for charlatans' tricks. Why is that? Why is the lure of charlatans so difficult to resist? Why do things that sound good to us sound *so* good? Why are they so powerful that we'll set our lives on fire to pursue them?

When we're urged to reflect that something is "too good to be true," we're being urged to use slow thinking, to engage our critical thinking abilities and subject the claim in front of us to scrutiny.

Charlatans know the power our dreams have over us. That is why they go to great pains to make sure they are speaking to us in the language of our dreams. Few of us are willing or able to "think slow," to think genuinely critically, about the things that, deep down, we feel *must* be true, because those are the kinds of beliefs that *define* us. Connect with someone's dreams and you connect with *them*.

Charlatans know this, and they exploit it ruthlessly.

To protect yourself from a charlatan, to actually spot the thing that's "too good to be true," you have to keep just a bit of distance between *your dreams* and *who you are*—that tiny bit of critical distance between what *feels true* and what *you can trust*.

This is incredibly difficult. It is asking us to run against the grain of HumanOS—doing the effortful, slow thinking it takes to seek to falsify our beliefs, rather than looking for reasons to confirm them. It's asking us to use reason not only to come up with arguments to support our intuition but also to have critical insight into them. It's asking us to remember that the people we look up to can be wrong, and we shouldn't interpret the fact that our peers believe a thing as reason to believe it ourselves.

None of this is easy. Hearing someone championing our dreams and keeping our guard up anyway will never come naturally.

We know it's a big request. Of anyone. Young or old, rich or poor, Black, brown, or white. Most of us can't manage it—not consistently, anyway. When times are tough, when we are isolated or stressed or depressed, when we are vulnerable, we lapse. We grab onto the beliefs we *need* to be true if the world is to make any sense to us, the beliefs our dreams are built on. And that's when they get us.

In today's world, the charlatans out to prey on us at that moment are everywhere: digital, viral, scalable, and global. To protect ourselves from them, to keep our ability to notice when something really is too good to be true, we need to keep a measure of healthy skepticism pointed at our own dreams.

We need to do this at all times. That's incredibly hard. But it's an indispensable survival skill for the twenty-first century.

Three Ideas to Take Away

So far, you've come on a wild ride with us through some of the seedier parts of the modern attention economy. What we have learned has often been ugly, but we hope it will also prove useful. What should you take away from this book?

Everybody Is at Risk from Charlatans

Charlatans target vulnerabilities written deep into HumanOS, turning features of the way we think into weapons against us. Pretty much everyone prefers to have their ideas confirmed than refuted. All of us actively look for reasons to believe in our most cherished beliefs and ignore reasons to doubt them. Everyone finds it uncomfortable to question their dreams. And everyone is of a mind to follow the herd, assuming that if trusted people believe something, it must be right. These biases are universal and inescapable, products of fast thinking that take place before we're even aware of it. This is why, even though many charlatans will strike you as ludicrous, the charlatans who address themselves to you in particular will always be tricky to spot.

Charlatans Are a Threat in Every Aspect of Life

Back when charlatans relied on their voices from the top of a soapbox, they had to limit themselves to a few tried-and-true paths. Most of them specialized in quack medicines and get-rich-quick schemes, because the dreams of health and wealth are so widespread. Today, technology allows charlatans to target much narrower niches. As a result, charlatanry has exploded across the spectrum of human activity. Once, having a quirky dream protected you from exploitation. No more. New charlatans arise all the time, aiming at dreams as niche as Turkish city dwellers' nostalgia for rural living, or the quest for your one, unique "twin flame" for love. With algorithms becoming ever more sophisticated at matching media consumers to the thing they most long to hear, the scope for charlatanry continues to expand.

Technology Tips the Scales in Charlatans' Favor

Today's charlatans push grifts that are digital, viral, scalable, and potentially even global. They take in the world's most sophisticated investors as well as the voters of the most advanced democracies. They can lay waste to a once-prosperous nation's economy, as they did in Britain, and take on even the world's most powerful corporations, as Baba Ramdev has done in India. Using the increasingly sophisticated tools the internet makes available for matching people with their interests, their impact is hugely magnified. And as charlatans begin to experiment with the potential that artificial intelligence has for expanding their reach even further, all bets are off.

One thing we're sure of: the upcoming cohort of AI-enabled charlatans can only be that much more destructive than the last.

This may all feel daunting, but it ought not to. Becoming cognizant of the challenge in front of us is always the first step in rising to it. We can't help carrying with us the vulnerabilities that are built into HumanOS, but we can turn our understanding of those vulnerabilities into a shield to protect us.

This is vital work because our dreams are who we are: to protect them is to defend our truest selves.

Acknowledgments

A book like this one could not have been written without the dogged reporting of the journalists and researchers all around the world who uncovered the facts behind the stories of each of our charlatans. Our savvy sherpas are recognized throughout the text as well as in the notes at the end of the book. Some of them prefer to remain anonymous and we, of course, have honored their wishes.

This book is much better than what it would have been without the generous contributions of colleagues and friends who read earlier drafts of the manuscript and gave us invaluable comments and suggestions. We are immensely grateful to Anne Applebaum, Marie Arana, Bill Bradley, Gustavo Coronel, David Frum, James Gibney, Adan Grant, Jessica Mathews, Maurizio Molinari, Tom Rachman, Jose Juan Ruiz, Brian Winter, Dan Yergin, Fareed Zakaria, and Robert Zoellick.

We are indebted especially to Lara Heimert, the president and publisher of Basic Books, who has offered her enthusiastic support for this project since its inception. Thank you, Lara! An excellent team of professionals at Basic Books made things happen speedily and effectively. Our thanks to Jessica Breem, Angie Messina, and their teams. We are also grateful to Pilar Reyes and Miguel Aguilar, our publishers in the Spanish-speaking world.

Over the almost four years that it took us to do the research and writing, we counted on the support of two extraordinary assistants: Angie Estevez and Andrea Guerra. Our thanks to them. We are indebted to Sena Deniz Töreli for helping us translate some of Farm Bank's Turkish material.

Notes

Preface

1. Grete De Francesco, *The Power of the Charlatan* (New Haven, CT: Yale University Press, 1939).

2. Hillary Rodham Clinton, "The Weaponization of Loneliness," *Atlantic*, August 7, 2023, www.theatlantic.com/ideas/archive/2023/08/hillary-clinton-essay-loneliness-epidemic/674921.

3. Vivek H. Murthy, "Our Epidemic of Loneliness and Isolation: The U.S. Surgeon General's Advisory on the Healing Effects of Social Connection and Community," U.S. Department of Health and Human Services, accessed October 22, 2024, www.hhs.gov/sites/default/files/surgeon-general-social-connection-advisory.pdf.

4. Yuval Noah Harari, "What Happens When the Bots Compete for Your Love?," *New York Times*, September 4, 2024, www.nytimes.com/2024/09/04/opinion/yuval-harari-ai-democracy.html.

5. Shoshana Zuboff, *The Age of Surveillance Capitalism: The Fight for a Human Future at the New Frontier of Power* (New York: PublicAffairs, 2019).

Chapter 1. Hacking HumanOS

1. P. C. Wason, "On the Failure to Eliminate Hypotheses in a Conceptual Task," *Quarterly Journal of Experimental Psychology* 12, no. 3 (1960): 129–140, https://doi.org/10.1080/17470216008416717.

2. Karl Raimund Popper, *The Logic of Scientific Discovery* (London: Routledge, 2002).

3. Raymond S. Nickerson, "Confirmation Bias: A Ubiquitous Phenomenon in Many Guises," *Review of General Psychology* 2, no. 2 (1998): 177.

4. Daniel Kahneman, *Thinking, Fast and Slow* (New York: Farrar, Straus and Giroux, 2013).

5. Tamas Madl, Bernard J. Baars, and Stan Franklin, "The Timing of the Cognitive Cycle," *PLOS One* 6, no. 4 (2011): e14803.

6. Alleen Oeberst and Roland Imhoff, "Toward Parsimony in Bias Research: A Proposed Common Framework of Belief-Consistent Information Processing for a Set of Biases," *Perspectives on Psychological Science* 18, no. 6 (2023), https://doi.org/10.1177/17456916221148147.

7. Patrick W. Kraft, Milton Lodge, and Charles S. Taber, "Why People 'Don't Trust the Evidence': Motivated Reasoning and Scientific Beliefs," *Annals of the American Academy of Political and Social Science* 658, no. 1 (2015), https://doi.org/10.1177/0002716214554758.

8. Jonathan Haidt, *The Righteous Mind: Why Good People Are Divided by Politics and Religion* (New York: Knopf Doubleday, 2013).

9. Thomas J. Leeper and Kevin J. Mullinix, "Motivated Reasoning," Political Science, Oxford Bibliographies, last modified February 22, 2018, www.oxfordbibliographies.com/display/document/obo-9780199756223/obo-9780199756223-0237.xml.

10. Leeper and Mullinix, "Motivated Reasoning."

11. Nicholas Epley and Thomas Gilovich, "The Mechanics of Motivated Reasoning," *Journal of Economic Perspectives* 30, no. 3 (Summer 2016): 133–140.

12. Epley and Gilovich, "Mechanics of Motivated Reasoning."

13. Charles G. Lord, Lee Ross, and Mark Lepper, "Biased Assimilation and Attitude Polarization: The Effects of Prior Theories on Subsequently Considered Evidence," *Journal of Personality and Social Psychology* 37, no. 11 (1979): 2098–2109, https://doi.org/10.1037/0022-3514.37.11.2098.

14. Briony Swire-Thompson et al., "The Backfire Effect After Correcting Misinformation Is Strongly Associated with Reliability," *Journal of Experimental Psychology: General* 151, no. 7 (2022): 1655–1665, https://doi.org/10.1037/xge0001131.

15. Oliver James and Gregg G. Van Ryzin, "Motivated Reasoning About Public Performance: An Experimental Study of How Citizens Judge the Affordable Care Act," *Journal of Public Administration Research and Theory* 27, no. 1 (2017): 197–209, https://doi.org/10.1093/jopart/muw049.

16. Martin Baekgaard et al., "The Role of Evidence in Politics: Motivated Reasoning and Persuasion Among Politicians," *British Journal of Political Science*, August 18, 2017, Cambridge University Press, www.cambridge.org/core/journals/british-journal-of-political-science/article/role-of-evidence-in-politics-motivated-reasoning-and-persuasion-among-politicians/6813A080C058E1BB4920661FF60BED6F.

17. Stanley Milgram, Leonard Bickman, and Lawrence Berkowitz, "Note on the Drawing Power of Crowds of Different Size," *Journal of Personality and Social Psychology* 13, no. 1 (1969): 79–82, https://doi.org/10.1037/h0028070.

18. Noah J. Goldstein, Robert B. Cialdini, and Vladas Griskevicius, "A Room with a Viewpoint: Using Social Norms to Motivate Environmental Conservation in Hotels," *Journal of Consumer Research* 35, no. 3 (2008): 472–482, https://doi.org/10.1086/586910.

19. Alan Gerber, Donald Green, and Christopher Larimer, "Social Pressure and Voter Turnout in the United States," The Abdul Latif Jameel Poverty Action Lab, 2006, www.povertyactionlab.org/evaluation/social-pressure-and-voter-turnout-united-states.

20. Robert B. Cialdini et al., "Managing Social Norms for Persuasive Impact," *Social Influence* 1, no. 1 (2006): 3–15, https://doi.org/10.1080/15534510500181459.

Chapter 2. The Dark Side of Entrepreneurship

1. Paul Harrison and Serter Akyol, "Farm Bank: Founder Accused of Defrauding Gamers," BBC, March 16, 2018, www.bbc.com/news/blogs-trending-43430363.

2. Mehmet Aydın, "Çiftlikbank Mehmet Aydın Rap," Güvercin Dünyası Hünkari, posted March 14, 2018, YouTube video, www.youtube.com/watch?v=boR2vn5zfyU.

3. Paul Benjamin Osterlund, "Fraud on the Farm: How a Baby-Faced CEO Turned a FarmVille Clone into a Massive Ponzi Scheme," Rest of World, July 20, 2021, https://restofworld.org/2021/farmbank-turkey-scam-jail-time.

4. "Çiftlik Bank ın Yayınladığı tüm reklam filmleri," Vine official, posted March 22, 2018, YouTube video, www.youtube.com/watch?v=gFgbHY5h-A8&t=228s, translation courtesy of Sena Deniz Töreli.

5. Osterlund, "Fraud on the Farm."

6. "Police Start to Question Founder of Çiftlik Bank," *Hürriyet Daily News* (Istanbul), July 6, 2021, www.hurriyetdailynews.com/police-start-to-question-founder-of-ciftlik-bank-166081; Emre İlkan Saklıca, "Fotoğrafın Çiftlik Bank'ın kurucusu Mehmet Aydın'ın ölümünü gösterdiği iddiası," Teyit, December 17, 2019, https://teyit.org/analiz/fotografin-ciftlik-bankin-kurucusu-mehmet-aydinin-olumunu-gosterdigi-iddiasi.

7. Osterlund, "Fraud on the Farm."

8. "Çiftlik Bank CEO'su Mehmet Aydın Ferrari almış," Ulusal Kanal, posted March 21, 2018, YouTube video, www.youtube.com/watch?v=hLCkkp4Ho-k.

9. Osterlund, "Fraud on the Farm."

10. Daily Sabah with Agencies, "Turkish 'Farm Bank' Ponzi Founder Gets over 45,370 Years in Prison," *Daily Sabah*, February 3, 2025, www.dailysabah.com/business/economy/turkish-farm-bank-ponzi-founder-gets-over-45370-years-in-prison.

11. FüL (@Ful2live), "Grilled eggplant, roasted red pepper, arugula, fresh mozzarella, grated Parmesan, baguette. Calories: 474," X, April 10, 2011, 3:54 p.m., https://x.com/Ful2live/status/120980147598929920; Ari Bendersky, "FÜL Opening Saturday to Offer Healthy Food Options," Eater Chicago, July 22, 2011, https://chicago.eater.com/2011/7/22/6667599/ful-opening-saturday-to-offer-healthy-food-options.

12. Anita Busch, "1inMM Prods. Raises $5M in Funds for Genre Films," *Deadline*, August 21, 2017, https://deadline.com/2017/08/1inmm-5-million-film-fund-genre-movies-1202153140.

13. Jennie Punter, "SXSW: 1inMM, Alebrije Team to Form One Key Entertainment," *Variety*, March 7, 2013, https://variety.com/2013/film/markets-festivals/sxsw-1inmm-alebrije-team-to-form-one-key-entertainment-1200005507.

14. *Shifter*, directed by Diego Hallivis (1inMM Productions, 2014), accessed October 22, 2024, www.imdb.com/title/tt3271174.

15. Evan Osnos, "Master of Make-Believe," Annals of Crime, *New Yorker*, May 27, 2024, www.newyorker.com/magazine/2024/06/03/master-of-make-believe.

16. Edward Helmore, "Hollywood Grifter: The Actor Who Took Tinseltown for a Ponzi Scheme Ride," *Guardian* (US edition), October 11, 2021, www.theguardian.com/money/2021/oct/10/hollywood-ponzi-scheme-zachary-horwitz-zach-avery; Sarah Hagi and Scaachi Koul, "The Talented Mr. Avery," January 16, 2023, in *Scamfluencers*, produced by Bryan Taylor White, podcast, https://wondery.com/shows/scamfluencers/episode/10539-encore-the-hollywood-ponzi-scheme-the-talented-mr-avery.

17. Osnos, "Master of Make-Believe."

18. Hagi and Koul, "Talented Mr. Avery."

19. *Last Moment of Clarity*, directed by Colin Krisel and James Krisel, featuring Samara Weaving, Carly Chaikin, and Zach Avery (Metalwork Pictures, Rogue Black, 2020), accessed October 22, 2024, www.imdb.com/title/tt1929297.

20. Osnos, "Master of Make-Believe."

21. Leslie Felperin and Stuart Murdoch, "Last Moment of Clarity Review—Neo-Noir in Double Trouble," *Guardian* (US edition), March 2, 2021, www.theguardian.com/film/2021/mar/02/last-moment-of-clarity-review-neo-noir-brian-cox-udo-kier.

22. Osnos, "Master of Make-Believe."

23. Helmore, "Hollywood Grifter."

24. Rob McLean, "Hollywood Actor Sentenced to 20 Years for Multimillion-Dollar Ponzi Scheme," CNN, February 14, 2022, https://edition.cnn.com/2022/02/14/media/ponzi-scheme-zachary-horwitz-sentenced/index.html.

25. Osnos, "Master of Make-Believe."

26. Obama White House, "A New Beginning: Presidential Summit on Entrepreneurship Participant Bios," National Archives, accessed October 22, 2024, https://obamawhitehouse.archives.gov/sites/default/files/rss_viewer/entrepreneurship_summit_participant_bios.pdf.

27. Landon Thomas Jr., "Leading Private Equity Firm Accused of Misusing Funds," *New York Times*, February 2, 2018, www.nytimes.com/2018/02/02/business/abraaj-naqvi-world-bank.html.

28. Simon Clark and Will Louch, *The Key Man: How the Global Elite Was Duped by a Capitalist Fairy Tale* (New York: Harper Business, 2021).

29. Fadi Ghandour, "How I Did It: The CEO of Aramex on Turning a Failed Sale into a Huge Opportunity," *Harvard Business Review*, March 2011, https://hbr.org/2011/03/how-i-did-it-the-ceo-of-aramex-on-turning-a-failed-sale-into-a-huge-opportunity.

30. Elizabeth MacBride, "The Story Behind Abraaj Group's Stunning Rise in Global Private Equity," *Forbes*, November 4, 2015, www.forbes.com/sites/elizabethmacbride/2015/11/04/the-story-behind-abraajs-stunning-rise; Sara Hamdan, "Mideast Private Equity Pioneer Looks Beyond the Unrest," *New York Times*, April 27, 2011, https://archive.nytimes.com/dealbook.nytimes.com/2011/04/27/mideast-private-equity-pioneer-looks-beyond-the-unrest.

31. Josh Lerner, Asim Ijaz Khwaja, and Ann Leamon, "Abraaj Capital and the Karachi Electric Supply Company," Harvard Business School Strategy Unit case no. 812-019, February 1, 2012, https://hbsp.harvard.edu/product/812019-PDF-ENG.

32. Clark and Louch, *The Key Man*.

33. "List of Abraaj Group's 16 Acquisitions," Crunchbase, accessed October 22, 2024, www.crunchbase.com/search/acquisitions/field/organizations/num_acquisitions/abraaj-capital.

34. Clark and Louch, *The Key Man*.

35. Clark and Louch, chap. 8.

36. Simon Clark, "The Strange Case of the Cricket Match That Helped Fund Imran Khan's Political Rise," *Financial Times*, July 28, 2022, www.ft.com/content/de29dd83-8fa9-40a2-aff6-5996f1557d0d.

37. Clark and Louch, *The Key Man*.

38. The Abraaj Group, "The Abraaj Group Appoints Kito de Boer as Managing Partner," press release, September 18, 2017, www.zawya.com/en/press-release/the-abraaj-group-appoints-kito-de-boer-as-managing-partner-g8tpzlad.

39. Clark and Louch, *The Key Man*.

40. Clark and Louch.

41. "Case Studies," AlixPartners, accessed October 22, 2024, www.alixpartners.com/what-we-do/case-studies.

42. Clark and Louch, *The Key Man*.

43. *Billion Dollar Downfall: The Dealmaker*, directed by Victoria James, aired January 11, 2023, on BBC Two, www.bbc.co.uk/programmes/m001h1nd.

44. Clark and Louch, *The Key Man*, chap. 10.

45. Clark and Louch, *The Key Man*.

46. *Billion Dollar Downfall*.

47. Clark and Louch, *The Key Man*.

48. Clark and Louch.

49. William Louch, Ed Ballard, and Simon Clark, "Abraaj Investors Hire Auditor to Trace Money," *Wall Street Journal*, February 2, 2018, www.wsj.com/articles/abraaj-investors-hire-auditor-to-trace-money-1517598630.

50. Adveith Nair and Archana Narayanan, "Abraaj's Naqvi Handed $136 Million Fine over Firm's Collapse," *Bloomberg*, January 28, 2022, www.bloomberg.com/news/articles/2022-01-27/abraaj-s-naqvi-handed-136-million-fine-over-firm-s-collapse.

51. Simon Clark, "Interpol Foundation Suspends Embattled Founder of Private-Equity Firm," *Wall Street Journal*, updated July 5, 2018, www.wsj.com/articles/interpol-foundation-suspends-embattled-founder-of-private-equity-firm-1530791106.

Chapter 3. Star Power: The World's Oldest Grift

1. *Mucho Mucho Amor: The Legend of Walter Mercado*, directed by Cristina Constantini and Kareem Tabsch, starring Walter Mercado and featuring Lin-Manuel Miranda (Netflix, 2020).

2. Taylor Orth, "One in Four Americans Say They Believe in Astrology," YouGov, April 26, 2022, https://today.yougov.com/entertainment/articles/42292-one-four-americans-say-they-believe-astrology.

3. Research Co., "One-in-Five Canadians Currently Pay Attention to Astrology," press release, January 1, 2020, https://researchco.ca/wp-content/uploads/2019/12/Release_Astrology_CAN_01Jan2020.pdf.

4. "Europeans, Science and Technology," Eurobarometer, December 2001, https://europa.eu/eurobarometer/surveys/detail/209.

5. Centro de Estudios e Investigaciones Laborales, "Segunda Encuesta Nacional Sobre Creencias y Actitudes Religiosas en Argentina," Sociedad y Religión en Movimiento, CONICET-CEIL, 2019, accessed October 22, 2024, www.bahia.gob.ar/wp-content/uploads/2021/12/Segunda-Encuesta-Nacional-CEIL-CONICET-2019.pdf.

6. William Jordan, "8% of Britons Believe Horoscopes Can Predict the Future," YouGov, July 3, 2015, https://yougov.co.uk/politics/articles/12731-8-of-Britons-believe-horoscopes-predict-the-future.

7. "Voyance, sorcellerie, astrologie . . . La croyance dans les parasciences au plus fort," L'Express, updated December 3, 2020, www.lexpress.fr/sciences-sante/sciences/voyance-sorcellerie-astrologie-la-croyance-dans-les-parasciences-au-plus-fort_2139898.html.

8. Stephanie Pappas, "New Zodiac Signs 2011: Why Astrology Is Even Sillier Than We Thought," *Christian Science Monitor*, January 13, 2011, www.csmonitor.com/Science/2011/0113/New-zodiac-signs-2011-Why-astrology-is-even-sillier-than-we-thought.

9. Shawn Carlson, "A Double-Blind Test of Astrology," *Nature* 318 (1985): 419–425.

10. William Hunter, "Bad News for Horoscope Readers! Astrology Doesn't Work, Scientists Say," *Daily Mail*, August 20, 2024, www.msn.com/en-ae/news/other/bad-news-for-horoscope-readers-astrology-doesnt-work-scientists-say/ar-AA1p6gnu.

11. Walter Mercado, "Comerciales mexicanos: Walter Mercado 2003," ric rdz alva, posted November 14, 2018, YouTube video, www.youtube.com/watch?v=spEUXDatC2o.

12. Walter Mercado, "Walter Mercado Comercial de TV YouTube," Guilherme Maia, posted December 27, 2016, YouTube video, www.youtube.com/watch?v=ovmLL_Q6ipI&t=4s.

13. "Suit Against Astrologist Is Granted Class Status," *Tampa Bay Times*, December 4, 1999, www.tampabay.com/archive/1999/12/04/suit-against-astrologist-is-granted-class-status.

14. Walter Mercado Salinas Astromundo Inc. v. BART Enterprises International LTD, 1st Cir. R. 32.1.0 (2011), https://caselaw.findlaw.com/court/us-1st-circuit/1589009.html.

15. Jennifer Robertson, "Hemato-Nationalism: The Past, Present, and Future of 'Japanese Blood,'" *Medical Anthropology* 31, no. 2 (2012): 93–112, https://doi.org/10.1080/01459740.2011.624957.

16. Waka Kanda and Shinden Tetsugu, *The Instruction Manual for Blood Type of Man* (Tokyo: Asa Publishing, 2013).

17. Toshitaka Nomi and Alexander Besher, *You Are Your Blood Type: The Biochemical Key to Unlocking the Secrets of Your Personality* (New York: Pocket Books, 1988).

18. Amelia Fruzzetti, "Early Nintendo DS Prototype Contained Blood Type Setting, Preservationists Find," *Nintendo Wire*, December 27, 2022, https://nintendowire.com/news/2022/12/27/early-nintendo-ds-prototype-contained-blood-type-setting-preservationists-find.

19. Jake Adelstein and Mari Yamamoto, "Un-True Blood: Japan's Weird Taste for Discrimination Against 'Type Bs,'" *Daily Beast*, May 29, 2017, www.thedailybeast.com/un-true-blood-japans-weird-taste-for-discrimination-against-type-bs.

20. Shigeyuki Yamaoka, "How Television Programs Amplify Blood Type Discrimination," *Psychological World / Japanese Psychological Association* 52 (January 2011), 5–8, https://psych.or.jp/wp-content/uploads/old/52-5.pdf.

21. "This Zodiac Sign Voted Most Undateable by Americans Across the Nation—Digitalhub US," SWNS Digital, September 6, 2021, https://swnsdigital.com/us/2021/02/this-zodiac-sign-voted-most-undateable-by-americans-across-the-nation.

22. Jessica Weisberg, "Joan Quigley, Ronald Reagan's Guide to the Stars," *Paris Review*, June 4, 2018, www.theparisreview.org/blog/2018/06/04/joan-quigley-ronald-reagans-guide-to-the-stars.

23. Mary Kay Linge, "How Ronald Reagan's Wife Nancy Let Her Astrologer Control the Presidency," *New York Post*, October 18, 2021, https://nypost.com/article/ronald-reagans-wife-nancy-astrologer-joan-quigley.

24. Michael Wilson, "At the Trial of a Psychic, It's Awkward for Her Clients," *New York Times*, October 4, 2013, www.nytimes.com/2013/10/05/nyregion/at-the-trial-of-a-psychic-its-awkward-for-her-clients.html.

25. Michael Wilson, "Fortuneteller in Manhattan Is Sentenced to 5 to 15 Years in Prison," *New York Times*, November 14, 2013, www.nytimes.com/2013/11/15/nyregion/5-to-15-year-prison-sentence-for-manhattan-fortuneteller.html.

26. "'Psychic' Gets Vision of Prison," *Martha's Vineyard Times*, January 17, 2018, www.mvtimes.com/2018/01/17/psychic-gets-vision-prison.

27. Ariana Igneri, "Meet the Woman Bringing Social Justice to Astrology," *Rolling Stone*, June 1, 2018, www.rollingstone.com/culture/culture-features/meet-the-woman-bringing-social-justice-to-astrology-629153.

28. The Social, "Oprah Magazine's Resident Astrologer Gives Us a Lesson in Astrology," Facebook video, January 14, 2020, www.facebook.com/watch/?v=600268550518392.

29. *CHANI*, v. 2.2.1 (Chani Nicholas Incorporated, 2021), accessed December 28, 2024.

30. *CHANI*, v. 2.2.1.

31. Bertram R. Forer, "The Fallacy of Personal Validation: A Classroom Demonstration of Gullibility," *Journal of Abnormal and Social Psychology* 44, no. 1 (1949): 118–123, https://doi.org/10.1037/h0059240. Copyright ©1949, American Psychological Association; all content is in the public domain.

32. "About Chani," CHANI, accessed January 7, 2025, https://chaninicholas.com/about-chani-nicholas.

33. *CHANI*, Ratings and Reviews, App Store (Apple Inc.), accessed June 23, 2023.

34. Tonya Mosley and Cristina Kim, "Finding Meaning in the Stars: Astrologer Chani Nicholas on Why More People Are Turning to Their Horoscopes," WBUR, December 31, 2019, www.wbur.org/hereandnow/2019/12/31/astrologer-chani-nicholas-self-acceptance.

35. Natalie Kitroeff, "Astrologer Chani Nicholas Doesn't Care If You Approve of Her," *Los Angeles Times*, January 1, 2017, www.latimes.com/business/la-fi-himi-astrologer-chani-nicholas-20170101-story.html.

Chapter 4. Megachurches and Megabucks: Turning God into Mammon

1. Matt. 6:24 (English Standard Version).

2. Leah MarieAnn Klett, "Prosperity Gospel Is a 'Damning Heresy That Paves the Road to Hell,' Says Benny Hinn's Nephew," *Christian Today*, December 11, 2018, www.christiantoday.com/article/prosperity-gospel-is-a-damning-heresy-that-paves-the-road-to-hell-says-benny-hinns-nephew/131184.htm.

3. M. L. Shettle Jr., *United States Marine Corps Air Stations of World War II* (Schaertel Publishing, 2001).

4. Kenneth Copeland, "01 Kenneth Copeland Lasciviousness," Symbools, posted March 2, 2021, YouTube video, www.youtube.com/watch?v=8Ie0UVF-w7U.

5. Copeland, "01 Kenneth Copeland Lasciviousness."

6. Kenneth Copeland and Gloria Copeland, "How We Got Started . . . ," Kenneth Copeland Ministries, https://kcmcanada.ca/kenneth-gloria-copeland-how-we-got-started.

7. Ken Copeland, "1957 HITS ARCHIVE: Pledge of Love—Ken Copeland," The-45Prof, posted June 14, 2019, YouTube video, www.youtube.com/watch?v=XZramw8nay4.

8. Kenneth Copeland, "1971 Word of Faith Broadcasts—Message 1—Kenneth Copeland," 1971, KCM Europe, posted May 26, 2022, YouTube video, www.youtube.com/watch?v=1tecgFubRkk&t=3151s; Kenneth Copeland Ministries Europe, "The Founding of a Ministry," Issuu, accessed October 29, 2024, https://issuu.com/kcmeurope/docs/bvov_01-22_digital_issuu/s/14341898.

9. Believers Stand United, "Believers Stand United FAQ," The Internet Archive, November 4, 2013, https://web.archive.org/web/20131104010640/http://www.believersstandunited.com/faq/#Sect1.

10. Federal Aviation Administration, "Kenneth Copeland Airport (4T2) Information," Airport-Data.com, accessed October 29, 2024, https://airport-data.com/airport/4T2.

11. "VICTORY Channel—Another Available Voice!," Victory Channel, August 10, 2016, www.govictory.com/victory-network-another-available-voice.

12. Jay Root, "Kenneth Copeland Is the Wealthiest Pastor in America: So Why Does He Live in a Tax-Free Texas Mansion?," *Houston Chronicle*, updated December 15, 2021, www.houstonchronicle.com/news/investigations/unfair-burden/article/kenneth-copeland-wealth-pastor-tax-free-mansion-16662283.php.

13. Root, "Kenneth Copeland."

14. Steven Kozar, "The Kenneth Copeland Cornucopia of False Doctrine, Word of Faith Sorcery and Big Piles of Money," The Messed Up Church, November 8, 2017, www.themessedupchurch.com/blog/the-kenneth-copeland-cornucopia-of-false-doctrine-word-of-faith-sorcery-and-big-piles-of-money.

15. Leonardo Blair, "'I'm a Very Wealthy Man,' Says Kenneth Copeland; He Couldn't Help but Buy Jet from Tyler Perry," *Christian Post*, May 28, 2019, www.christianpost.com/news/prosperity-preacher-kenneth-copeland-says-ministry-brought-122-million-people-jesus-christ.html.

16. Alex Woodward, "Coronavirus: Televangelist Kenneth Copeland 'Blows Wind of God' at Covid-19 to 'Destroy' Pandemic," *Independent*, April 6, 2020, www.independent.co.uk/news/world/americas/kenneth-copeland-blow-coronavirus-pray-sermon-trump-televangelist-a9448561.html.

17. Ed Mazza, "Right-Wing Preacher Cooks Up the Most Bonkers Plea Yet for a Private Jet," *Huffington Post*, September 23, 2021, www.huffpost.com/entry/kenneth-copeland-private-jet-plea_n_614c24f7e4b03d83baceff5d.

18. James Ojo, "Don't Stop Tithing Even If You Lose Your Job Because of Coronavirus, Says Kenneth Copeland," Lifestyle, *Cable*, March 20, 2020, https://lifestyle.thecable.ng/dont-stop-tithing-even-if-you-lose-your-job-because-of-coronavirus-says-kenneth-copeland.

19. "Our Experiences with Kenneth Copeland," *Ex Word of Faith* (blog), February 20, 2008, https://exwordoffaith.blogspot.com/2008/02/our-experiences-with-kenneth-copeland.html.

20. Maud Newton and Aymann Ismail, "My Mom Won't Stop Donating to the Victory Channel: I'm Not Sure What to Do," *Slate*, September 17, 2023, https://slate.com/human-interest/2023/09/kenneth-copeland-victory-channel-donations.html.

21. Alicia Cohn, "Former Trump Faith Adviser Holding In-Person Event for More Than 2,000," *The Hill*, August 3, 2020, https://thehill.com/homenews/state-watch/510313-former-trump-faith-adviser-holding-in-person-event-for-more-than-2000.

22. Kenneth Copeland, "Pro-Trump Evangelical Kenneth Copeland Laughs Manically over Media Calling Biden's Win," The Independent, posted November 9, 2020, YouTube video, www.youtube.com/watch?v=VBkegy4aDvk.

23. Rebecca Speare-Cole, "Pro-Trump Televangelist Kenneth Copeland Says Devil Is Trying to Steal Election, Kill Babies," *Newsweek*, December 21, 2020, www.newsweek.com/trump-televangelist-kenneth-copeland-devil-steal-election-kill-babies-1556305.

24. Michael Gryboski, "TBN Drops Kenneth Copeland from Programming Lineup amid Upcoming Changes," *Christian Post*, August 19, 2020, www.christianpost.com/news/tbn-to-drop-kenneth-copeland-from-programming-lineup-amid-upcoming-changes.html.

25. Alexander Zaitchik, "How a Demon-Slaying Pentecostal Billionaire Is Ushering in a Post-Catholic Brazil," *New Republic*, February 7, 2019, https://newrepublic.com/article/153083/demon-slaying-pentecostal-billionaire-ushering-post-catholic-brazil.

26. "Dilma participa da inauguração de templo da Igreja Universal," Jornal da Gazeta, posted July 31, 2014, YouTube video, www.youtube.com/watch?v=nVvQ7JKdrUQ.

27. Katie Mark, "Igreja Universal: Investigação da BBC mostra pastor dizendo expulsar 'espírito maligno' de adolescentes em Londres," BBC (Brazil), December 11, 2023, www.bbc.com/portuguese/articles/cxe12nmvlzxo.

28. Rodrigo Soberanes, "Los secretos de la millonaria iglesia brasileña que vende milagros en Chile," CIPER Chile, December 11, 2015, www.ciperchile.cl/2015/12/11/los-secretos-de-la-millonaria-iglesia-brasilena-que-vende-milagros-en-chile.

29. Zaitchik, "Demon-Slaying Pentecostal Billionaire."

30. Iglesia Universal del Reino de Dios, "La Hora del Milagro—Telefe—Programa de la Familia," VARIADOS FABRI, posted March 28, 2013, YouTube video, www.youtube.com/watch?v=x7a1ACQj9fM&list=PL1PN7S7NycU81bYeqM5qXs1DxHl_YE1dt.

31. "Ex Miembro de la Iglesia Universal (Pare de Sufrir) lo cuenta todo," Disrupción Espiritual, streamed live June 2, 2022, YouTube video, www.youtube.com/watch?v=LmSXKdMrXDA.

32. Soberanes, "Secretos de la millonaria iglesia."

33. "Edir Macedo and Family," *Forbes*, accessed October 31, 2024, www.forbes.com/profile/edir-macedo.

34. Edir Macedo and Carlos Oliveira, *Plano de poder: Deus, os cristãos e a política* (Rio de Janeiro: Vida Melhor, 2011).

35. "Ranking de Instituições por Índice de Reclamações," Banco Central do Brasil, accessed October 23, 2024, www.bcb.gov.br/ranking/index.asp.

36. Associated Press, "Brazil Evangelical Leader Accused of Fraud," NBC News, August 11, 2009, www.nbcnews.com/id/wbna32380136.

37. Tom Phillips, "Brazilian Evangelical Leader Charged with Fraud," *Guardian*, August 13, 2009, www.theguardian.com/world/2009/aug/13/brazil-evangelical-leader-charged-fraud.

38. "Governo concede novo passaporte diplomático a Edir Macedo e esposa," *UOL Notícias*, March 25, 2022, https://noticias.uol.com.br/politica/ultimas-noticias/2022/03/25/governo-concede-novo-passaporte-diplomatico-a-edir-macedo.htm.

39. Anfibia Podcasts, "En nombre de Dios," March 2, 2021, in *Podimo*, podcast, https://podimo.com/latam/shows/en-nombre-de-dios.

40. "Who We Are," Universal Church of the Kingdom of God, accessed October 23, 2024, www.uckg.org.au/who-we-are.

41. Gabriel Sherman, "Inside Jerry Falwell Jr.'s Unlikely Rise and Precipitous Fall at Liberty University," *Vanity Fair*, January 24, 2022, www.vanityfair.com/news/2022/01/inside-jerry-falwell-jr-unlikely-rise-and-precipitous-fall.

42. Michael Cohen, *Disloyal: A Memoir; The True Story of the Former Personal Attorney to President Donald J. Trump* (New York: Skyhorse, 2020).

43. Sherman, "Inside Jerry Falwell Jr.'s Unlikely Rise."

44. Alec MacGillis, "How Liberty University Built a Billion-Dollar Empire Online," *New York Times Magazine*, April 17, 2018, www.nytimes.com/2018/04/17/magazine/how-liberty-university-built-a-billion-dollar-empire-online.html.

45. MacGillis, "How Liberty University Built a Billion-Dollar Empire."

46. MacGillis.

47. MacGillis.

48. MacGillis.

49. MacGillis.

50. MacGillis.

51. MacGillis.

52. Giancarlo Granda and Mark Ebner, "Inside the Jerry Falwell Love Triangle: Pool Boy Tells All," *Rolling Stone*, October 15, 2022, www.rollingstone.com/politics/politics-features/pool-boy-jerry-falwell-love-triangle-1234610995.

53. Granda and Ebner, "Inside the Jerry Falwell Love Triangle."

54. Sherman, "Inside Jerry Falwell Jr.'s Unlikely Rise."

55. Sherman.

56. Cohen, *Disloyal*.

57. Sherman, "Inside Jerry Falwell Jr.'s Unlikely Rise."

58. Dori Zook, "Liberty University, Jerry Falwell Jr. Settle Legal and Personal Disputes," CVille Right Now, July 29, 2024, https://cvillerightnow.com/news/208802-liberty-university-jerry-falwell-jr-settle-legal-and-personal-disputes.

59. Sean Watts and Tanya Munir, "The Role of Religious Capital in Shaping Wellbeing of Individuals," *Discover Social Science and Health*, April 11, 2024, www.semanticscholar.org/paper/The-role-of-religious-capital-in-shaping-wellbeing-Watts-Munir/340f58d811c068a4c4d4d006e3a3d3cea85b7964; Jakub Pawlikowski et al., "Religious Service Attendance, Health Behaviors and Well-Being—an Outcome-Wide Longitudinal Analysis," *European Journal of Public Health* 29, no. 6 (2019): 1177–1183, https://doi.org/10.1093/eurpub/ckz075; D. B. Yaden et al., "A Meta-Analysis of Religion/Spirituality and Life Satisfaction," *Journal of Happiness Studies* 23 (2022): 4147–4163, https://link.springer.com/article/10.1007/s10902-022-00558-7; C. C. Borges et al., "Association Between Spirituality/Religiousness and Quality of Life Among Healthy Adults: A Systematic Review," *Health and Quality of Life Outcomes* 19, no. 242 (2021), https://doi.org/10.1186/s12955-021-01878-7; Jeff Levin, "Religion and Happiness Among Israeli Jews: Findings from the ISSP Religion III Survey," *Journal of Happiness Studies* 15 (2014): 593–611, https://link.springer.com/article/10.1007/s10902-013-9437-8; Hisham Abu-Raiya and A. Ayten, "Religious Involvement, Interpersonal Forgiveness and Mental Health and Well-Being Among a Multinational Sample of Muslims," *Journal of Happiness Studies* 21 (2020): 3051–3067.

60. Gallup, "Religion: Gallup Historical Trends," accessed October 23, 2024, https://news.gallup.com/poll/1690/religion.aspx.

Chapter 5. Born Digital: Dawn of the AI Grift

1. Bentinho Massaro (@bentinhomassaro), "Bentinho Massaro," Instagram, accessed October 23, 2024, www.instagram.com/bentinhomassaro.

2. Oscar Schwartz, "My Journey into the Dark, Hypnotic World of a Millennial Guru," *Guardian*, January 9, 2020, www.theguardian.com/world/2020/jan/09/strange-hypnotic-world-millennial-guru-bentinho-massaro-youtube.

3. Bentinho Massaro, "Free Yourself from Any Pattern," posted August 2, 2022, YouTube video, www.youtube.com/watch?v=lyZZOJ6Of-w&t=1179s.

4. Bentinho Massaro, "You Are Source," posted April 13, 2018, YouTube video, www.youtube.com/watch?v=ZTJn9ysm_gM&t=3607s.

5. Bentinho Massaro, "Powerful Third Eye and Pineal Gland Activation | Guided Meditation," posted October 27, 2016, YouTube video, www.youtube.com/watch?v=BLQBx5v5L1o&t=9s.

6. "Bentinho Massaro," YouTube video, accessed October 23, 2024, www.youtube.com/@BentinhoMassaro.

7. "The Controversial Guru Who Wants to 'Upgrade Civilization,'" Vice, posted February 13, 2019, YouTube video, www.youtube.com/watch?v=RWUZnYCe0QA&t=23s.

8. "Controversial Guru," 21:36.

9. Sarah Edmondson and Anthony Ames, "Bentinho Massaro Sucks Part 1," February 2022 in *A Little Bit Culty*, podcast, https://alittlebitculty.com/episode/bentinho-massaro-sucks-part-1.

10. Edmondson and Ames, "Bentinho Massaro Sucks."

11. Edmondson and Ames.

12. Edmondson and Ames.

13. Matt Bruenig, "I Have Filed Unfair Labor Practice Charges Against Cult Leader Bentinho Massaro," NLRB Edge, May 13, 2024, www.nlrbedge.com/p/i-have-filed-unfair-labor-practice-063.

14. "Welcome to the Philia Center," The Philia Center, accessed October 23, 2024, https://philiacenter.com.

15. Lebo Diseko, "Teal Swan: The Woman Encouraging Her Followers to Visualise Death," BBC, November 22, 2019, www.bbc.com/news/world-us-canada-50478821.

16. Teal Swan, "The Story of Flavors," *Teal Swan* (blog), September 25, 2013, https://tealswan.com/teals-blog/the-story-of-flavors.

17. Chris Oswalt, "Teal Swan's Story Part 1," Idaho News 6, posted October 30, 2014, YouTube video, www.youtube.com/watch?v=fVpsMBeTjHY.

18. Teal Swan, *The Completion Process: The Practice of Putting Yourself Back Together Again* (Carlsbad, CA: Hay House, 2016).

19. *The Deep End*, directed by Jon Kasbe, featuring Teal Swan and Molly Monahan (Hulu, 2022).

20. Jennings Brown, "The Dark Origin Story of Internet Spiritual Guru Teal Swan," *Gizmodo*, June 6, 2018, https://gizmodo.com/the-dark-origin-story-of-internet-spiritual-guru-teal-s-1826598620.

21. Jennings Brown, "Gizmodo Launches 'The Gateway,' an Investigative Podcast About a Controversial Internet Spiritual Guru," *Gizmodo*, May 30, 2018, https://gizmodo.com/weve-launched-an-investigative-podcast-about-a-controve-1826416613.

22. Jennings Brown, "Part 1: Catalyst," May 30, 2018, in *The Gateway: Teal Swan*, produced by Jessica Glazer and Emily Pontecorvo, podcast, https://player.megaphone.fm/PPY5389954534, 28:10.

23. Brown, "Part 1: Catalyst."

24. Mormon Stories Podcast, "Leaving Mormonism to Join a Cult?—an Ex-Follower of Teal Swan—Jared Dobson," Facebook video, September 5, 2020, www.facebook.com/mormonstories/videos/2707354986154732.

25. Teal Swan, 2012, YouTube video (since deleted).

26. Teal Swan, "What to Do If You Are Suicidal," posted January 19, 2020, YouTube video, www.youtube.com/watch?v=g86hreIWfqQ.

27. "Teal Swan," Facebook, accessed October 23, 2024, www.facebook.com/tealswanofficial.

28. "Teal Swan," YouTube video, accessed October 23, 2024, www.youtube.com/@TealSwanOfficial.

29. Amy Kepferle, "Local PI Molly Monahan Is on the Case in New Documentary on Hulu," *Cascadia Daily News*, May 24, 2022, www.cascadiadaily.com/2022/may/24/local-pi-molly-monahan-is-on-the-case-in-new-documentary-on-hulu.

30. *The Deep End*, episode 2, 37:00.

31. *The Deep End*, episode 3, 34:15.

32. Stephanie Beatriz, "Lost It," February 14, 2022, in *Twin Flames*, produced by Wondery, podcast, https://wondery.com/shows/twin-flames.

33. Beatriz, "Lost It."

34. Stephanie Beatriz, "Honey Badger of Love," February 21, 2022, in *Twin Flames*, podcast, 26:00, https://wondery.com/shows/twin-flames.

35. Alice Hines, "'Everywhere I Went, They Went with Me, Because They Were on My Phone': Inside the Always Online, All-Consuming World of Twin Flames Universe," *Vanity Fair*, December 3, 2020, www.vanityfair.com/style/2020/12/inside-the-all-consuming-world-of-twin-flames-universe.

Chapter 6. Trust Me, I'm a Charlatan

1. Grete De Francesco, *The Power of the Charlatan* (New Haven, CT: Yale University Press, 1939), 82.

2. De Francesco, *Power of the Charlatan*, 81.

3. Robert J. Blendon, John M. Benson, and Joachim O. Hero, "Public Trust in Physicians—U.S. Medicine in International Perspective," *New England Journal of Medicine* 371, no. 17 (2014): 1570–1572, www.nejm.org/doi/full/10.1056/nejmp1407373.

4. *Dr. Joseph Mercola: The Misinformation 'Superspreader,'* directed by Lora Moftah, streamed August 16, 2022, *New York Times*, 8:56, www.nytimes.com/2022/08/16/NYT-Presents/joseph-mercola-coronavirus-misinformation.html.

5. *Dr. Joseph Mercola*.

6. *Dr. Joseph Mercola*.

7. "Organic Ashwagandha," Mercola Market, accessed January 31, 2025, www.mercolamarket.com/product/2811/1/organic-ashwagandha-180-per-bottle-90-day-supply.

8. *Dr. Joseph Mercola*, 2:24.

9. "FDA Warns Mercola: Stop Selling Fake COVID Remedies and Cures," Alliance for Science, March 15, 2021, https://allianceforscience.org/blog/2021/03/fda-warns-mercola-to-stop-selling-fake-covid-remedies-and-cures.

10. Shannon Bond, "Just 12 People Are Behind Most Vaccine Hoaxes on Social Media, Research Shows," NPR, May 13, 2021, www.npr.org/2021/05/13/996570855/disinformation-dozen-test-facebooks-twitters-ability-to-curb-vaccine-hoaxes.

11. Gerrit De Vynck, "YouTube Is Banning Prominent Anti-Vaccine Activists and Blocking All Anti-Vaccine Content," *Washington Post*, September 29, 2021, www.washingtonpost.com/technology/2021/09/29/youtube-ban-joseph-mercola; Brendan Pierson and Husch Blackwell, "Google Sued by Anti-Vax Doctor over YouTube Ban," Reuters, September 29, 2022, www.reuters.com/legal/litigation/google-sued-by-anti-vax-doctor-over-youtube-ban-2022-09-29.

12. "Mercola.com, LLC—607133—02/18/2021," Food and Drug Administration, February 18, 2021, www.fda.gov/inspections-compliance-enforcement-and-criminal-investigations/warning-letters/mercolacom-llc-607133-02182021; "Doctor Removing Health Articles After Misinformation Claims," Fox 4 News, August 4, 2021, www.fox4now.com/news/coronavirus/local-doctor-removing-health-articles-after-claims-of-misinformation.

13. Joann L. Porter and Prashanth Rawla, "Hemochromatosis," StatPearls, NCBI, October 6, 2024, www.ncbi.nlm.nih.gov/books/NBK430862.

14. Joseph Mercola, "The Poorly-Understood Role of Copper in Anemia—Discussion Between Morley Robbins and Dr. Mercola," September 11, 2022, in *Dr. Joseph Mercola—Take Control of Your Health*, podcast, 32:27, https://mercola.libsyn.com/the-poorly-understood-role-of-copper-in-anemia-discussion-between-morley-robbins-dr-mercola.

15. Henrik Ullum et al., "Blood Donation and Blood Donor Mortality After Adjustment for a Healthy Donor Effect," *Transfusion* 55, no. 10 (June 2015): 2479–2485, https://pubmed.ncbi.nlm.nih.gov/26098293.

16. Abdul H. Kebalo et al., "Lipid and Haematologic Profiling of Regular Blood Donors Revealed Health Benefits," *Journal of Blood Medicine* 4, no. 13 (July 2022): 385–394, https://pmc.ncbi.nlm.nih.gov/articles/PMC9270008.

17. Joseph Mercola, *Dr. Joseph Mercola—Take Control of Your Health*, podcast, 2017–2024, https://mercola.libsyn.com.

18. Joseph Mercola, "The Most Important Stealth Factor to Improve Your Health—Discussion Between Morley Robbins and Dr. Mercola," April 3, 2022, in *Dr. Joseph Mercola—Take Control of Your Health*, podcast, https://mercola.libsyn.com/the-most-important-stealth-factor-to-improve-your-health-discussion-between-morley-robbins-dr-mercola; Joseph Mercola, "The War on Ivermectin—Discussion Between Fr. Pierre Kory and Dr. Mercola," October 12, 2022, in *Dr. Joseph Mercola—Take Control of Your Health*, podcast, https://mercola.libsyn.com/the-war-on-ivermectin-discussion-between-fr-pierre-kory-dr-mercola; Joseph Mercola, "Best of Series—COVID-19 and the Global Predators," September 7, 2022, in *Dr. Joseph Mercola—Take Control of Your Health*, podcast, https://mercola.libsyn.com/best-of-series-covid-19-and-the-global-predators.

19. Neena Satija and Lena H. Sun, "A Major Funder of the Anti-Vaccine Movement Has Made Millions Selling Natural Health Products," *Washington Post*, December 20, 2019, www.washingtonpost.com/investigations/2019/10/15/fdc01078-c29c-11e9-b5e4-54aa56d5b7ce_story.html.

20. Chip Brown, "The Experiments of Dr. Oz," *New York Times*, July 30, 1995, www.nytimes.com/1995/07/30/magazine/the-experiments-of-dr-oz.html.

21. MitraClip patient website, accessed October 25, 2024, https://mitraclip.com.

22. *Second Opinion with Dr. Oz*, directed by Adam Sorota (Discovery Channel, 2003–2004), accessed October 25, 2024, www.imdb.com/title/tt0459632.

23. Shannon Power, "Oprah and Dr. Oz's TV Relationship: A Timeline," *Newsweek*, November 4, 2022, www.newsweek.com/oprah-dr-oz-timeline-relationship-pennsylvania-1756893.

24. Adam S. Cifu, "Why Dr. Oz Makes Us Crazy," *Journal of General Internal Medicine* 29, no. 2 (2013): 417–418, https://pmc.ncbi.nlm.nih.gov/articles/PMC3912308.

25. Chie Morimoto et al., "Anti-Obese Action of Raspberry Ketone," *Life Sciences* 77, no. 2 (2005), https://pubmed.ncbi.nlm.nih.gov/15862604; Kyoung Sik Park, "Raspberry Ketone Increases Both Lipolysis and Fatty Acid Oxidation in 3T3-L1 Adipocytes," *Planta Med* 76, no. 15 (2010): 1654–1658, https://pubmed.ncbi.nlm.nih.gov/20425690.

26. Kris Gunnars, "Do Raspberry Ketones Really Work? A Detailed Review," *Healthline*, July 31, 2023, www.healthline.com/nutrition/do-raspberry-ketones-work.

27. Fiitto Singapore HQ, "Here's What Dr. Oz Featured About Raspberry Ketones (Pure Focus) Supplements and How It Benefits Consumers," Facebook video, June 12, 2022, www.facebook.com/watch/?v=1107735589803913.

28. "Raspberry Ketones Frenzy Follows Dr. Oz Show," ABC News, April 5, 2012, https://abcnews.go.com/Health/Diet/raspberry-ketones-frenzy/story?id=16074044.

29. Nicole Bootsman, David F. Blackburn, and Jeff Taylor, "The Oz Craze," *Canadian Pharmacists Journal* 147, no. 2 (2014): 80–82, https://pmc.ncbi.nlm.nih.gov/articles/PMC3962061.

30. Philip Seo, "Neti Pots, Nurse Ambassadors and American Healthcare," *Rheumatologist*, March 15, 2021, www.the-rheumatologist.org/article/neti-pots-nurse-ambassadors-american-healthcare; Alice G. Walton, "The Oz Effect: Medicine or Marketing?," *Forbes*, June 6, 2011, www.forbes.com/sites/alicegwalton/2011/06/06/the-oz-effect-medicine-or-marketing.

31. Mehmet Oz, "Written Testimony of Dr. Mehmet Oz, M.D. Hearing on 'Protecting Consumers from False and Deceptive Advertising of Weight-Loss Products,'" Senate Commerce Committee, June 17, 2014, www.commerce.senate.gov/services/files/EB6D07FF-1307-4220-9BAE-381EC3220B30.

32. Joe A. Vinson, Bryan R. Burnham, and Mysore V. Nagendran, "Randomized, Double-Blind, Placebo-Controlled, Linear Dose, Crossover Study to Evaluate the Efficacy and Safety of a Green Coffee Bean Extract in Overweight Subjects," *Diabetes, Metabolic Syndrome and Obesity: Targets and Therapy* 5 (2012): 21–27, https://pubmed.ncbi.nlm.nih.gov/22291473, retracted article.

33. "Dr. Oz-Endorsed Diet Pill Study Was Bogus, Researchers Admit," CBS News, updated October 21, 2014, www.cbsnews.com/news/dr-oz-endorsed-green-coffee-bean-diet-study-retracted.

34. Derek Lowe, "A New Low for Dr. Oz," *Science*, June 7, 2018, www.science.org/content/blog-post/new-low-dr-oz.

35. Gabby Bernstein, "The Mysterious Ways Our Loved Ones Communicate from Beyond | Dr. Oz," DoctorOz, posted September 13, 2023, YouTube video, www.youtube.com/watch?v=iPDleQmEZSI.

36. Christina Korownyk, "Televised Medical Talk Shows—What They Recommend and the Evidence to Support Their Recommendations: A Prospective Observational Study," *British Medical Journal* 349 (2014), www.bmj.com/content/349/bmj.g7346.

37. Bootsman, Blackburn, and Taylor, "The Oz Craze."

38. Robert F. Worth, "The Billionaire Yogi Behind Modi's Rise," *New York Times*, July 26, 2018, www.nytimes.com/2018/07/26/magazine/the-billionaire-yogi-behind-modis-rise.html.

39. Priyanka Pathak-Narain, "The Yogi and His Epic Story," *Hindu*, July 28, 2017, www.thehindu.com/books/the-yogi-and-his-epic-story/article19377742.ece.

40. "How a Penniless Yoga Guru Built a Consumer Goods Empire by Tapping into Indian Nationalism," *Bloomberg*, video, January 30, 2020, www.bloomberg.com/news/videos/2020-01-30/how-a-penniless-yoga-guru-built-a-consumer-goods-empire-by-tapping-into-indian-nationalism-video.

41. Rahul Bhatia, "The Origins of Ramdev," *Open Magazine*, June 30, 2011, https://openthemagazine.com/features/india/the-origins-of-ramdev.

42. Vinay Patil, "Kapalbhati Pranayam with English Subtitles," posted February 4, 2011, YouTube video, www.youtube.com/watch?v=6ZwgFiQuZME&t=342s.

43. "Homosexuality Is a Disease, Yoga Can Cure It: Ramdev," *Deccan Chronicle*, December 11, 2013, www.deccanchronicle.com/131211/news-current-affairs/article/homosexuality-disease-yoga-can-cure-it-ramdev.

44. "Patanjali Shilajit Capsule 11 G," Patanjali Ayurved, accessed October 25, 2024, www.patanjaliayurved.net/product/natural-health-care/health-and-wellness/patanjali-shilajeet-capsule/786.

45. Ami Patel, "9 Benefits of Shilajit," Healthline, updated February 19, 2024, www.healthline.com/health/shilajit; Vikas Kumar et al., "Amalaki Rasayana, a Traditional Indian Drug Enhances Cardiac Mitochondrial and Contractile Functions and Improves Cardiac Function in Rats with Hypertrophy," *Scientific Reports* 7, no. 1 (2017): 8588, https://doi.org/10.1038/s41598-017-09225-x.

46. Una Galani, "Indian Yogi Shows Power of Local Consumer Kings," Reuters, May 24, 2017, www.reuters.com/article/us-india-modi-ramdev-breakingviews-idUSKBN18K0JP.

47. "India's Richest: Acharya Balkrishna," *Forbes*, accessed September 10, 2024, www.forbes.com/profile/acharya-balkrishna.

48. Acharya Balkrishna, "'The Science of Ayurveda' Book by Acharya Balkrishna, Publised [*sic*] in 80 Countries," Bharat Swabhiman, posted July 13, 2017, YouTube video, www.youtube.com/watch?v=fAcu5nydzmo.

49. Shambhavi Anand and Ratna Bhushan, "Baba Ramdev Alleges Adulteration of Patanjali Products by FMCG Companies," *Economic Times*, February 2, 2016, https://economictimes.indiatimes.com/news/politics-and-nation/baba-ramdev-alleges-adulteration-of-patanjali-products-by-fmcg-companies/articleshow/50811763.cms.

50. Anand and Bhushan, "Baba Ramdev Alleges Adulteration."

51. "Revenue for Colgate-Palmolive India," Companies Market Cap, accessed October 26, 2024, https://companiesmarketcap.com/colgate-palmolive-india/revenue.

52. "Inside Patanjali: Here's What Life Is Like in Baba Ramdev's Company," *Economic Times*, July 30, 2017, https://economictimes.indiatimes.com/industry/cons-products/fmcg/inside-patanjali-heres-what-life-is-like-in-baba-ramdevs-company/articleshow/59824892.cms; see also "Baba Ramdev Wants Employees to Work for Free: A Former CEO Reveals the Patanjali Story," *New Indian Express*, August 4, 2017, https://web.archive.org/web/20210418135632/https:/www.newindianexpress.com/business/2017/aug/04

/baba-ramdev-wants-employees-to-work-for-free-a-former-ceo-reveals-the-patanjali-story-1638376.html.

53. "How a Penniless Yoga Guru Built a Consumer Goods Empire."

54. Sukirti Dwivedi, "Ramdev Draws Doctors' Fury, Legal Trouble Over 'Allopathy Is Stupid' Video," NDTV, updated May 23, 2021, www.ndtv.com/india-news/ramdev-draws-doctors-fury-legal-trouble-over-allopathy-is-stupid-video-2447485.

55. Sneha Mordani, "IMA Appeals PM Modi to Stop Baba Ramdev's 'Misinformation Campaign' Against Vaccination," *India Today*, May 26, 2021, www.indiatoday.in/coronavirus-outbreak/story/ima-letter-pm-narendra-modi-ramdev-misinformation-campaign-vaccination-1807248-2021-05-26.

56. "Indian Medical Association Writes to PM Modi, Demands Action Against Baba Ramdev," *Hindu*, May 26, 2021, www.thehindu.com/news/national/other-states/indian-medical-association-serves-defamation-notice-on-ramdev/article34647942.ece.

57. "Patanjali Ayurved vs Supreme Court: A Timeline of the Misleading Ads Case," Storyboard18, April 25, 2024, www.storyboard18.com/quantum-brief/patanjali-ayurved-vs-supreme-court-a-timeline-of-the-misleading-ads-case-29896.htm.

58. "Arrest Warrant Issued Against Baba Ramdev and Acharya Balakrishna over Misleading Ads," Mathrubhumi, January 20, 2025, https://english.mathrubhumi.com/news/kerala/baba-ramdev-patanjali-arrest-warrant-1.10269695.

59. PTI, "Don't Talk of Money When Mics Are On: Ramdev to BJP Candidate," *Deccan Herald*, April 18, 2014, www.deccanherald.com/archives/dont-talk-money-mics-ramdev-2187714.

Chapter 7. Digital Alchemy: The Crypto Grift

1. Natalie Angier, "Moonlighting as a Conjurer of Chemicals," *New York Times*, October 11, 2010, www.nytimes.com/2010/10/12/science/12newton.html.

2. New Advent Catholic Encyclopedia, s.v. "Alchemy," accessed October 26, 2024, www.newadvent.org/cathen/01272b.htm.

3. Angus Berwick and Tom Wilson, "Crypto Exchanges Enabled Online Child Sex-Abuse Profiteer," Reuters, November 23, 2022, www.reuters.com/legal/government/crypto-exchanges-enabled-online-child-sex-abuse-profiteer-2022-11-23; Sankul Kabra and Saira Gori, "Drug Trafficking on Cryptomarkets and the Role of Organized Crime Groups," *Journal of Economic Criminology* 2 (December 2023), www.sciencedirect.com/science/article/pii/S294979142300026X; Joe Tidy, "74% of Ransomware Revenue Goes to Russia-Linked Hackers," BBC, February 14, 2022, www.bbc.com/news/technology-60378009; US Government Accountability Office, "As Virtual Currency Use in Human and Drug Trafficking Increases, So Do the Challenges for Federal Law Enforcement," *WatchBlog: Following the Federal Dollar* (blog), February 24, 2022, www.gao.gov/blog/virtual-currency-use-human-and-drug-trafficking-increases-so-do-challenges-federal-law-enforcement.

4. "Crypto Funds at Fidelity," Fidelity Investments, accessed October 26, 2024, www.fidelity.com/etfs/crypto-funds.

5. *Cointelegraph*, "PayPal Enables Business Accounts to Buy, Sell, and Trade Crypto," Trading View, September 25, 2024, www.tradingview.com/news/cointelegraph:4613da862094b:0-paypal-enables-business-accounts-to-buy-sell-and-trade-crypto; Visa,

"'Digital Gold': Spending on Visa Crypto-Linked Cards Tops $1 Billion in the First Half of the Year," press release, August 7, 2020, www.visasoutheasteurope.com/about-visa/newsroom/press-releases/prl-08072020.html.

6. Kyle Torpey, "Where Does Jamie Dimon Stand on Crypto?," Investopedia, December 8, 2023, www.investopedia.com/first-he-hates-it-then-he-s-ok-with-it-now-he-hates-it-again-where-does-jamie-dimon-stand-on-crypto-8411584.

7. "Smart Contracts Launch on Stellar with $100M Allocated to Soroban Adoption Fund," Stellar, March 19, 2024, https://stellar.org/press/smart-contracts-launch-on-stellar.

8. James Chen, Charles Potters, and Yarilet Perez, "Chicago Mercantile Exchange: Definition, History, and Regulation," Investopedia, updated July 11, 2022, www.investopedia.com/terms/c/cme.asp; "Digital Assets," Intercontinental Exchange, accessed October 26, 2024, www.ice.com/digital-assets.

9. Andrew Beattie and JeFreda R. Brown, "The SEC: A Brief History of Regulation," Investopedia, updated September 23, 2021, www.investopedia.com/articles/07/secbeginning.asp.

10. Barbara H. Fried, "Beyond Blame," *Boston Review*, June 28, 2013, www.bostonreview.net/forum/barbara-fried-beyond-blame-moral-responsibility-philosophy-law.

11. Nikou Asgari and Joshua Oliver, "'It Just Kinda Went Crazy': FTX's Lavish Spending Highlights Lack of Controls," *Financial Times*, November 29, 2022, www.ft.com/content/7cfbb894-a332-4629-a417-4bcda27eb6e7.

12. Derek Andersen, "SEC Charges Crypto Investment Manager Titan with Misleading Advertising Claims," *Cointelegraph*, August 21, 2023.

13. Emma Newbery, "What We Can Learn from OneCoin, Crypto's Biggest Scam," The Motley Fool, October 23, 2021, www.fool.com/the-ascent/cryptocurrency/articles/what-we-can-learn-from-onecoin-cryptos-biggest-scam.

14. Rob Byrne, "Fugitive 'Cryptoqueen' Hit by Asset Freeze," BBC, August 7, 2024, www.bbc.com/news/articles/c9d1y0z4z9no.

15. Rich Stanton, "Crypto CEO Behind $2.5B 'Rug Pull' Arrested, Faces 40,564 Years in Prison," *PC Gamer*, September 26, 2022, www.pcgamer.com/crypto-ceo-behind-dollar25b-rug-pull-arrested-faces-40564-years-in-prison; Arijit Sarkar, "AnubisDAO's Rug-Pulled 13.5K ETH Washes Away on Tornado Cash," *Cointelegraph*, July 17, 2023, https://cointelegraph.com/news/anubis-dao-rug-pull-money-washes-away-on-tornado-cash; Rob Behnke, "Explained: The StableMagnet Rugpull (June 2021)," Halborn, July 3, 2021, www.halborn.com/blog/post/explained-the-stablemagnet-rugpull-june-2021; Sebastian Sinclair, "Solana's Luna Yield Goes Dark with Some Fearing a 'Rug Pull' Involving $6.7M," CoinDesk, August 20, 2021, www.coindesk.com/markets/2021/08/20/solanas-luna-yield-goes-dark-with-some-fearing-a-rug-pull-involving-67m.

16. James Dator, "Did De'Aaron Fox Really Defraud People for $1.5M in an NFT 'Rug Pull' Scheme?," *SBNation*, February 25, 2022, www.sbnation.com/nba/2022/2/25/22950186/deaaron-fox-defraud-nft-swipathefox-nba-kings.

17. Kevin Hurler, "What's Happening with Logan Paul, Coffeezilla, and CryptoZoo?," *Gizmodo*, January 9, 2023, https://gizmodo.com/youtube-logan-paul-coffeezilla-cryptozoo-scam-1849965572.

18. Kevin Reynolds, "People Behind Crypto Protocol DeFi100 May Have Absconded with $32M in Investor Funds," CoinDesk, May 22, 2021, www.coindesk.com/markets/2021/05/22/people-behind-crypto-protocol-defi100-may-have-absconded-with-32m-in-investor-funds.

19. Mark Hunter, "DEFI100 Claims Website Hack Was Behind Exit Scam Message," FullyCrypto, May 24, 2021, https://fullycrypto.com/defi100-claims-website-hack-was-behind-exit-scam-message.

20. Emma Fletcher, "Reports Show Scammers Cashing In on Crypto Craze," Federal Trade Commission, June 3, 2022, www.ftc.gov/news-events/data-visualizations/data-spotlight/2022/06/reports-show-scammers-cashing-crypto-craze.

21. MacKenzie Sigalos, "Crypto Scammers Took a Record $14 Billion in 2021," CNBC, January 6, 2022, www.cnbc.com/2022/01/06/crypto-scammers-took-a-record-14-billion-in-2021-chainalysis.html.

22. Kim Komando, "Crooks Up Their Game in Pig Butchering Scams to Steal Money," *USA Today*, October 24, 2024, www.msn.com/en-us/news/technology/crooks-up-their-game-in-pig-butchering-scams-to-steal-money/ar-AA1sQ1cY.

23. Lauren Leffer, "Bankruptcy Judge Says Celsius Crypto Investors Don't Own Their Accounts," *Gizmodo*, January 6, 2023, https://gizmodo.com/crypto-celsius-earn-accounts-alex-mashinsky-1849957843.

24. Steven Zeitchik, "Bad News for Thousands of Crypto Investors: They Don't Own Their Accounts," *Washington Post*, January 5, 2023, www.washingtonpost.com/technology/2023/01/05/celsius-crypto-bankruptcy-ruling.

25. Nikhilesh De, "Celsius 'Earn' Assets Belong to Bankrupt Crypto Lender, Judge Rules," CoinDesk, updated January 4, 2023, https://finance.yahoo.com/news/celsius-earn-assets-belong-bankrupt-065147013.html.

26. Kate Selig, "Stanford-Connected Fundraising Group Wants to Raise $140 Million for Democrats in 2020," *Stanford Daily*, January 16, 2020, https://stanforddaily.com/2020/01/16/stanford-connected-fundraising-group-wants-to-raise-140-million-for-democrats-in-2020.

27. Samuel Bankman-Fried, "Crypto CEOs Testify Before House Financial Services Hearing," Rev, transcript, December 8, 2021, www.rev.com/blog/transcripts/crypto-ceos-testify-before-house-financial-services-hearing-transcript#.

28. "The Entirely Predictable Collapse of FTX Exposes the Failures of Regulators and Journalists," *Current Affairs*, November 14, 2022, www.currentaffairs.org/news/2022/11/the-entirely-predictable-collapse-of-ftx-exposes-the-failures-of-regulators-and-journalists.

29. Steven Ehrlich and Chase Peterson-Withorn, "Meet the World's Richest 29-Year-Old: How Sam Bankman-Fried Made a Record Fortune in the Crypto Frenzy," *Forbes*, 2021, www.forbes.com/sites/stevenehrlich/2021/10/06/the-richest-under-30-in-the-world-all-thanks-to-crypto.

30. Randall Lane, "Operation Wealth Speed," *Forbes*, April 6, 2021, www.forbes.com/sites/randalllane/2021/04/06/operation-wealth-speed-what-a-record-number-of-new-self-made-billionaires-says-about-capitalism.

31. "The Cointelegraph Top 100: Sam Bankman-Fried #3," *Cointelegraph*, 2021, accessed October 26, 2024, https://cointelegraph.com/top-people-in-crypto-and-blockchain-2021/sam-bankman-fried.

32. Michelle Chan, "Hong Kong's 29-Year-Old Crypto Billionaire: FTX's Sam Bankman-Fried," *Nikkei Asia*, June 25, 2021, https://asia.nikkei.com/Business/Business-Spotlight/Hong-Kong-s-29-year-old-crypto-billionaire-FTX-s-Sam-Bankman-Fried.

33. Leo Schwartz, "Inside Sam Bankman-Fried's Extravagant Penthouse Lifestyle in the Bahamas, Where the T-Shirt-Clad FTX Founder Lived Like Royalty," *Fortune*, November 22, 2022, https://fortune.com/crypto/2022/11/22/sbf-ftx-bahamas-house-lifestyle.

34. Samantha Delouya, "Sam Bankman-Fried Disputed Reports That FTX and Alameda Employees Were Fueled by Drugs: 'This Has Been Totally On-Label Use of Medication,'" *Business Insider*, November 30, 2022, www.businessinsider.com/sam-bankman-fried-drug-use-ftx-alameda-caroline-ellison-amphetamines-2022-11; Tracy Wang, "Bankman-Fried's Cabal of Roommates in the Bahamas Ran His Crypto Empire—and Dated: Other Employees Have Lots of Questions," CoinDesk, November 10, 2022, www.coindesk.com/business/2022/11/10/bankman-frieds-cabal-of-roommates-in-the-bahamas-ran-his-crypto-empire-and-dated-other-employees-have-lots-of-questions; Alex Hern, "Polyamory, Penthouses and Plenty of Loans: Inside the Crazy World of FTX," *Guardian* (UK edition), November 19, 2022, www.theguardian.com/technology/2022/nov/19/polyamory-penthouses-and-plenty-of-loans-inside-the-crazy-world-of-ftx.

35. Zeke Faux, "A 30-Year-Old Crypto Billionaire Wants to Give His Fortune Away," *Bloomberg*, April 3, 2022, www.bloomberg.com/news/features/2022-04-03/sam-bankman-fried-ftx-s-crypto-billionaire-who-wants-to-give-his-fortune-away.

36. Seth Meyers, "FTX Super Bowl Don't Miss Out with Larry David," The World's Best Ads, posted February 14, 2022, YouTube video, www.youtube.com/watch?v=hWMnbJJpeZc.

37. Jamie Crawley, "Crypto Exchange FTX Secures Naming Rights for Miami Heat Arena for $135M," CoinDesk, March 24, 2021, www.coindesk.com/markets/2021/03/24/crypto-exchange-ftx-secures-naming-rights-for-miami-heat-arena-for-135m.

38. Mustafa Khalifa and Jimmy Kimmel, "All 3 Tom Brady FTX Commercial | FTX Tom Brady and Gisele Bundchen," Mustafa Khalifa, posted November 20, 2022, YouTube video, www.youtube.com/watch?v=_aCGMyrFn-8; Rohan Goswami, "FTX's Venture Backers Included Patriots Owner Robert Kraft and Billionaire Paul Tudor Jones, New Filings Show," CNBC, January 10, 2023, www.cnbc.com/2023/01/10/ftx-investors-included-robert-kraft-paul-tudor-jones-new-filings.html.

39. Nina Bambysheva, "Royal Flush: Inside Crypto's Most Exclusive Gathering," *Forbes*, May 3, 2022, www.forbes.com/sites/ninabambysheva/2022/05/03/royal-flush-inside-cryptos-most-exclusive-gathering.

40. "Ontario Teachers' Statement on FTX," Ontario Teachers' Pension Plan, November 17, 2022, www.otpp.com/en-ca/about-us/news-and-insights/2022/ontario-teachers--statement-on-ftx.

41. Temur Durrani, "FTX FOMO: How Big-Name Investors, Including Canadian Pension Funds, Bought into a Crypto Craze That Ended Up with Criminal Charges," *Globe and Mail*, December 24, 2022, www.theglobeandmail.com/business/article-ftx-crypto-canadian-investors-oleary-teachers.

42. Steven Ehrlich and Chase Peterson-Withorn, "The Croesus of Crypto: How Sam Bankman-Fried Built a $22.5 Billion Fortune Without Really Believing in Cryptocurrency,"

Forbes India, November 20, 2021, www.forbesindia.com/article/cross-border/the-croesus-of-crypto-how-sam-bankmanfried-built-a-225-billion-fortune-without-really-believing-in-cryptocurrency/71659/1.

43. Lakshmi Varanasi et al., "Who Is Caroline Ellison? The Mind Behind FTX's Collapse," *Business Insider*, September 25, 2024, www.businessinsider.com/who-is-caroline-ellison-the-mind-behind-ftx-collapse#ive-been-into-math-since-i-was-probably-a-little-kid-she-said-on-an-episode-of-ftxs-podcast-in-2020-adding-that-shes-been-thinking-about-it-a-lot-from-an-early-age-4.

44. United States of America v. Samuel Bankman-Fried, 22 Cr. 0673 (LAK) (S.D.N.Y. 2023), www.justice.gov/usao-sdny/press-release/file/1557571/dl.

45. Yong Li Khoo et al., "Blockchain Analysis: The Collapse of Alameda and FTX," Nansen, November 17, 2022, www.nansen.ai/research/blockchain-analysis-the-collapse-of-alameda-and-ftx.

46. Antoine Gara et al., "FTX Held Less Than $1bn in Liquid Assets Against $9bn in Liabilities," *Financial Times*, November 13, 2022, www.ft.com/content/f05fe9f8-ca0a-48d5-8ef2-7a4d813af558.

47. Kelsey Piper, "Sam Bankman-Fried Tries to Explain Himself," *Vox*, November 16, 2022, www.vox.com/future-perfect/23462333/sam-bankman-fried-ftx-crypto currency-effective-altruism-crypto-bahamas-philanthropy.

48. Luke Barr, "New FTX CEO Says He's Never Seen 'Complete Failure' of Corporate Controls in His Career, Including at Enron," ABC News, November 17, 2022, https://abcnews.go.com/Business/ftx-ceo-complete-failure-corporate-controls-career-including/story?id=93488990.

49. Eric Wallerstein, "New FTX CEO Says Firm Approved Payments Using Emojis," *Wall Street Journal*, November 17, 2022, www.wsj.com/livecoverage/stock-market-news-today-11-17-2022/card/new-ftx-ceo-says-firm-approved-payments-using-emojis-AZ1zJYUZED6xk2sp58cd.

50. "New FTX CEO Reveals the Company Had No Board of Directors or Accounting Department," Forbes Breaking News, posted December 26, 2022, YouTube video, www.youtube.com/watch?v=f31FzhMdhFY.

51. Ava Benny-Morrison, Hannah Miller, and Chris Dolmetsch, "Alameda's Former CEO Ellison Said She, Bankman-Fried Misled FTX Lenders," *Bloomberg*, December 23, 2022, www.bloomberg.com/news/articles/2022-12-23/ellison-said-she-bankman-fried-agreed-to-mislead-ftx-lenders.

52. Allison Morrow, "Sam Bankman-Fried Found Guilty of Seven Counts of Fraud in Stunning Fall for Former Crypto Billionaire," CNN, November 3, 2023, www.cnn.com/2023/11/02/business/ftx-sbf-fraud-trial-verdict/index.html.

53. "Exhibit B: Victim Impact Statements," document 411-2, United States of America v. Samuel Bankman-Fried, 22 Cr. 0673 (LAK) (S.D.N.Y. 2023), https://storage.courtlistener.com/recap/gov.uscourts.nysd.590940/gov.uscourts.nysd.590940.411.2.pdf.

54. "Sam Bankman-Fried Sentenced to 25 Years in Prison," CNN, March 28, 2024, https://edition.cnn.com/business/live-news/sam-bankman-fried-sentencing-03-28-24/index.html.

55. Allison Morrow and Kara Scannell, "Caroline Ellison, Whose Testimony Helped Convict Sam Bankman-Fried, Sentenced to Two Years in Prison," CNN, September 24,

2024, https://edition.cnn.com/2024/09/24/business/caroline-ellison-sentencing-nightcap/index.html.

56. Fried, "Beyond Blame."

Chapter 8. Charlatans in High Places

1. Alexander Hamilton, "The Federalist Papers: No. 1," October 27, 1787, The Avalon Project, Lillian Goldman Law Library, Yale Law School, https://avalon.law.yale.edu/18th_century/fed01.asp.

2. Andrew T. Little, Keith E. Schnakenberg, and Ian R. Turner, "Motivated Reasoning and Democratic Accountability," *American Political Science Review* 116, no. 2 (2020): 751–767, www.semanticscholar.org/paper/Motivated-Reasoning-and-Democratic-Accountability-Little-Schnakenberg/215ad8bd0da4f789549da1ef90cb460c4eb96e45.

3. Ronald Schnackenberg, "Declaration of Ronald Schnackenberg in Support of Plaintiffs' Motion for Class Certification," September 16, 2012, United States District Court for the Southern District of California, https://s3.documentcloud.org/documents/2850043/Schnackenberg.pdf.

4. Schnackenberg, "Declaration of Ronald Schnackenberg."

5. "Learn Trump's Secret to Success, Only $1,495," *Columbus Dispatch*, June 29, 2008, www.dispatch.com/story/business/2008/06/29/learn-trump-s-secret-to/23465908007.

6. Ryan Lotman, "Trump University 2010 Playbook: One Company. One Culture. One Goal; Achieving Sustained Profitability in 2010," *Politico*, December 7, 2009, https://static.politico.com/25/88/783a0dca43a0a898f3973da0086f/trump-university-playbook.pdf.

7. Lotman, "Trump University 2010 Playbook."

8. Libby Nelson, "Trump University, Explained," *Vox*, updated February 26, 2016, www.vox.com/2015/7/29/9067429/trump-university.

9. Schnackenberg, "Declaration of Ronald Schnackenberg."

10. John Cassidy, "The Enduring Scandal of Trump University," *New Yorker*, November 20, 2016, www.newyorker.com/news/john-cassidy/the-enduring-scandal-of-trump-university.

11. Camila Domonoske, "Judge Approves $25 Million Settlement of Trump University Lawsuit," NPR, March 31, 2017, www.npr.org/sections/thetwo-way/2017/03/31/522199535/judge-approves-25-million-settlement-of-trump-university-lawsuit.

12. Shane Goldmacher, "How Trump Moved Money to Pay $100 Million in Legal Bills," *New York Times*, March 27, 2024, www.nytimes.com/interactive/2024/03/27/us/politics/trump-cases-legal-fund.html.

13. Lazaro Gamio, "Election 2020: The Two Americas Financing the Trump and Biden Campaigns," *New York Times*, October 25, 2020, www.nytimes.com/interactive/2020/10/25/us/politics/trump-biden-campaign-donations.html.

14. Zach Everson, "Trump's D.C. Hotel Hosted Officials from These 33 Countries After He Won the 2016 Election," *Forbes*, April 21, 2022, www.forbes.com/sites/zacheverson/2021/10/10/trumps-dc-hotel-hosted-foreign-officials-from-these-33-countries-while-he-was-in-office.

15. Anna Schecter, "Trump D.C. Hotel Receipts Reveal $10,500-a-Night Rooms for Foreign Officials Seeking to Influence U.S. Policy," NBC News, November 14, 2022, www.nbcnews.com/politics/donald-trump/trump-dc-hotel-10500-night-rooms-foreign-officials-rcna57027.

16. Mark Landler and Eric Lichtblau, "Jeff Sessions Recuses Himself from Russia Inquiry," *New York Times*, March 2, 2017, www.nytimes.com/2017/03/02/us/politics/jeff-sessions-russia-trump-investigation-democrats.html; Pamela Brown, "Comey Documented 'Everything He Could Remember' After Trump Conversations," CNN, updated May 16, 2017, https://edition.cnn.com/2017/05/16/politics/james-comey-trump-memo-documents/index.html; Chris Cillizza, "Here's the Real Reason Why Donald Trump Fired James Comey," CNN, updated May 19, 2017, https://edition.cnn.com/2017/05/19/politics/trump-comey-fired/index.html.

17. Alexander Stille, *The Sack of Rome: Media + Money + Celebrity = Power = Silvio Berlusconi* (New York: Penguin, 2007).

18. Alexander Stille, "How Silvio Berlusconi Wrecked Italy—and, Sort of, America," *New Republic*, June 13, 2023, https://newrepublic.com/article/173537/silvio-berlusconi-wrecked-italy-america.

19. Stille, "How Silvio Berlusconi Wrecked Italy."

20. Paolo Mancini and Matteo Gerli, "Media Legislation—Italy," Italy, *Media Landscapes*, accessed October 26, 2024, https://medialandscapes.org/country/italy/policies/media-legislation.

21. Cory Doctorow, "Italy Proposes Mandatory Licenses for People Who Upload Video," *BoingBoing*, January 16, 2010, https://boingboing.net/2010/01/16/italy-proposes-manda.html.

22. Roberto Di Quirico, "Italy and the Global Economic Crisis," *Bulletin of Italian Politics* 2, no. 2 (2010): 3–19, www.gla.ac.uk/media/Media_191024_smxx.pdf.

23. Joe Sommerlad, "What Happened in Silvio Berlusconi's Notorious 'Bunga Bunga' Sex Party Scandal?," *Independent*, June 13, 2023, www.independent.co.uk/news/world/europe/silvio-berlusconi-bunga-bunga-party-b2356544.html.

24. Agence France Presse, "Italy's Berlusconi Acquitted in 'Bunga Bunga' Bribe Case," *Le Monde*, February 15, 2023, www.lemonde.fr/en/international/article/2023/02/15/italy-s-berlusconi-acquitted-in-bunga-bunga-bribe-case_6015908_4.html.

25. "Italy: Ex-PM Silvio Berlusconi Laid to Rest at State Funeral," *DW* (Bonn, Germany), June 14, 2023, www.dw.com/en/former-italian-pm-silvio-berlusconi-laid-to-rest-at-state-funeral/a-65910988.

26. "Brexit Polls 2024," Statista, accessed October 26, 2024, www.statista.com/statistics/987347/brexit-opinion-poll.

27. Moisés Naím, *The Revenge of Power: How Autocrats Are Reinventing Politics for the 21st Century* (New York: St. Martin's, 2022).

28. Naím, *The Revenge of Power.*

29. Mark D'Arcy, "Nigel Farage: The Story of 'Mr Brexit,'" BBC, November 28, 2019, www.bbc.com/news/election-2019-50565543.

30. Henry Mance, "Britain Has Had Enough of Experts, Says Gove," *Financial Times*, June 3, 2016, www.ft.com/content/3be49734-29cb-11e6-83e4-abc22d5d108c.

31. "The Misinformation That Was Told About Brexit During and After the Referendum," *Independent*, July 28, 2018, www.independent.co.uk/news/uk/politics/final-say-brexit-referendum-lies-boris-johnson-leave-campaign-remain-a8466751.html.

32. Liam Fox, "EU Trade Deal 'Easiest in Human History,'" BBC, July 20, 2017, www.bbc.com/news/av/uk-40667879.

33. Katrin Forster-van Aerssen and Tajda Spital, "The Impact of Brexit on UK Trade and Labour Markets," *ECB Economic Bulletin*, March 2023, www.ecb.europa.eu/press/economic-bulletin/articles/2023/html/ecb.ebart202303_01~3af23c5f5a.en.html.

34. Dharshini David, "What Impact Has Brexit Had on the UK Economy?," BBC, January 31, 2023, www.bbc.com/news/business-64450882.

35. Toby Helm, "Brexit Has Completely Failed for UK, Say Clear Majority of Britons—Poll," *Guardian* (UK edition), December 30, 2023, www.theguardian.com/politics/2023/dec/30/britons-brexit-bad-uk-poll-eu-finances-nhs.

Chapter 9. QAnonsense: Where We Go One, We Go Nuts

1. Ryan Bort, "A Ridiculous QAnon Conspiracy Forced a Small Charter School to Cancel a Fundraiser," *Rolling Stone*, May 10, 2019, www.rollingstone.com/politics/politics-news/qanon-conspiracy-comey-forced-charter-school-cancel-fundraiser-834050.

2. Mike Rothschild, "The Inside Story of How QAnon Derailed a Charter School's Annual Fundraiser," *Daily Dot*, updated May 20, 2021, www.dailydot.com/debug/qanon-grass-valley-charter-school-foundation.

3. Mike Rothschild, *The Storm Is Upon Us: How QAnon Became a Movement, Cult, and Conspiracy Theory of Everything* (New York: Melville House, 2021).

4. Rothschild, *The Storm Is Upon Us.*

5. Emily Rauhala and Loveday Morris, "QAnon Conspiracy Theories Spread Around the World," *Washington Post*, November 13, 2020, www.washingtonpost.com/world/qanon-conspiracy-global-reach/2020/11/12/ca312138-13a5-11eb-a258-614acf2b906d_story.html.

6. Rothschild, *The Storm Is Upon Us.*

7. Rothschild.

8. Nicky Woolf, *Finding Q: My Journey into QAnon*, produced by Audible, podcast, 2021, www.audible.com/podcast/Finding-Q-My-Journey-into-QAnon/B09BVZRLCN?msockid=2aeb06ab76316ce81cbd15f677246d3c.

9. Dan Evon, "Qurious About QAnon? Get the Facts About This Dangerous Conspiracy Theory," Snopes, August 21, 2020, www.snopes.com/news/2020/08/21/qanon-2020-election.

10. Woolf, *Finding Q.*

11. Drew Harwell and Timothy McLaughlin, "From Helicopter Repairman to Leader of the Internet's 'Darkest Reaches': The Life and Times of 8chan Owner Jim Watkins," *Washington Post*, September 12, 2019, www.washingtonpost.com/technology/2019/09/12/helicopter-repairman-leader-internets-darkest-reaches-life-times-chan-owner-jim-watkins.

12. Craig Silverman and Jane Lytvynenko, "The Owner of 8chan Has Created a News Source for Internet Trolls," *BuzzFeed News*, February 22, 2017, https://archive.ph/KSIM0.

13. Woolf, *Finding Q.*

14. Tom Sykes, "Ron Watkins Slips Up, Suggests He Is Q, in HBO QAnon Documentary Series," *Daily Beast*, April 5, 2021, www.thedailybeast.com/ron-watkins-slips-up-suggests-he-is-q-in-hbo-qanon-documentary-series.

15. Sykes, "Ron Watkins Slips Up."

16. Patrick Malone, "Seattle Man Wonders If His Childhood Friend Is the Leader of Q-Anon," *Seattle Times*, April 13, 2021, www.seattletimes.com/seattle-news/seattle-man-wonders-is-his-childhood-friend-the-leader-of-q-anon.

17. Davey Alba, "'Q' Has Been Quiet, but QAnon Lives On," *New York Times*, December 20, 2021, www.nytimes.com/2021/12/20/technology/qanon-conspiracy-movement.html.

18. *The Matrix*, directed by Lana Wachowski and Lilly Wachowski (Warner Bros., 1999).

19. Hunter S. Thompson, *Fear and Loathing in Las Vegas* (New York: Knopf Doubleday, 1998).

20. "Understanding QAnon's Connection to American Politics, Religion, and Media Consumption," Public Religion Research Institute, May 27, 2021, www.prri.org/research/qanon-conspiracy-american-politics-report.

21. "Understanding QAnon's Connection to American Politics."

22. Grete De Francesco, *The Power of the Charlatan* (New Haven, CT: Yale University Press, 1939).

23. Richard Ruelas, "QAnon Interpreter, Praying Medic, off Facebook After Q Crackdown," *Arizona Republic*, October 8, 2020, www.azcentral.com/story/news/local/arizona-investigations/2020/10/08/qanon-interpreter-praying-medic-off-facebook-after-q-crackdown/5917183002.

24. "Q! Intelligence Drops," Q Alerts, accessed October 26, 2024, https://qalerts.app.

25. Hawthornemoon22, "I'm so angry . . . and I don't know how to let it go," r/QAnonCasualties, Reddit, November 3, 2022, www.reddit.com/r/QAnonCasualties/comments/ylkgrm/im_so_angryand_i_dont_know_how_to_let_it_go.

26. NeverQ4Me, "Is There Any Hope?," r/QAnonCasualties, Reddit, November 3, 2022, www.reddit.com/r/QAnonCasualties/comments/yl263i/is_there_any_hope.

Chapter 10. How Charlatans Took Over the Culture Wars

1. Claudia Koerner and Brianna Sacks, "The Veteran Who Has Raised Over $12 Million to Fund Trump's Wall Made Money Off Peddling Conspiracy Theories and Fake News," *BuzzFeed News*, December 21, 2018, www.buzzfeednews.com/article/briannasacks/veteran-gofundme-border-wall-fake-news.

2. "Breaking: Muslim Teen Refugee Charged with Murder for Beating 97-Yr-Old WWII Veteran to Death," Freedom Daily, January 7, 2016, https://freerepublic.com/focus/news/3381786/posts.

3. "Bad News for Barack After What Malia's Caught Doing in Chicago—No Hiding Her NASTY Secret Now," Freedom Daily, posted August 6, 2017, YouTube video, www.youtube.com/watch?v=wYl898f6CQE.

4. Bree Burkitt, "Meet the Veteran Who Has Raised $16 Million for Trump's Border Wall," *USA Today*, December 13, 2018, www.usatoday.com/story/news/politics/2018/12/24/brian-kolfage-veteran-started-border-wall-gofundme/2405770002.

5. Ben Feuerherd and Lia Eustachewich, "Inside the 'Lavish' Life of Alleged 'We Build the Wall' Scammer Brian Kolfage," *New York Post*, August 20, 2020, https://nypost.com/2020/08/20/the-lavish-life-of-alleged-border-wall-scammer-brian-kolfage.

6. "Steve Bannon Pleads Not Guilty in Scheme to Defraud Donors to Campaign Pledging to Build Border Wall," CBS News, August 21, 2020, www.cbsnews.com/news/steve-bannon-arrested-fraud-charges-border-wall-scheme-brian-kolfage-we-build-the-wall.

7. US Attorney's Office, Southern District of New York, "Two Sentenced to Prison for 'We Build the Wall' Online Fundraising Fraud Scheme," press release, US Department of Justice, April 26, 2023, www.justice.gov/usao-sdny/pr/two-sentenced-prison-we-build-wall-online-fundraising-fraud-scheme.

8. Chloe Atkins and Tom Winter, "Steve Bannon's Border Wall Fraud Trial Set for December," NBC News, July 24, 2024, www.nbcnews.com/politics/politics-news/steve-bannons-border-wall-fraud-trial-set-december-rcna163558.

9. Tucker Higgins, "Alex Jones: 5 Most Disturbing and Ridiculous Conspiracy Theories," CNBC, September 14, 2018, www.cnbc.com/2018/09/14/alex-jones-5-most-disturbing-ridiculous-conspiracy-theories.html.

10. Tyrone B. Hayes et al., "Atrazine Induces Complete Feminization and Chemical Castration in Male African Clawed Frogs (*Xenopus laevis*)," *Biological Sciences* 107, no. 10 (2010): 4612–4617, https://doi.org/10.1073/pnas.0909519107; Higgins, "Alex Jones."

11. "Preparedness—Ready for Any Fight," Infowars Store, accessed October 26, 2024, www.infowarsstore.com/preparedness.

12. Sebastian Murdock, "Alex Jones' Infowars Store Made $165 Million over 3 Years, Records Show," *Huffington Post*, January 7, 2022, www.huffpost.com/entry/infowars-store-alex-jones_n_61d71d8fe4b0bcd2195c6562.

13. The Associated Press, "More Sandy Hook Families Tell Stories of Harassment by Deniers," NBC Connecticut, September 28, 2022, www.nbcconnecticut.com/news/local/testimony-to-continue-in-alex-jones-defamation-trial/2880997.

14. Lauren del Valle, "Sandy Hook Parent Recounts Years of Harassment After Alex Jones Called Him a Crisis Actor," CNN, September 29, 2022, https://edition.cnn.com/2022/09/29/tech/sandy-hook-parent-harassment/index.html.

15. Dave Collins and Pat Eaton, "Sandy Hook Families Testify About Threats, Fear of Deniers," AP News, September 21, 2022, https://apnews.com/article/shootings-school-connecticut-alex-jones-waterbury-782e495a3ece4753d857a9b47d444385.

16. Patrick Skahill, "Father of Sandy Hook Victim Found Dead in Newtown," Connecticut Public Radio, www.ctpublic.org/news/2019-03-25/father-of-sandy-hook-victim-found-dead-in-newtown.

17. "Alex Jones Ordered to Pay Nearly $1 Billion to Sandy Hook Families in Connecticut Trial," CBS News, October 12, 2022, www.cbsnews.com/news/alex-jones-verdict-sandy-hook-trial-damages-2022-10-12.

18. The Associated Press, "Alex Jones Ordered to Pay Another $473M to Sandy Hook Families on Top of the Billion Ordered Last Month," CBC, November 10, 2022, www.cbc.ca/news/world/alex-jones-verdict-damages-hoax-1.6647707.

19. Jesse Singal and Katie Herzog, "Kevin Kruse and Rebekah Jones Are the Heroes and/or Villains a Divided America Needs," July 2, 2022, in *Blocked and Reported*, podcast, 32:00, www.blockedandreported.org/p/episode-121-kevin-kruse-and-rebekah.

20. Lawrence Mower and Mary Ellen Klas, "Rebekah Jones Jailed, Accused of Illegally Accessing Emergency Message System," *Tampa Bay Times*, January 18, 2021, www.tampabay.com/news/florida-politics/2021/01/18/rebekah-jones-jailed-accused-of-illegally-accessing-emergency-message-system.

21. Rachel Martin, "Florida Scientist Says She Was Fired for Not Manipulating COVID-19 Data," NPR, June 29, 2020, www.npr.org/2020/06/29/884551391/florida-scientist-says-she-was-fired-for-not-manipulating-covid-19-data.

22. Emily Bloch, "Rebekah Jones Tried to Warn Us About COVID-19: Now Her Freedom Is on the Line," *Cosmopolitan*, March 11, 2021, www.cosmopolitan.com/politics/a35714647/rebekah-jones-florida-covid-19-data-whistleblower-arrest.

23. "40 Under 40: Rebekah Jones," *Fortune*, 2020, https://fortune.com/ranking/40-under-40/2020/rebekah-jones; Tiffany Razzano, "Rebekah Jones Honored as Forbes 'Technology Person of the Year,'" Yahoo! News, December 30, 2020, www.yahoo.com/news/rebekah-jones-honored-forbes-technology-190714541.html; Helen A. S. Popkin, "Forbes Technology Awards 2020: Geeks Step Up When Governments Fail," *Forbes*, December 26, 2020, www.forbes.com/sites/helenpopkin/2020/12/26-forbes-technology-awards-2020-geeks-step-up-when-governments-fail.

24. Stephany Matat, "Stalking Case Against Fired Health Data Scientist Delayed," *Gainesville Sun*, July 22, 2020, www.gainesville.com/story/news/state/2020/07/22/stalking-case-against-fired-health-data-scientist-delayed/112691612.

25. Charles C. W. Cooke and Noah Rothman, "Rebekah Jones, the COVID Whistleblower Who Wasn't," *National Review*, May 13, 2021, www.nationalreview.com/2021/05/rebekah-jones-the-covid-whistleblower-who-wasnt.

26. Jemima Kelly, "Now You Too Can 'Dismantle White Supremacy,' for Just $48," *Financial Times*, September 3, 2021, www.ft.com/content/7980fc65-1ebf-4519-b741-74d35af53ca7.

27. Naomi Schaefer Riley, "Dinner Party from Hell," American Enterprise Institute, November 20, 2022, www.aei.org/op-eds/dinner-party-from-hell.

28. Isabel Vincent, "Exclusive | Anti-Racism Dinner Club Race2Dinner Appears like Charity—but Rakes in Profits for Its Two Leaders," *New York Post*, November 10, 2022, https://nypost.com/2022/11/10/anti-racism-dinner-club-race2dinner-appears-like-charitybut-rakes-in-profits-for-its-two-leaders.

Chapter 11. Ten Million Psychopaths

1. "*DSM-IV-TR* Diagnostic Criteria for Antisocial Personality Disorder (301.7)," Psychiatry Online, January 2, 2004, https://psychiatryonline.org/doi/full/10.1176/pn.39.1.0025a.

2. *APA Dictionary of Psychology*, s.v. "Machiavellianism," American Psychiatric Association, updated November 11, 2023, https://dictionary.apa.org/machiavellianism; *APA Dictionary of Psychology*, s.v. "Narcissism," American Psychiatric Association, updated November 15, 2023, https://dictionary.apa.org/narcissism.

3. David J. Cooke, "Psychopathy Across Cultures," in *Psychopathy: Theory, Research and Implications for Society*, ed. David J. Cooke, Adelle E. Forth, and Robert D. Hare (Princeton: Springer, 1991), 249, https://link.springer.com/chapter/10.1007/978-94-011-3965-6_2.

4. Andrea L. Glenn, Robert Kurzban, and Adrian Raine, "Evolutionary Theory and Psychopathy," *Aggression and Violent Behavior* 16, no. 5 (2011): 371–380, https://ir-api.ua.edu/api/core/bitstreams/3e732a96-df34-4cf3-9e25-6e6f2ab27d6d/content.

5. Kepios, "Global Social Media Statistics," *DataReportal*, accessed October 26, 2024, https://datareportal.com/social-media-users.

6. Tori DeAngelis, "A Broader View of Psychopathy," *Monitor on Psychology* 53, no. 2 (2022), www.apa.org/monitor/2022/03/ce-corner-psychopathy.

7. Daniel Kahneman, *Thinking, Fast and Slow* (New York: Farrar, Straus and Giroux, 2013).

8. David Ingram, "Google Is Trying Out 'Pre-Bunking' to Counter Misinformation," NBC News, August 24, 2022, www.nbcnews.com/tech/misinformation/google-trying-pre-bunking-effort-counter-misinformation-rcna43818.

Index

Credit: Photo courtesy of the author

Moisés Naím is distinguished fellow at the Carnegie Endowment for International Peace. He was the editor in chief of *Foreign Policy* magazine for more than a decade, and his column on global affairs is syndicated to dozens of publications worldwide. Naím is the author of *Illicit*, *What Is Happening to Us?*, and *The New York Times* bestseller *The End of Power*. He is based in Washington, DC.

Credit: Audrey Legerot

Quico Toro is a writer and editor who serves as the global opinion columnist for *The Washington Post*. He is based in Tokyo, Japan.